Conor Husbands
Klossowski's Semiotic of Intensity

Conor Husbands

Klossowski's Semiotic of Intensity

―

Time, Language and the Vicious Circle

DE GRUYTER

ISBN 978-3-11-077769-7
e-PDF 978-3-11-065976-4
e-PUB 978-3-11-065914-6

Library of Congress Control Number: 2020934093

Bibliographic information published by the Deutsche Nationalbibliothek
The Deutsche Nationalbibliothek lists this publication in the Deutsche Nationalbibliografie;
Detailed bibliographic data are available in the Internet at http://dnb.dnb.de.

© 2021 Walter de Gruyter GmbH, Berlin/Boston
This volume is text- and page-identical with the hardback published in 2020.
Print and binding: CPI books GmbH, Leck

www.degruyter.com

Acknowledgements

I would acknowledge the support and guidance of the following in the completion of this work, with gratitude and humility: Christian Kerslake, Daniel W. Smith, Joni Lewis, Manuel Dries, Ruth Broadbent, Alice Housset.

Contents

1	Introduction — 1	
2	**The Semiotic of Intensity — 13**	
2.1	Intensity in Thermodynamics and Philosophy — 15	
2.2	Intensity and Signs — 18	
2.3	Signifying Edifices — 20	
2.4	The Three-fold Structure of Signification: Klossowski and Peirce — 27	
2.5	Infinite Semiosis — 28	
2.6	Metasemiosis and Order — 29	
2.7	Final Interpretant, Mediate Phantasm — 31	
2.8	Klossowski and Peirce: A Comparison — 34	
2.9	Abbreviation — 34	
2.10	Signs and Genesis — 42	
2.11	Conclusion: Thought and Representation — 44	
3	**The Sign of the Self — 48**	
3.1	The Homonym of the Self — 53	
3.2	Resolution — 56	
3.3	Two Images of the Unconscious — 59	
3.4	Cohesion and Fortuity — 62	
3.5	Fluctuation and Discontinuity — 72	
3.6	Conclusion: Discontinuity and Selfhood — 79	
4	**Possibility and Fortuity in the Vicious Circle — 80**	
4.1	Definition of the Circle — 80	
4.2	Receptivity and Displacement — 84	
4.3	Economy of Interpretation — 86	
4.4	The Vicious Circle and Necessity — 92	
4.5	Conclusion: Actuality and Representation — 98	
5	**Temporality of the Vicious Circle — 106**	
5.1	The Inversion of Temporality — 109	
5.2	Permanence and Relationism — 113	
5.3	Palingenesis and Kenogenesis in the Circle — 116	
5.4	Asynchrony — 117	
5.5	Asynchronous Time: Forgetting — 122	

5.6	Reversal of Anachronism —— 126
5.7	Distinction of the Nietzschean and Kantian Positions —— 134
5.8	Parody —— 136
5.9	Forgetting and Memory: Coalescence —— 141
5.10	Consistency and Repetition —— 147
5.11	The Excentric Calendar —— 151
5.12	Order and Disorientation —— 154
5.13	From Intention to Intensity —— 158
5.14	Conclusion: Summary of Propositions —— 165

6 Conclusion —— 167

References —— 183

Index of Names —— 187

Index of Subjects —— 189

1 Introduction

> At the end of it the reader ... experiences utter vertigo ... Reading the text afresh in translation in 1999 I had the distinct feeling that its readers still lie in the future.[1]

> Klossowski has a rare understanding of the details of Nietzsche's thinking and of what is truly at stake in it. His book takes us further into the treacherous depths of Nietzsche's thought than any other study I know.[2]

When Ansell-Pearson states of Klossowski's work that its true readers lie in the future, we must declare that he is in this regard profoundly, and doubly, correct. Not only is this current study doubtless as incomplete as the scant scholarly attention committed thus far to reaching an understanding of *Nietzsche and the Vicious Circle*. It is incomplete also because of the latter's fundamental contentions, and what they imply for *any* possible reading of this text.

In Ansell-Pearson's description, futurity has a dual role. First of all, it refers to a contingent fact: the absence of scholarly attention directed at Klossowski's work, which might one day be redressed with a more sustained treatment than has yet appeared – a treatment which in turn might engage with the myriad aspects of the text which have escaped most commentators, namely the conception of intensity, the theory of signs, and the logical relations between this theory and the metaphysics of causality and time. This construal of futurity arises from even a cursory survey of any philosophical literature which seeks to respond to Klossowski's interpretation of Nietzsche. Despite its reverberation through a generation of Continental thinkers, and the overt attention of some of the most recognisable among them, such as Foucault and Deleuze, there have been no sustained or systematic attempts to engage with it over more than a few pages within a work with a broader focus. *Nietzsche and the Vicious Circle* has been addressed sporadically, in short sections and articles which discuss particular themes in isolation, and which do not typically aim to deliver analytical exegesis.

Even putting aside breadth and depth of engagement, from a thematic standpoint, few if any of these emphasise the semiotic underpinning of the work and the importance of these principles for both Klossowski and Nietzsche. Daniel W. Smith, following Deleuze, rightly emphasises the central notions of impulses and phantasms, and their relations to simulacra and stereotypes.

---

1 Ansell-Pearson, K. (2000). p. 249
2 Ansell-Pearson, K. (2000). p. 249

https://doi.org/10.1515/9783110659764-001

James and Faulkner, by contrast, emphasise Klossowski's philosophy of the body, and its relation to the principle of identity.³ Ansell-Pearson himself leverages the distinction between intensity and culture in order to argue for an unavowed kinship between Klossowski and Bergson.⁴ It is the contention of the present work, by contrast, that any conscientious account of *Nietzsche and the Vicious Circle*, and its concomitant thematic recapitulations in *Such a Deathly Desire*, *Sade My Neighbour* and other texts in Klossowski's philosophical writings, must fulfil three conditions:

(i) Grounding the metaphysical content of Klossowski's work in his theory of signs, in whose terms this content is defined;
(ii) Stating and explaining this metaphysical content, including its implications for the philosophical categories of individuality, chance, causality and time;
(iii) Expositing the fundamental commitments and theses advanced by Klossowski in analytically transparent fashion, to the maximum extent possible.

The motivation for the present work is the observation that, considering all of these important readings tendered thus far, it is impossible to avoid the conclusion that no project fulfilling these conditions yet exists. Thus, in the first sense of Ansell-Pearson's term, it lies ahead, in the future. However, as we have already stated, this term is subject to a double meaning: it refers not only to a contingent state of scholarship or academia, but to a *necessary* result of the Nietzschean experience and doctrines.

Although they must be defended from synopsis according to the "fashionable tropes" of "the incompleteness of meaning" and "the infinite play of interpretation," meaning, signification and interpretation are notions which stand in a close connection to the vicious circle which is the subject of Klossowski's work, underwriting just the kind of futurity Ansell-Pearson predicates of Klossowski's authentic reader. The infinite semiosis of signs, the indeterminacy of the position of events corresponding to them, the discontinuity of the moments in which these events inhere, and the deactualisation of the individual living them –all of these phenomena Nietzsche experienced as manifestations of the vicious circle, and all of these phenomena contribute to the kind of futurity which befits all possible readings of Klossowski's work, including the currently attempted reading, as it would even the most fastidious reading.

---

3 James, I. (2001). pp. 59–70; Faulkner, J. (2007). pp. 43–69
4 Ansell-Pearson, K. (2000). pp. 248–256

Following this introduction, the second chapter of this work elaborates what it takes to be the central principles of Klossowski's theory of signs. Signs are generated from fluctuations of intensity – a notion with a rich philosophical lineage which Klossowski will modify and develop. Fluctuations of intensity obey a tripartite dynamic: in fluctuating, an intensity divides, separates from itself, and eventually rejoins itself.[5] This is what is experienced in the "moments of rise and fall"[6] which, for Klossowski as for Smith[7] and others, populate the Nietzschean experience. The second chapter analyses this description of Klossowski's semiotic, and explores its main consequences. It situates the underlying conception of intensity in contrast to its predominant forerunners, both philosophical and scientific. This will lead us to five marks of intensity:

(i) as the unity of a sensation;
(ii) as quality;
(iii) as confused (in the Leibnizian sense);
(iv) as divisible only with qualitative change;
(v) as a hierarchy.

We shall then argue that if this intensity is to give rise to a theory of signs, it can only be understood in relation to what Klossowski refers to as the semiotic of the institutional code. The institutional code is parasitic on fluctuations, but modifies them in two main ways: it *abbreviates* and *falsifies* them with its representations. This code, he claims, is responsible for the experience of space, by virtue of the way in which signs are indexed to specific locations (in spatial experience, and indeed in time conceived as spatial). In itself, by contrast, intensity accommodates none of these features. This conclusion will also explain the critique of intentionality which is a constant refrain of *Nietzsche and the Vicious Circle:*

> The day human beings learn how to behave as phenomena devoid of intention – for every intention at the level of the human being always implies its own conservation, its continued existence – on that day, a new creature would declare the integrity of existence.[8]

> The forces we improperly name 'Chaos' have no intention whatsoever. Nietzsche's unavowable project is to act without intention: the impossible morality. Now the total economy of this intentionless universe creates intentional beings. The species 'man' is a creation of this kind – pure chance – in which the intensity of forces is inverted into intention: the work of

---

5 Klossowski, P. (1997). pp. 60–61
6 Klossowski, P. (1997). p. 61
7 Smith, D. (2005). p. 9
8 Klossowski, P. (1997). p. 139

morality. The function of the simulacrum is to lead human intention back to the intensity of forces, which generate phantasms.[9]

Subsequent to the analysis of this semiotic, these statements will form the basis for the esoteric typology of morals Klossowski attributes to Nietzsche – the notions of singular and gregarious forces, robust and decadent types, and the many other oppositional pairs of symptoms which allowed Nietzsche to formulate speculative diagnoses of his own physical state, and by analogy his prognosis for the species.

Klossowski's semiotic of intensity, whilst doubtless among the eccentricities of recent decades' philosophy of language, is not entirely without precedent. In particular, we will see several analogies begin to emerge between it and the work of C. S. Peirce, that of Eco, and even that of Wittgenstein. Both Peirce and Klossowski endorse the principle of infinite semiosis, as well as the premise that signs relate to the objects which determine them through a *hierarchy* of interpretation: chains of signs forming a hierarchy. But whereas in Peirce's semiotic these objects are rigorously determinative of the meanings of these signs, that of Klossowski replaces such objects with the "phantasmic coherence"[10] of the impulses – ultimately, that is, with no determinative object at all, and only deferment and indeterminacy.

If these semiotic considerations are indeed the foundation of *Nietzsche and the Vicious Circle* and its counterparts such as *Polytheism and Parody*, how do they entail the metaphysical content which comprises the remainder of the book? If Kellner is correct in taking each doctrine as "a translation into language"[11] of Nietzsche's "most profound experiences which further put in question major philosophical concepts such as the self, life, fate, necessity, causality, and other key conceptions in the Western philosophical arsenal,"[12] then the question inevitably arises as to the provenance of these attacks on the tradition. The remaining chapters of the current study take this question as their guiding line of enquiry.

First of all, fluctuations of intensity, the starting point of the semiotic, force us to reevaluate our conception of the subject, self, or ego. The self Klossowski defines in the following way: "There is *one* sign ... that always corresponds to

---

[9] Klossowski, P. (1997). p. 140
[10] Klossowski, P. (1997). p. 260
[11] Kellner, D. (1998).
[12] Kellner, D. (1998).

either the highest or lowest degree of intensity: namely, the *self*, the I, *the subject of all our propositions.*"[13]

This definition, and its ramifications, governs Klossowski's position as an interpreter of the Nietzschean critique of the self relative to the interpretations of Heidegger or Deleuze, for instance, or relative to psychoanalytical construals. The third chapter of this study discusses this position.

As an initial prerequisite for this discussion, it is necessary to resolve the apparent antinomy inherent in this definition: the self, according to Klossowski, corresponds simultaneously to opposite extremes of intensity (its "highest" as well as "lowest degree"), with opposite characteristics. The self is both the highest and lowest degree of intensity. Providing an explanation of this strange predicament will lead us to elucidate the relationship between intensity, impulses and forces, the body which they constitute and the self which is parasitic on them. Specifically, we will examine two of the most important propositions in Klossowski's account: (i) that a *non-homonymic* relation obtains between the body and the self, and (ii) that the intellect is the obverse of any impulse in general. In addition, the third chapter compares the notions of the unconscious in psychoanalysis and in *Nietzsche and the Vicious Circle*, and decomposes Klossowski's seven-step proof of the conclusion that the unconscious and conscious cannot coexist in the way defunct psychoanalytic theories presuppose. Rather, such theories point to an elliptical dichotomy: "Either everything in us is unconscious, or everything in us is conscious."[14]

Klossowski's formulation of the Nietzschean critique of selfhood and subjectivity also facilitates the first appearances of his metaphysics of chance, chaos or fortuity. The self, for Klossowski, is a combative arena of fortuitously reconciled instinctual forces, vying for command of the organism:

Intensity is subject to a moving chaos without beginning or end.[15]

Chance is but one thing at each of the moments (the individual, singular and hence fortuitous existences) of which it is composed.[16]

All that remains, then, is for me to re-will myself ... as a fortuitous moment whose very fortuity implies the integral return of the whole series.[17]

---

13 Klossowski, P. (1997). p. 62
14 Klossowski, P. (1997). p. 39
15 Klossowski, P. (1997). p. 62
16 Klossowski, P. (1997). p. 72
17 Klossowski, P. (1997). p. 58

The examination of the self, therefore, will also involve an examination of a conceptual patchwork of notions such as chance, chaos and fortuity which are predominant features of Klossowski's reading, as even the limited commentary has consistently acknowledged.[18] The usages of these notions, clearly indebted to the later Nietzsche's researches in the physical sciences, his flirtation with the metaphysics of Boscovich and his disparagement of the mechanism he assigns to Boyle and Kelvin, evoke the combinatorial and statistical foundations of thermal physics. Fortuity, for example, evokes the statistical-mechanical concept of ergodicity. In turn, this will prove an important determinant of the way in which the self, as fortuitous, can be considered cyclic, dissolving and re-emerging from the fluctuating impulses which make it up. In the third chapter, we will show why this cyclic dissolution and re-emergence of the self must be, for Klossowski, perpetual. Most importantly as regards the theory of the self, however, fortuity is characterised as a decentring or "centrifugal"[19] force, a description which cements his view of the subject, ego and person.

Posed in these terms, however, this account of fortuity, as a basic facet of the self, depends upon precisely the tropes Ansell-Pearson disparages – those of perpetual becoming, interpretative experimentation and latitude, and the other devices which could be employed cavalierly enough to risk blunting such theories' subversive potential. We will duly undertake to avoid confining our explanation in this way. "The Sign of the Self," the second chapter after this introduction, will try to go beyond these terms, concluding that *discontinuity* is a further, necessary commitment of Klossowski's, in the context of his account of fortuity. This discontinuity, a term drawn from the mathematical language of functions and appropriated throughout *Nietzsche and the Vicious Circle*, refers not only to the periodic breaks which intervene in lived experience, between the moments of its illusory steadiness and consistency. It refers also to breaks which, more fundamentally, exist between the coherence of the intellect and incoherence of the impulses, or between silence and declarations. Declarations and representations are *non-contiguous* with intensity. This proposition reiterates the fundamental distinction between the semiotic of intensity and that of the institutional code: there is no sense in which the latter is a continuation of the former. As the second chapter will demonstrate, this statement can be made clearer by contrasting it with the Kantian theory of subjectivity, and we will show how it undermines Kant's doctrine of the unity of apperception, by way of illustration. These are the preliminary explanations of the semiotic of intensity and its implications.

---

[18] Ansell-Pearson, K. (2000). p. 252; James I. (2001). pp. 248–256
[19] Klossowski, P. (1997). p. 216

Klossowski proposes a theory of signs which this study attempts to interpret and justify, and to compare to other the work of scholars. It also reveals Klossowski's position on the self. However, these considerations make no mention of the true subject of Klossowski's study: the vicious circle. The fourth chapter turns to this central theme. Here, under the title "Possibility and Fortuity in the Vicious Circle," the vicious circle is defined as *the identity between intensity and its own trace*. The circle is, as intensity, the trace of itself. The immediate consequence of this definition is an event which Klossowski terms deactualisation: the subject of the vicious circle no longer occupies a particular place and time and instead becomes multiple, forming a series. Initially, this is a simple result of the tendency of intensity to incorporate multiple competing impulses, and the tendency of different fluctuations to inter-mix. Posed more fully, in the vicious circle, immediate access to phenomena is replaced by infinite semiosis, and the determinate particulars which populate the world in, for instance, the Cartesian account of experience are replaced by a recursive structure. Further, Klossowski argues that the tendency of impulses to interpret one another, which becomes especially pronounced with their intensification in the circle, is responsible for the provenance of this structure, and the serialisation of the ego. Thus Klossowski refers to the "interpretative availability"[20] which befell Nietzsche's evacuated persona in Turin:

> The euphoria of Turin led Nietzsche to maintain, in a kind of interpretive availability, the residues of everything that constituted the past in the context of his present experience.[21]

Accordingly, this contention grounds Klossowski's insistence that *nothing is ever constituted in a single meaning, once and for all*.[22] Any meaning becomes conditional on interpretation and this interpretative availability. The notion of interpretation does, therefore, play an important role in the economy of the vicious circle, in spite of Ansell-Pearson's prudent attempts to stave off its vulnerability to philosophical cliché and platitude.

Further, this important role played by interpretation in Klossowski's theory leads to an equally important role for possibility, by dint of the following argument which we will extract from various opaque passages.

No interpretation is once and for all (Axiom)
All events are given a signification only by interpretation (Axiom)
Signification is the signification of an event (Definition)

---

20 Klossowski, P. (1997). p. 251
21 Klossowski, P. (1997). p. 251
22 Klossowski, P. (1997). p. 64

>   No signification is once and for all (Thesis)
>   Actuality is once and for all (Definition)
>   Possibility is never once and for all (Definition)
>   Signification is the signification of possibility (Conclusion)

With this argument, Klossowski endorses a variant of the Heideggerian dictum that possibility stands higher than actuality. This thesis is developed and explained in this same chapter, which will also defend Klossowski's iterated modal thesis that the possibilities, into which the individual decomposes in the vicious circle, are themselves necessary events, in the sense that they are the results of a law:

P) "Every identity must pass through a series of individualities in order for the fortuitousness of a particular identity to render them all necessary."[23]

The fourth chapter offers a logical formalisation of this principle, and also states its view on the way in which the concepts of fortuity and totality, respectively explicit and implicit in this proposition, are best understood.

We will also, however, see the ways in which Klossowski's conception of possibility stretches beyond traditional accounts, including the Heideggerian position. Whereas traditionally possibility is a feature of sentences, determined by the variation of their truth values with those of the arguments of which they are functions, and is opposed to real states of affairs, with Klossowski, there is no categorical distinction between possibility and actuality, and no exclusive postulation of the reality of the latter (but not the former). Rather, actuality is epiphenomenal in relation to possibility. To the extent that they are distinguishable at all, it is as excitations incorporated to varying degrees into the organism, that they are distinguished.

However, of all the subjects central to Klossowski's tract, the temporality of the vicious circle stands at the forefront, as both the lived and experienced impetus for Nietzsche's philosophical proclamations, and their theoretical foundation. Indeed, the entirety of *Nietzsche and the Vicious Circle* can be read – and repeatedly re-read – as an attempt to technically formalise Nietzsche's inchoate theories of time, first adumbrated in the theory of signs, ramified through the many categories that Nietzsche barraged in both his published and unpublished work, and finally finding intermittent expression as a philosophy of time.

Just as temporality stands in a close relationship to causality, it is to these two categories that the penultimate chapter of this work is dedicated. By way

---

[23] Klossowski, P. (1997). pp. 216–217

of testament to the importance of the relationship between these two concepts, the notion of inversion, the lynchpin of Klossowski's presentation of temporality – seemingly deliberately stationed at the very end of *Nietzsche and the Vicious Circle* – is presented as a revision to a traditional causal schema. Rather than the external world causing its effects on us, it is through these effects that the world is projected as a causal agent. Klossowski denies the thesis that, in a given series of events, each is the cause of its action on its successor. In doing so, we will show, he is committed to denying in turn both the permanence of events, and the completeness of any empirical presentation of events: their characteristics, the qualities they present, also vary with time. In this way, in this, the fifth chapter, the signs which are the subject of his semiotic give way to the events which make up time.

This dramatic crystallisation of Nietzsche's fragmented critique of mechanism, under the influence of his researches in experimental science, can be most clearly grasped with the aid of the notion of asynchrony, or, in Klossowski's terms, anachronism. Present conditions, which are determinately located, with a given origin, and comprise successions of moments, are asynchronous or anachronistic with respect to the time of singular impulses, which lack all of these characteristics. This distinction, it will be argued, relies further on the conception of forgetting which is employed throughout *Nietzsche and the Vicious Circle*, and we will state the organising logical principle of this aspect of Klossowski's work: the denial that, given a series of events, the order of their appearance and their temporal order can be equated, so that the order of events and the ordering process are fundamentally distinct. It is this principle that is most distinctive about Klossowski's position. Thus seemingly abstract thesis will be made more concrete by translation into the context of Klossowski's biographical citations, such as Nietzsche's afflictions, and biological reflections, including the notion of *intelligent synthetic interaction*. We will also attempt a comparative reading of Klossowski's view of time as a mnemonic "parody," invoking both *Nietzsche and the Vicious Circle* and *Such a Deathly Desire*.

The second major stratum of the theory of temporality is the coalescence of memory and forgetting. In one of the text's culminating sequences, Klossowski's explicitly avows the principle that forgetting itself "amounts to" a memory. Assimilating these categories to modes of time, such is to affirm the unification of past and future, and their reduction to one another. The fifth chapter amasses the justification for these remarkable claims, appealing once again to the distinction between the order of events and their ordering process. The order in which an agent ranks events at a given moment need not reflect the order in which they appear, are given, or acquire determinacy. For Klossowski, these considerations effectively refute the possibility of prising the contents of a moment in which past and future may occur into separate groups. The following part of this section argues for two resultant claims:

Y) Recurrences of events in present series cannot be assigned an original fluctuation
Z) Recurrences of events in present series occur at variable distances from other events

The fifth chapter which concerns itself with the temporality of the vicious circle, concludes by reconsidering Nietzsche's attack on intentionality in light of these reflections on temporality and causality. Building upon the Nietzschean analogy between causality and ostensibly intentional agency – the former of which couple he asserts to be a disingenuous manifestation of the latter – and following Klossowski's dictum that intentionality must be led back to intensity,[24] we will demonstrate that this attack can be characterised by the following five assertions:

Q) Intention is an epiphenomenon.
R) Purpose and means are strictly dependent on the events which produce them.
S) No intended outcome is ever realised.
T) No realised outcome is ever intended.
U) No action is caused by a purpose.

In this way, this current work seeks to explore the manifold contentions and consequences of Klossowski's iconoclasm, as it sits both within and beyond the world of Nietzsche studies, and all of which arises out of this esoteric semiotic of intensity, with its strange movement of division which he posits as an originary dynamic. Fluctuations of intensity, monsters of energy,[25] produce the signs which are the world. In fluctuating, intensity divides, separates, and reunifies, in an intrinsically circular movement which repeats throughout *Nietzsche and the Vicious Circle*, and which is latent in its postulation of fluctuation as a metaphysical category, the loss of permanence from signs and events, the infinity of semiosis, the division of the self into series of series and never a single moment, the discontinuity of experience and the discontinuity between intensity and lan-

---

24 Klossowski, P. (1997). p. 112
25 KSA 11, 38[12] = WP 1067. Here and hereafter, KSA refers to the *Kritische Studienausgabe* (Nietzsche 1999), and WP refers to *The Will to Power* (Nietzsche 1968).

guage, and the inverted time and causality which follows, in the argument of the final chapter. The semiotic of intensity and the critique which derives from it all rest upon this division of intensity.

Division, in spite of being a strange and unfamiliar term with little philosophical or semiological precedent is, in this way, the underpinning of the entire work. Albeit hardly well established, there is one prominent work in which this foundational notion is discussed at some length, and which serves as an insightful foil for Klossowski's interpretation.

In the eponymous Platonic dialogue, Parmenides employs the notion of division to derive what he regards as an absurd conclusion. This he attributes to Socrates as a rejoinder or refutation. For Parmenides (and Zeno), Being is one because it cannot be many, lest it be both "like and unlike."[26] For Socrates, however, beings *participate* in the *ideas* of likeness and unlikeness to *varying degrees*. Degrees of participation in ideas enable diversity: Being being many does not imply Being being like and unlike, since Being may then be many by dint of beings participating in ideas, in virtue of which like and unlike beings can coexist, without the incompatible ideas coexisting. That being is many is a defensible proposition, for Socrates, since does not require the claim that the like is unlike, nor the reverse. To this explanation, however, Parmenides and Zeno will object as follows:

> Each individual partakes either of the whole of the idea or else of a part of the idea … The whole idea is one, and yet, being one, is in each of the many … One and the same thing will exist as a whole at the same time in many separate individuals and will therefore be in a state of separation from itself … The ideas themselves will be divisible, and the things which participate in them will have a part of them only and not the whole idea existing in each of them.[27]

If each being participates in ideas of likeness and unlikeness, they must participate in either the whole or in parts. If they participate in parts, the idea is divisible into parts. Otherwise, they participate in the whole, and so the whole exists in a state of separation from itself.

The state of separation from itself, a purported absurdity according to this dialogue, is precisely the state in which intensity exists when generating signs in the semiotic of intensity: it divides and separates from itself, before rejoining. This dynamic is explicit in the foundation of Klossowski's work. He builds a theory of signs from this self-separation of intensity, and its recursive semiotic, and

---

26 Jowett, B. (2015). p. 36
27 Jowett, B. (2015). pp. 39–40

on top of this the many metaphors of displacement, deferment, indeterminacy, inversion, lack of a specific location and symmetry in time which define the text's metaphysical profile. Whereas in *Parmenides* divisibility is cognate with having parts, in *Nietzsche and the Vicious Circle* it does not quite imply the existence of parts – in the way that, for instance, the desires stoked up by intensity and their objects would be parts separate from one another – but rather an intensity which refers only to itself. Divisibility, for Klossowski, does not lead to separate parts, but to a circular movement of intensity which aims to rejoin itself, and thus signs which do not refer to anything determinate, sensations which cannot be affixed a location in time, and premonitions which are no different from memories. In the vicious circle, these correspond to the divisibility of intensity into itself and its trace. This principle, undoubtedly an abuse of the term "division," and which contrasts with the usages in the *Parmenides*, is nonetheless expressed by Parmenides himself in his fragments, attesting to the compatibility of something which is "one" and therefore not separate from itself, but divisible, by facilitating its return back into itself, a harbinger of the Nietzschean image:

> It is all one to me where I begin; for I shall come back again there.[28]
>
> Ought one to pour the most precious wines and salves into the sea? My consolation is that ... the sea will cast it up again.[29]

---

28 Burnet, J. (1920). Fragment 5
29 WP 1065 = KSA 13, 11[94]

2 The Semiotic of Intensity

> When a sentence is called senseless,
> it is not as it were its sense that is senseless.[30]

In Wittgenstein's *Philosophical Investigations*, we are confronted with a distinction between two linguistic fields: The field of properly formed syntax, exposited in the *Tractatus*, and a deeper, symbolic field of inscriptions. Elements of the former obey structural rules which qualify them as propositions with semantic content. They stand in a relation to the world by virtue of their linkages to atomic propositions, expressing facts independent of the structure of the language. Propositions or sentences, however, not only have a sense in this sense, but another kind of sense – as inscriptions whose absence Wittgenstein names "senseless." Such inscriptions, by contrast, may or may not be well formed, and may or may not stand in a connection to the world, the sign S among them. Where, then, does this sense originate, and how can they take on a signification?

It is not only the prosaic form of aphorism that Wittgenstein's work shares with Nietzsche's; just as the question of sense preoccupied the obsessive researches of the former's later years, the latter's life and thought must also be interpreted as, in part, a response to this very question. As Klossowski demonstrates throughout his work, we attain a staid and stereotyped view of Nietzsche when we interpret his thought as a metaphysical theory or ontology among arbitrary numbers of others. These ontological descriptions are the principal exegetical tools in Heidegger's decisive treatment, bestowing upon Nietzsche the epithet "the last metaphysician of the West"[31] and naming his thought the "consummation of metaphysics."[32] By contrast, it will be argued in this text that the primacy of *competing semiotics* in Nietzsche is what sets him apart from this theoretical lineage. Klossowski's work demonstrates that his work cannot be understood as a meta-ethical system, nor as a biologism, nor a materialist voluntarism, but only as a semiotic theory. Nietzsche's diagnostic or symptomatological approach, to his own physical afflictions as much as to the predicament of the species, which produces genealogies and moralistic reflections, is a product of this theory, together with its abundance of consequences – including that nothing ever succeeds in getting constituted once and for

---

30 Wittgenstein, L. (2001). p. 118e
31 Heidegger, M. (1991c). p. 8
32 Heidegger, M. (1991c). p. ix

all[33] – even Nietzsche's own phantasm, as we will see. The groundwork of Klossowski's study *Nietzsche and the Vicious Circle* is this question concerning the origin of signification: "From this point of view, the first question we must ask concerns the function of the signs of language; or rather, in an even more rudimentary fashion: how and *where* are signs born?"[34]

The connection between Wittgenstein and Nietzsche, or Klossowski as Nietzsche's archaeologist, may seem faint, straddling separate traditions. However, there is evidence that Klossowski engaged meaningfully with the work of Wittgenstein, as the first French translator of *Philosophical Investigations* in 1961, just a few years before the culmination of his work on Nietzsche and the publication of his major study.[35] The quietist tendencies, among the few commonalities between Wittgenstein's earlier and later philosophies, are ubiquitous in Klossowski's writings, as well as his post-philosophical outward life. It is less surprising, then, that Wittgenstein's work opens up a fundamentally Nietzschean problem: Regardless of its formal characteristics and prior to any relation to a linguistic system or totality, what imparts signification to a sign?

Consider Wittgenstein's argument concerning private language, which contends that signs connected with strictly private sensations cannot be rigorously defined. Concerning such a connection, such a sign cannot be such that it "brings it about that I remember the connexion *right* in the future,"[36] so there are no criteria for the correctness of the application of such a sign to a sensation, or an impulse. In order for an application to be correct, it must be repeatable in the sense that all future and past usages of this association must cohere with the current one, and thus must be both "habitual and specific."[37] There can be no language and no communication without this minimum of repeatability, yet no private sensation could establish such a consistent regime. Rather, under the force of Wittgenstein's argumentation the hypothesised singularity of the symbol S gives way to a totality: the socio-cultural matrix of language and its use, analogous to Klossowski's anthropocentric "code of everyday signs."

In this regard, Klossowski's study approaches Wittgenstein's research quite directly, concerning itself with *fluctuations of intensity* and their signifying edifices. If well-formed formulae or propositions obey structural criteria for signification, inscriptions – any marks or traces whatsoever, any sensations or impulses, any mental content or representations, and *any experience as such* – bearing dif-

---

33 Klossowski, P. (1997). p. 43
34 Klossowski, P. (1997). p. 45
35 Helgeson, J. (2011). p. 346
36 Wittgenstein, L. (2001). p. 258
37 Klossowski, P. (1997). p. 26

ferent criteria of sense were the fluctuations which populated Nietzsche's lifeworld: roughly, oscillatory and unstable changes in state, exciting psychic and corporeal forces, conscious and unconscious, and eventually signs – the data of representation. The inchoate kind of sign constituted by sensations, precluded from definition in Wittgenstein's analysis, parallels the object of Klossowski's study: intensity and its fluctuations. Just as, in Wittgenstein's work, the exteriority of private experience to forms of life disqualifies them from manifesting sense, Klossowski locates intensity firmly outside traditional regimes of signification, and dedicates the majority of his study to the analysis of its broader consequences for the philosopher, as opposed to the linguist. But whereas the scope of Wittgenstein's attack on private sensation can be defined by comparison and contrast with the positions of Russell, Locke and Descartes, that of Klossowski is defined by the concept of *intensity*. This notion will play a profoundly important role in *Nietzsche and the Vicious Circle*. But what exactly is intensity, and where does this notion originate?

2.1 Intensity in Thermodynamics and Philosophy

The modern notion of intensity was elaborated by and imported into philosophy from thermodynamics, partly under the influence of Klossowski, Bergson and Deleuze.[38] However, long before, Kant's *Critique of Pure Reason* introduces a forerunner of this concept, containing several competing determinations of the distinction between the predicates "extensive" and "intensive." In the Axioms of Intuition, Kant defines a magnitude as extensive insofar as the representation of its parts makes possible and precedes that of the whole, in contrast to intensive magnitudes which are only ever apprehended as a unity. Thus, sensations are elements in the field of appearances (undetermined objects of an empirical intuition) and thus the *real* element in such intuitions, according to the Axioms of Intuition. Since they are not themselves intuitions, these sensations are apprehended as wholes, as opposed to spatial parts in space, or temporal parts in time. Equivalently, Kant expresses these characteristics as resulting from a difference in the remit of synthesis: when synthesis applies to the manifold of intuition, the objects are considered as whole only after combination from parts. Thus, "As sensation is that element in the [field of] appearance the apprehension of which does not involve a successive synthesis proceeding from parts to

---

38 Tolman, R. (1917). pp. 237–253

the whole representation, it has no extensive magnitude."[39] The intensive, then, is an aspect of experience seemingly unintuited, apart from the formal conditions of space and time.

Common to both these marks of intensivity or extensivity is the following: Kant is explicit about the possibility of quantitatively reducing a given intensity.

> Between reality in the [field of] appearance and negation there is therefore a continuity of many possible intermediate sensations, the difference between any two of which is always smaller than the difference between the given sensation and zero or complete negation.[40]

Here, anticipating Klossowski's attribution of *degrees* to intensities (as intensive sensations), magnitude in its quantitative aspect is imputed fully to intensity, no less than to extensity. Yet, before Klossowski, many lengthy chapters of the work of Bergson turn this very imputation against Kant. In *Time and Free Will*, Bergson argues that intensities – roughly, sensations – do not admit of magnitude. *Apparent* differences in the magnitude of sensations are not real. Rather, they correspond to the multiplication and metastatisation of sensations, producing a difference in *quality* which masquerades as a quantitative one. Sensations of pain, for instance, intensify as they multiply and spread over the body, consuming a greater part of its functions – and not insofar as they induce a cathexis, or a concentration of energy at the one same point. This intensification cannot be explained as a series of differences in magnitude of one qualitatively identical, localised sensation. Bergson's subordination or, in Nietzschean terms, appropriation of the organism's functions as a result of intensification amounts to a variation in *quality*. Although Bergson follows Kant in affirming the *continuity* of such a variation, he diverges on the question as to whether these variations are numerical. According to this view, the description "intensive quantity" verges on a misnomer; an intensity is less a quantity or a magnitude and more a structure. Indeed, this more rigid position articulated in *Time and Free Will* allows no quantitative determination of intensity. Accordingly, it is impossible for sensations to increase or diminish, since this would require them to contain lesser supposed quantities.

The proof Bergson assembles for the thesis that sensations do not admit of magnitude is the following. All magnitudes must be greater or lesser than other magnitudes. A magnitude is greater than another only if it contains this other. Any containment of one by another involves attributing one of two spaces, unequal in size, to each of the pair. But since sensations can never be assimilated

---

39 Kant, I. (1929). A167/B209
40 Kant, I. (1929). A168/B210

to a space, defining an adequate notion of containment for sensations comes to be seen by Bergson as implausible. As a result, the essential mark of an intensive sensation, with its quality, is therefore its intractability to space. Accordingly, the variation of sensations always involves a *qualitative* change in the sensation, in which other, heterogeneous sensations become distorted as they begin to gravitate around it.

Intensities are thus *confused*, according to the Leibnizian taxonomy.[41] They are clear, either in the sense that they are capable of signification, or in the sense that we are capable of recognising the objects they signify. They are nevertheless confused in a double sense: not only do we lack the criteria by means of which to distinguish them from others; we are also not conscious of their entire composition or membership. "At every moment there is in us an infinity of perceptions ... too tiny and too numerous"[42] to be consciously apperceived, but which remains perceptible nonetheless. The complexity and incomparability of our sensations means that we are ignorant, not only of what distinguishes them from any others, but of some of their very elements. Bergson therefore imparts to intensity the *indistinctness* proper to confusion, as well as placing into doubt its capacity to accommodate determinations of magnitude.

Following Bergson and Kant, Deleuze offers two separate characterisations of the intensive: the divisibility of a quantity, and the analysability of a quantity.

Intensivity as divisibility: A quantity which can be divided without undergoing qualitative change is regarded as extensive. One which cannot is intensive. Extensive characteristics such as volumes and enthalpy can be divided producing no qualitative variation. A volume, being homogeneous, can be cut into sections whose qualities are identical before and after, just as a measure of enthalpy, or total thermodynamic internal and external energy, can be separated into subsystems each with the same characteristics as before. Such variables thus scale with the size of the system considered. Intensive quantities such as specific heat capacity, temperature and pressure are independent of system size. In order to divide a region of defined quantity into different quantities thereof (regions of variable pressure or temperature), a qualitative change must be introduced (supplying power over time on a gradient over the volume).

Intensity as analysability: An intensive quantity is analysable into couples of different elements. Every element of the quantity in turn refers to elements of another order.[43] The notion of order thus establishes a hierarchy of reference: each

---

41 Wilson, M. (1977).
42 Leibniz, G. (2005). p. 5
43 Deleuze, G. (2004). p. 222

element refers to all elements related to it of the subjacent order and below, hence Deleuze's schema E-E', E: e-e', e: ε-ε',... – a composition by virtue not only of the heterogeneity of the members of each couple, but also of that of the subjacent elements or children.[44]

Thus, the tradition prior to and following Klossowski's *Nietzsche and the Vicious Circle*, in which experience, construed as signs, is described (and diagnosed) in terms of intensity, develops a notion of intensity with several aspects – intensity (i) as the unity of a sensation; (ii) as quality, unassimilable to space; (iii) as confused; (iv) as divisible only with qualitative change; (v) as subsuming a hierarchy; (vi) as, nevertheless, quantitative and gradated.

These characteristics, inherited by Klossowski's meticulous exposition of the concept of intensity, will become the key interpretative tools in unlocking Nietzsche's philosophy, as a set of propositions about the conditions of an intensity's signification, leading to an attack on some of the chief pillars of Western philosophy – attacks which culminate in the diffuse Nietzschean temporality. Intensities are unassimilable to space, following Bergson; but, following Kant, they admit of degree – yet privileged degrees of intensity, such as its highest and lowest points, exert dramatic and incommensurable effects on the artifices of signification. A marriage of quantity and quality thus results from this approach, in which intensity has degrees, despite being pre-spatial. On top of this marriage of degree and quality, what is added to the *propria* of intensity in *Nietzsche and the Vicious Circle* is captured in the concept of fluctuation – seemingly a familiar trope of the scholarly reception of Nietzsche, insofar as it parallels the notion of *becoming* – but one which Klossowski articulates in terms of a singular and specific dynamic, together with an account of the economy of significations it generates.

2.2 Intensity and Signs

Klossowski does not attribute just one semiotic to Nietzsche, but two, beginning with the institutional code of everyday signs. This code applies to thought, language and ordinary experience. On the other hand, there is the semiotic of fluctuating intensity, which inhabits authentic instinctual experience. The two semiotics correspond to differing degrees of intensity, one everyday and one

---

[44] This definition apparently formalises many of the features of intensivity as divisibility, insofar as a division of such quantities leads to a qualitative change given the differences between the members of each couple and their descendants.

exceptional – attesting to the innovation of Klossowski's usage of this term: differences in degree support structurally and categorically different systems of interpretation. These differences do not, therefore, imply a qualitative similarity between the two, and one of the principal achievements of *Nietzsche and the Vicious Circle* is to provide a detailed account of how these two edifices, seemingly irreconcilable, in fact derive only from different *degrees* of the *same* movement – an account which in parts resembles a hypostasised monism, and which oscillates between two views of the relation between these semiotics. On the one hand, the exceptional semiotic is the most immediate expression of intensity, of which Nietzsche was the privileged exponent, and the institutional code of everyday signs a corrupted epiphenomenon. It is to this view that the text inclines when it claims this semiotic to be the result of the fullest, strongest or highest feeling, that is, of extremal intensity – *hohe Stimmung, höchste Gefühl*.[45] Yet, elsewhere, this relationship is complicated by the institutional code: "the sign of the self in the code of everyday communication ... corresponds to the strongest or weakest intensity."[46] Additionally, in the "Attempt at a Scientific Explanation of the Eternal Return," Klossowski appears to conceive of intensity as a *disruption* to the prevailing semiotic, not as its direct expression.

> Now if a fluctuation of intensity can take on a signification only in the trace it leaves – that is, in the meaning of a sign – then the sign of the Circle is at once the trace (in the mind), the meaning, and the intensity itself. In this sign (*circulus vitiosus Deus*), everything becomes merged with the movement itself, which by turns resuscitates and abandons the trace, empty, to itself.[47]

Here, it is not at all obvious that different configurations of intensity lead to different forms of signification. The sign of the circle, defined as the peak of intensity, modifies the very dynamic of fluctuation, and seems to vitiate all distinctions between different semiotics – a unitary intensity. So how can the sheer *degree* of an intensity be said to generate two different semiotics, with all their qualitative and structural differences? What are the marks of these two, which apparently coalesce at the height of intensity when, at the same time, the height of intensity is thought to be what separates them? In search of an answer, we are inevitably led back to the foundations of these fluctuations of intensity, and the groundwork of this theory.

---

45 Klossowski, P. (1997). p. 60
46 Klossowski, P. (1997). p. 63
47 Klossowski, P. (1997). p. 114

2.3 Signifying Edifices

Klossowski provides a detailed, sequential account of the birth of signs from intensity, which any exploration of the groundwork of the semiotic must cognise.
1. *The tonality of the soul is a fluctuation of intensity.*
2. *In order for it to be communicable, the intensity must take itself as an object, and thus turn back on itself.*
3. *In turning back on itself, the intensity interprets itself. But how can it interpret itself? By becoming a counter-weight to itself; for this, the intensity must divide, separate from itself, and come back together. Now this is what happens to the intensity in what could be called moments of rise and fall; however, it is always the same fluctuation, a wave in the concrete sense (we might note, in passing, the importance of the spectacle of sea waves in Nietzsche's contemplations).*
4. *But does an interpretation presuppose the search for a "signification"? Rise and fall: these are "designations" and nothing else. Is there any signification beyond this observation of a rise and fall? Intensity never has any meaning other than that of being an intensity. In itself, the intensity seems to have no meaning. What is a meaning? And how can it be constituted? What is the agent of meaning?*
5. *The agent of meaning, and thus of signification, once again seems to be the intensity, depending on its various fluctuations. If intensity by itself has no meaning, other than that of being an intensity, how can it be the agent of signification, or be signified as this or that tonality of the soul? We asked above how it could interpret itself, and we answered that, in its risings and fallings, it had to act as a counterweight. But this was nothing more than a simple observation. How then does it acquire a meaning, and how is meaning constituted in the intensity? Precisely by turning back on itself, even in a new fluctuation! By turning back on itself and, as it were, repeating and, as it were, imitating itself, it becomes a sign.*
6. *But a sign is first of all the trace of a fluctuation of intensity. If a sign retains its meaning, it is because the degree of the intensity coincides with it; it signifies only through a new afflux of intensity, which in a certain manner joins up with its first trace.*
7. *But a sign is not only the trace of a fluctuation. It can also mark an absence of intensity – and here too, a new afflux is necessary, if only to signify this absence.*[48]

---

48 Klossowski, P. (1997). p. 61

What do these elaborate movements which appear in this passage – movements of rising and falling, of separation and rejoining – describe? Moments of rise and fall – peaks and troughs of fluctuating intensity – are the moments where signification is brought about. However, like objects, they do not in themselves signify anything, and cannot account for the self-interpreting or reflective aspect of intensity without anthropomorphism. Intensity is processual, and must "take itself as an object," declares Klossowski. As the foregoing passage states, any fluctuation of intensity in fact signifies through a triad: division, separation and rejoining. This is, however, a triad which establishes a quite unusual process. All three aspects of signification are relations of intensity to itself: it divides *itself*, separates *from itself* and rejoins *itself* once more.

Considering these aspects which appear within the text, we are confronted by the tension between two competing movements, which remain to be reconciled. On the one hand, signification is effected by division, separation and rejoining. On the other, it is established by repetition, the sign "repeating and, as it were, imitating itself."[49] Now, in the latter case, the intensity signifies only through repetition and self-imitation. Initially, then, there would seem to be no difference between the repetition and the repeated object: any sign is the closed repetition of a determinate element, and thus the recurrence of an identity. But with the proposition (6), this repetition is described as that of a *trace*. Since every trace instantiates, in whatever particular way, the *past* nature of its subject, there can be no question of a truly *identical* fluctuation appearing in the form of a trace. A completely, that is numerically, identical fluctuation would have to refuse any distinction between the trace and its provenance. For the trace to be a contentful notion, there must surely be some minimal difference between the fluctuation and its trace. This difference must be clarified, if the dynamic of division, separation and rejoining is to be reconciled with this vestigial repetition, for on the surface it is far from obvious how these two movements (which describe signification) might converge.

How, then, might this difference be clarified? Is a sign distinguished as a trace simply by its atrophied degree of "force" and "vivacity,"[50] just as Hume characterises a sensory impression in contrast to the idea which follows it? If so, the repetition of an element in and with the trace is simply marked by the relative faintness of its quality. Such would be an analogical conception of the relation between the trace and that of which it is the trace, in terms of their re-

---

49 Klossowski, P. (1997). p. 61
50 Hume, D. (1969). pp. 49–50

semblance. The two are in this sense continuous, in that they differ only in how faint they are, not by virtue of quality.

Klossowski does not provide an explicit definition of the term "trace" which plays such a central role in his theory of signs, but we find at least two remarks in the text of *Nietzsche and the Vicious Circle* in which a sign's appearance as a trace is explained in terms of its *incorporation* into an organised body: "The new excitations are filtered through the traces of prior excitations, which have already been absorbed."[51] "Every meditation that happens to us is only the trace of something prior, a 'pre-meditation' incorporated into ourselves – namely, a *pre-meditation of the now-useless acts* that have constituted us."[52] These remarks can shed useful light on our present examination of the trace. Here, the notion of a trace is distinguished from that of its subject by its incorporation into a body, a reservoir of fluctuations, gradually obsolescing. This explanation of the semiotics of the trace appeals to physiological factors which specify its role in structuring new excitations, in the manner of the neo-Kantianism of Muller and Helmholtz,[53] whereby the conditions of experience are prolonged into the sensory apparatus, qua physical, as opposed to transcendental, conditions. More importantly, however, is the chief implication of this physiological metaphor: All traces lie together dormant within the organism, but a fluctuation of intensity re-activates these traces *provided its degree* "coincides" with them, according to proposition (6). From this thesis it follows that if these signs and their traces populate Nietzsche's life-world and our reality, then the variety and diversity of our experience – from the visual to the sonorous, and tonalities and emotions – arises as a result of the *degree* of the intensity of the body in which they are incorporated. The intensity's degree, and thus its magnitude or quantity, produces quality; different degrees produce different qualities – a dynamic dramatised recognisably in Nietzsche's own life: the degree of intensity of his physical afflictions converted themselves into mental antagonisms, moods, attitudes and perceptual colourations, such as the unrelenting migraines which prompted sweeping re-evaluations of the premises of his entire existence. Thus, in one way following Bergson and in another way against him, we see in Klossowski the possibility of a quantity which engenders quality, and thus a fluctuation which is capable of activating any and all of experience depending on its degree. The degree of a fluctuation engenders experience itself. *The degree of the intensity is not merely quantity but its quality, and intensity is not of itself quality.*

---

51 Klossowski, P. (1997). p. 31
52 Klossowski, P. (1997). p. 256
53 Crary, J. (1995). p. 92

Consequently, a trace is *not* a qualitatively identical vestige of a prior excitation, in the manner of Hume's atrophied impressions masquerading as innate ideas, contra Descartes and Leibniz among others. The trace's signification is variable. It depends, both for its quality and to be activated at all, on the degree of the new intensity which activates it. There is a variability or multiplicity of meaning implied by the trace of the sign, which is polysemic, depending entirely on the degree of this new intensity. As a result, the initial signification may or may not be retained in its later signification. The trace is plucked from its *dormant* incorporation into an organised body and reactivated by the degree of intensity; otherwise, it fails to signify.

Given this interpretation of the sign and the trace, how can we account for the tripartite dynamic of division, separation and rejoining which is at the origin of fluctuation and thus signification? Even if this goes some way towards explaining the tendency of the sign to repeat itself or imitate itself through traces, how can this be reconciled with the other, competing view of the signs which flow from intensity – namely just such a dynamic? Reconciling these two definitions, or interpretations, means grasping the basis of the semiotic of intensity, and it is in light of this that its primary implications are exposed.

Division of intensity: In order to understand Klossowski's topological allusions, we must first ask a rudimentary question. If intensity is subject to a division, what does it divide *into*? *Between* what and what is it divided? "The sign is first of all the trace of a fluctuation of intensity."[54] From the conjunction of proposition (6) with (5), a sign (generated by this division) is not only a trace of a fluctuation of intensity, but is "first of all"[55] and so *intrinsically* such a trace. If a sign is generated by the fluctuation of intensity, through its trace, and if it does so initially through division, then this division must be a division into its trace: the intensity divides into itself and its own trace. It divides itself – but not into parts external to each other. Thus, in dividing, degrees of intensity fluctuate *within* intensity itself, "fluctuation within fluctuation,"[56] subject to internal, not external, relation. In this vein, Orfali, in *Fiction érogène à partir de Klossowski* provides a number of visual schemas which illustrate the way in which "undulating"[57] intensities alternate and sometimes fluctuate simultaneously. The text's claim that, "it is always a question of the same intensity,"[58] in this way owes to the fact that these degrees arise within intensity itself.

---

54 Klossowski, P. (1997). p. 61
55 Klossowski, P. (1997). p. 61
56 Klossowski, P. (1997). p. 62
57 Orfali, I. (1983). p. 297
58 Orfali, I. (1983). p. 62

As we will shortly argue, this production of signs through traces which are somehow internal to fluctuations has an abundance of consequences, and can be contrasted with a plurality of other well-known theories of meaning or sense. According to a number of scholars, signs are produced through an appropriate relation to objects which determine them, whether these objects are ideal, as are the mental objects which (it is said) confer meaning upon the propositions contemplated by the subject, or whether these objects are worldly objects.[59] In both cases, these determining objects are distinct from and external to the signs. In S. Laurence's formulation of a Chomskian account of sense, a sign or "utterance has a certain syntactic structure in virtue of being associated with a representation which has that structure, so it has a certain content or meaning in virtue of being associated with a representation which has that content or meaning."[60] This association holds between mental representations and propositional or semantic content. The content of an utterance is bestowed by a representation. Representations, in turn, are products of a combination of psycho-physical processes, ultimately bracketed from the analysis as an object of "empirical psycholinguistic research,"[61] instead. These processes are of a different "level"[62] to the representations they produce and the propositions, signs or utterances owing sense to them, and are thus distinct from and external to one another.

Wittgenstein's early philosophy exhibits this externality differently, by virtue of the picturing relation between states of affairs and elementary propositions. "The sign through which we express the thought I call the propositional sign. And the proposition is the propositional sign in its projective relation to the world."[63] Signs have meaning through the relation to propositions, which relate appropriately to states of affairs in the world. Here as elsewhere, the production of sense involves two independent strata: both the signs and their *relata*. Despite Klossowski's own tendencies to analogise the production of signs from intensities and their traces to Freudian physiological mechanisms, such as the binding of sensory excitations and filtration of subsequent stimuli through them, there is *no* fundamental reliance in his work on such underlying mechanisms. These remain peripheral, admittedly speculative, features. Intensities do not give birth to signs by virtue of their connection with physiological processes. Nor does signification depend on relations between independent and completely separable

---

59 Laurence, S. (1996). pp. 269–301
60 Laurence, S. (1996). pp. 269–301
61 Laurence, S. (1996). p. 283
62 Laurence, S. (1996). p. 284
63 Wittgenstein, L. (1922). 3.12

terms. It is rather the internal relation of the intensity to its trace, the result of its division, which leads to signification.

Separation of intensity: In dividing itself between itself and its own trace, the intensity separates from itself. In separating from itself, the intensity acquires a degree (and later, Klossowski's text will analyse the critical points implied by these degrees, the highest and lowest degrees, together with their implications for the doctrine of return and beyond). But, initially, how does this separation lead to the traits of self-imitation, repetition and self-interpretation, and what are these traits? If separation is the result of division, and division occurs between the intensity and its own trace, intensity's separation from itself is the activation of this trace as a sign, and thus the intensity's own repetition by this sign. For Nietzsche, this separation lies at the origin of the organic world:

> Just as organs develop in multiple ways from a single organ, such as the brain and the nervous system from the epidermis, so it was necessary for all feeling, representing, and thinking to have been *one* at the beginning: sensation is thus an isolated *late* phenomenon. This *unity* must exist in the inorganic: for the organic begins by *separation*.[64]

Separation, moreover, seems to furnish an answer to the question posed at the beginning of this section: how can a difference of degree produce two *qualitatively* and *structurally* different semiotics? If Klossowski extols profound differences between the institutional code and the authentic expression of fluctuations – which ultimately produce differing ethical and metaphysical theses – then how can the mere degree of intensity explain the differences between them? Intensity's *separation* from itself provides a preliminary resolution. Although the semiotic of intensity initially undermines the external relation of signs to the source of their meaning, the dynamic of separation provides a natural account of this relation. With Wittgenstein's as with Laurence's expository view, a relation to an external determinant is needed, whether states of affairs which underwrite primitive logical propositions or psycho-physical processes which elicit mental representations. The separation of intensity from itself may seem to accommodate a similar view. Although intensity is not as distinct from the signs whose meaning it confers as are the determinants appealed to by these scholars – with signs being the traces of intensity to begin with, and accordingly not so strictly external and separate – it admits of one important parallel: it signifies relationally, by relating to a trace. By way of illustration, Nietzsche's recollections (traces) of stable health constituted the meaning of the urges he recorded in order to recuperate from his severe bouts of illness – as well as the meaning of

---

[64] Klossowski, P. (1997). p. 34

his descriptions of his suffering as his own, as opposed to those of a fleeting alter ego – as, perhaps, the trace of satiety underpins the meaning of the image of nourishment in the starving man's imagination. The notion of a trace thus embodies the relatedness commonly upheld to impart sense. Translated into the terms of the Nietzschean semiotic, then, Wittgenstein's relations of propositional "pictures" to the world become relations to traces of sensory excitations, as Laurence's mental representations are replaced by memories. *Prima facie*, separation thus suggests a bridge between the two semiotics, recovering features of traditional theories of sense whilst remaining embedded in the circular dynamic of intensity.

There is, however, an antinomy camouflaged in the discussion of separation and signification. Separation is, by Klosowski's hypothesis, the point at which intensity acquires a degree. Of the notions mobilised for this argument – division, separation and re-unification – the second is the only one immediately amenable to a determination of degree: two things, in the most general possible sense, which are separate can have the "degree" of their separation measured in a way that things which divide themselves or rejoin cannot (at least, not so readily). The indispensable role that the notion of degree commands in Klossowski's account might, then, be thought to enter at this point: the separation, however this is ultimately interpreted, of intensity from itself imparts to it its degree. Consider, however, the incompossible roles that this degree must play in the formation of two inconsistent kinds of signification. If the separation of intensity recreates an "ordinary" or representational semiotic, in which relations of external terms constitutes sense, the degree of intensity (as separation) correlates with this semiotic. Degree is proportional, so to speak, to the extent to which the institutional code is in effect. However, Klossowski is also explicit that, to the contrary, it is at the strongest moments of intensity that the authentic semiotic of fluctuations emerges, and is ultimately incarnated in the vicious circle. Degree is both proportional and inversely proportional to the institutional code, and both proportional and inversely proportional to the authentic semiotic – an incoherence which stymies the distinction between the two. Yet this distinction is the ground of Klossowski's entire method.

It is not until the elaboration of the vicious circle later on in the study that a resolution of these problems surfaces. At this stage, we can conclude only that the *separation* of intensity is the point of entry for the notion of degree or quantity in Klossowski's theory, and that it is at this point that his innovations to these notions begin.

Rejoining of intensity: Finally, the intensity subsides and vanishes into its own trace. In conclusion, if intensities are taken to be productive of signification, then Klossowski's semiotic is characterised by the *manifestation of the fluctua-*

tion as its own trace: insofar as it signifies, the fluctuation arises as the trace of itself.

2.4 The Three-fold Structure of Signification: Klossowski and Peirce

Klossowski was not the first to suggest that signification admits a triadic structure, as he does in evoking the three-fold dynamic of division, separation and rejoining. Decades prior, C. S. Peirce advanced such a structure in his theory of the sign as a medium of determination. The theory involves an object and an interpretant in a way that anticipates *Nietzsche and the Vicious Circle* in several surprising respects.

In order to grasp the relevant points of comparison between these two semiotics, we must consider the groundwork of Peirce's approach. Consider the following two remarks which define the Peircean sign, first of all as, "any medium for the communication or extension of a Form (or feature). Being medium, it is determined by something, called its Object, and determines something, called its Interpretant or Interpretand,"[65] or as that which "is so determined by something else, called its Object, and so determines an effect upon a person, which effect I call its interpretant, that the latter is thereby mediately determined by the former."[66]

There is a chain of determination passing from an object to the subject: the object determines the subject through the medium of the sign. The sign is determined by the object and the subject by the sign; the sign is both determined and determining. The effect of the sign on the subject, the interpretant, is the medium of the subject's determination. Nietzsche's semiotic is not, therefore, in any straightforward way analogical to Peirce's, for in that of the former the sign is in no way determined by an object – neither by virtue of a causal link, nor by virtue of truth functions. However, the theory of signs articulated in Klossowski's work has at least its triadic structure in common with this Peircean approach, and in both cases this structure leads to an additional commonality: infinite semiosis flows from the sign's self-interpreting tendency.

---

65 Peirce, C. S. (1998). pp. 477–478
66 Peirce, C. S. (1998). pp. 477–478

2.5 Infinite Semiosis

In Eco's exposition of Peirce, a prominent position is accorded to infinite semiosis, or infinite semiotic regression. The sign determines an interpretant, and is determined by the object. However, as much as the determination of the subject by the sign is itself subject to a mediation via the interpretant, it is less the sign than the *signification* of the sign that mediates this determination – that is, the sign insofar as it signifies. The determination of the subject is the interpretant of the sign, as an interpretant which interprets the sign's signification: "the sign not only determines the interpretant to represent (or to take the form of) the *object*, but also determines the interpretant to represent the sign."[67] The relation between the object and the subject requires a sign, but the sign in turn requires its own interpretation.

Further, Peirce is explicit that, by virtue of this interpretation undertaken by the interpretant, the interpretant itself becomes a sign. "A sign, or representamen ... creates in the mind of that person an equivalent sign, or perhaps a more developed sign. That sign which it creates I call the interpretant of the first sign."[68]

Peirce's description of the interpretant as a sign is the entry point of a noteworthy idiosyncrasy in his system, namely infinite semiosis. There are three distinct propositions which, taken together, imply this characteristic:[69]

(I)   A sign is a sign only if it determines an interpretant.
(II) All interpretants are signs.
(III) All signs are interpretants of prior signs.[70]

In case of scepticism about quite what the above triplet has to do with infinite semiosis, their relationship may be illustrated in the following way. Given these propositions, we may postulate a chain of signs, ordered by proximity to their determining object, of unknown length, finite or infinite. If finite, there will be both a first and last sign in the chain of signs. The last sign in the chain must determine a later sign by virtue of (I) and (II), yet it cannot if it is to count as the last. The first sign in the chain must interpret a previous sign by virtue of thesis (III), yet it cannot if it is to count as the first. Thus, not

---

67 Peirce, C. S. (1998). p. 478
68 Peirce, C. S. (1998). p. 228; Logos Group (2014)
69 Atkin, A. (2013).
70 Eco, U. (1983). p. 189

only must the chain fail to be finite in the prescribed sense; there can be neither an initial nor a final link which could limit its length: an infinite chain of signs.

In Klossowski, the role of such a chain is even more central than it is in Peirce, its existence guaranteed by the very definition of the sign. Every sign is a *trace* of a fluctuation of intensity.[71] It cannot signify outside of the constraint imposed by fluctuations of intensity, so it is intensity alone which fabulates meaning, once its degree coalesces with the trace:

> If a sign retains its meaning, it is because the degree of intensity coincides with it.[72]
>
> It signifies only through a new afflux of intensity, which in a certain manner joins up with its first trace.[73]

The first of these two theses states the conditions under which meaning is preserved: it must coincide with a degree of intensity. Without this coincidence, the sign means nothing, or anything at all, given another coincidence with another afflux. Signification is thus dependent entirely on the conditions of intensity, as fluctuations which each effect their own interpretation. Signs bear an unspecified, ultimate relation to intensity by virtue of which they are determined, just as do those of Peirce's theory to their objects, but there is no element in the signifying chain which is in a direct or one-to-one such relation. Each intensity which stirs up a prior intensity's trace brings about its signification, but has in turn its own trough which suppresses this signification. There is thus no element which terminates this chain, and signification is by nature dependent on the immanence and fortuity of fluctuation (a result which later in this work will be developed into a deflationary theory of selfhood). Thus, whereas Peircean semiosis is *countably* infinite, positing an unlimited chain of units, this semiosis is *uncountably* and indefinitely so.

2.6 Metasemiosis and Order

In both semiotics, we find a distinction of order between different kinds of signs, furnishing a conception of metasemiosis. In Peirce, this manifests itself as the organisation of signs in a hierarchy, in as much as "any interpretant of a given sign, being in its turn and under other circumstances a sign, becomes tem-

---

71 Klossowski, P. (1997). p. 61
72 Klossowski, P. (1997). p. 61
73 Klossowski, P. (1997). p. 61

porarily a metasemiotic construction acting (for that occasion only) as *explicans* of the interpreted *explicatum* and being in its turn interpreted by another interpretant."[74] All interpretants of given signs are signs themselves, but signs which explain the first signs' relations to their objects. The interpretant specifies a subclass of features proper to the sign it interprets which imbue the sign's relation to another sign, and thus the object. This specification is a necessary condition for signification, since, as A. Atkin notes, not all features of an object will be germane to its capacity as a sign – just as the various fortuitously juxtaposed afflictions Nietzsche experienced were to quite different degrees harbingers of his underlying condition, each illness a complex of more or less symptomatic afflictions.[75] "On the whole, I am happier now than I have ever been in my life. And yet, continual pain; for many hours of the day, a sensation closely akin to seasickness, a semi-paralysis that makes it difficult to speak, alternating with furious attacks."[76] The symptoms of illness manifested themselves as sensations: these sensations were signs – rhematic-iconic-qualisigns, according to the Peircean typology – determined by an object, namely the disease or affliction of which they were the results. The interpretant(s) of these signs, such as seasickness, serve to strip out other elements of the composite sensation and reduce it to a kind of nausea. In so doing, this interpretant focuses the subject – Nietzsche – on the peculiar sensation's connection to an enteric sickness, allowing it to function as a sign of a determinate illness. Thus, with each sign in the chain referring to elements of another order in order to sift germane from redundant features, a dynamic hierarchy is introduced – a dynamism which appears to Eco as a means of dispensing with a finite set of constructions whose permutations and combinations constitute an expression's content, in the mode of a compositional analysis.[77] Thus, the Peircean chain of signs, each functioning as interpretant of its predecessor, is no succession of appendices, but rather introduces metasemiosis through its hierarchisation of signs.

In Klossowski's approach, as we have seen, signification is the re-excitation of an intensity's trace. This re-excitation is effected by a new afflux of intensity. These affluxes depend on the degree of the intensity. Since it is, then, by the degree of this afflux that it "joins up"[78] with the trace, intensities are not *external* to one another in events of signification. All signification remains an internal element belonging to intensity: the nature of the signs generated by intensity de-

---

[74] Eco, U. (1983). p. 189
[75] Atkin A. (2013).
[76] Klossowski, P. (1997). p. 20
[77] Eco, U. (1983). p. 176
[78] Klossowski, P. (1997). p. 61

pends on the latter's degree. Nietzsche's sensations of illness, fluctuating with the degree of their intensity, merged with the traces of his previous kinetosis, thus forming an interpretation of the meaning of these sensations, as signs and therefore symptoms of an illness, enabling his self-diagnosis. Just as, in Peirce's system, each successive interpretant in the chain of signs which approaches their object *selects* a *subset* of its predecessor's features, and in doing so establishes its connection to the object – so, in Klossowski's system, the degree of the intensity determines which of its features signify, and thus merge with its trace. In both cases, the signifying elements are internal to the signs they interpret. Conversely, each sign depends on its descendant for its signification. This fact, the internality of signification to intensity, will become a rich source of metaphysical insight as Klossowski develops his argument and begins to apply the semiotic of intensity beyond the philosophy of language.

2.7 Final Interpretant, Mediate Phantasm

Despite that both semiotics avow in one way or another infinite semiosis, it is in the ramifications of this principle that they begin to diverge, as they confront the respective problems of how an infinite chain of signs can maintain a relation with an object, and a relation with an intensity. The infinite chains and infinite subdivisions, acknowledged by both to be a principal corollary of their theory, end up obscuring the way in which signs connect to their objects. First of all, according to Klossowski, signs are only ever traces of intensity. Intensity fluctuates, producing signs by virtue of its degree. Different degrees of intensity, different fluctuations, diversify sense and meaning. But if the signs produced by intensity are only ever traces of intensity, signs can never signify intensity itself – that is, in a direct or unmediated fashion, as elementary facts do states of affairs, or thoughts do mental representations. There is thus a cleft between the production or genesis of signs and the way in which they are, or are not, determined to signify this or that. Secondly, with the Peircean approach, the analogue of this cleft is the infinite length of the chain of interpretants interposed between subject and object. According to Peirce, the object determines the signs which interpret it, yet this chain seems never to terminate, either in a terminating interpretation or the final "dynamic" object. As Eco questions, "How can one link a sign to an object, since in order to recognize an object one needs a previous experience of it?"[79] The object endlessly recedes before endlessly supplementary interpretants.

---

[79] Eco, U. (1983). p. 191

Signs appear only to lead to further signs which they interpret, never to acquire such a determining relation to an object as would be required for reference or denotation. This is therefore a direct consequence of the infinite semiosis openly evinced by Peirce and, in the case of his 20th-Century Continental counterpart, a related claim – that the division of intensity yields traces internal to it, as opposed to referring to objects outside of it.

Remarkably, and by way of response to these difficulties, the conceptual role of the phantasm surfaces *in both* authors' texts as the form of perpetually *deferred signification*. The phantasm, one of the fundamental elements in Klossowski's conceptual arsenal, is not confined to his work. As Eco observes of Peirce's,

> What remains to be asked is how, in the philosophy of a thinker who calls himself a Scots realist, there can be something such as an infinite semiotic regression, the object which has determined the sign never being apparently determined by it, if not in the *phantasmatic* form of Immediate Object [emphasis added].[80]

Eco appeals to a distinction between two interpretations of the object in Peirce, and thus to two conceptions of the manner in which the sign relates to its determinant. The dynamic object of the outer world is the object "of which a sign is a sign."[81] By contrast, the immediate object is a semiotic construction and the mere object of a sign; this sign is a direct object, and thus possibly another sign. Were the latter object to be the only object determining a given sign, its determination would be purely *phantasmatic*, constituted in the endless deferment of signification in the chain, by virtue of succeeding signs' specification of their predecessors' signifying elements. But how could an infinite chain of interpretant-signs which never reach their dynamic object nonetheless be determined by it? Would they not be determined simply by the object which is most immediate or by nothing at all? And in Nietzsche a correlative question arises: how can a sign be a trace *of* intensity absent the fluctuation of this originary intensity? How can an infinite series of re-excitations of traces be anything more than traces of traces? Despite the contortions undergone by the impulses in their production of signification, the phantasm remains beyond signs.

> The phantasm – the phantasmic coherence of the agent with a determined impulse – is thus produced at the *limit-point* where this impulse is turned *into a thought (of this impulse)* ... But nothing of the phantasm remains in the *idea* thus transmitted, or rather created according to totally different dimensions.[82]

---

[80] Eco, U. (1983). p. 191
[81] Eco, U. (1983). p. 193
[82] Klossowski, P. (1997). p. 260

The obsessional tendency which compels the phantasm to signify can effect only ever a fraudulent exchange between impulse and sign, and even in this compulsion the phantasm remains a mute and obstinate singularity. "The singular case *disappears* as such as soon as it *signifies* what it is *for itself*."[83] The phantasm is thus depicted as incommunicable and unrepresentable in Klossowski's work.

With Peirce – at least, as relayed in Eco's account – the phantasm stands for the *replacement* of a direct relation to the *dynamic* object with an endlessly supplementary relation to the *immediate* object, thus a counterfeited objectivity. In Klossowski's account of Nietzsche, it stands for the ineluctable fraudulence and inadequacy of any sign which might attempt to give a faithful or final interpretation of intensity. In both cases, the phantasm marks the absence of the source of meaning. But whereas in Klossowski this absence is fundamental, in Eco it is surmounted by the final interpretant: an associative habit or tendency, acquired through repetition, which drives a series of reactions to an object: "In this way the apparent opposition between the intensional semantics of infinite semiotic regression and the extensional semantics of reference to Dynamic Objects is solved."[84]

The conciliation between the divergent conceptions of the phantasmic in these two texts is visible in Peirce's own writings. As far as the object of representation is concerned, Peirce states, "The meaning of a representation ... is nothing but the representation itself conceived as stripped of irrelevant clothing. But this clothing never can be completely stripped off; it is only changed for something more *diaphanous* [emphasis added]."[85] Diaphanousness is the characteristic of the decreasing ratio of unsignifying to signifying elements over successive signs in the chain – a characteristic Klossowski assigns to Nietzsche's euphoria of Turin, in which the vestiges of intensive fluctuations all underwent activation by the apparently unparalleled intensity of Nietzsche's phantasm of return: "The landscape of Turin, the monumental squares, the promenades along the Po River, were bathed in a kind of 'Claude Lorraine' luminosity, a diaphanousness that removed the weight of things."[86] Just as successive interpretants in the Peircean chain progressively specify its signifying features by stripping out redundant material, so the diaphanousness Nietzsche experienced reactivated other traces, and removed the resistance of the signs which, ordinarily, conceals their origin in prior fluctuations.

---

83 Klossowski, P. (1997). p. 261
84 Eco, U. (1983). pp. 192–193
85 Peirce, C. S. (1997). p. 339
86 Klossowski, P. (1997). p. 251

2.8 Klossowski and Peirce: A Comparison

What can we conclude from these analogies between the two semiotics? Both thinkers operate with a triadic model: in Peirce, with the sign, its object and its interpretant, and in Klossowski with intensity's division into traces, separation and rejoining. Despite undeniable differences in the ways in which these triads' members relate, they lead to a slew of shared results. Both are committed to infinite semiosis – the deferral of signification along an infinite chain of signs. They both posit a hierarchical structure to such a chain, which is described as metasemiosis by Eco. The signs' connection to their objects is labelled phantasmatic as a result. In all these cases, the signs and what determine them – polymorphous intensity in Klossowski, chains of interpretants in Peirce – in some way exchange positions with one another.

Returning to the framework of Klossowski, we have that the provenance of signs lies in fluctuations of intensity, which signify by dividing, separating and rejoining. Yet, as was noted before, this dynamic manifests itself in two *competing* semiotics, depending on its degree: not only the infinite metasemiosis verticalised in a hierarchy, nor the phantasmic deferment of signification – both shared with Peirce's model – but also the institutional code of everyday signs. If we accept the contention that "Nietzsche's obsessive thought had always been that events, actions, apparent decisions, and indeed the entire world have a completely different aspect from those that they have taken on, from the beginning of time, in the sphere of language"[87] it remains for this latter aspect, or aspects, to be clearly articulated in order to properly exhibit the difference between the two. Indeed, the emphasis Klossowski places on *communicability* and its origin is of critical significance, as it demonstrates the *philosophical* content of Nietzsche's project, as a theory capable of accounting for representation, thought, and the external world (albeit restyled as gregarious socialisation). How, then, does this institutional code emerge from intensity?

The text consistently describes the institutional code in terms of its two predominant effects on intensity: abbreviation and falsification.

2.9 Abbreviation

Principally, the code of everyday signs arises as an abbreviation of fluctuation. This abbreviation has what Klossowski describes as an intrinsically economic

---

87 Klossowski, P. (1997). p. 251

status, originating in exchange and assimilation. Given a certain fluctuation of intensity, the code specifies which signs stand in for the fluctuation. If we take the definition of a sign as a trace of a prior fluctuation, this economy of abbreviation is an obvious consequence, a trace being ossified, a distillation of the relevant fluctuation. Unequivocally, the criteria employed by the code as a basis for a given "selection" are the pure results of experiment, namely of fortuity – which will feature further on, in Nietzsche's attempt to bring about the collapse of deterministic metaphysics. But if, for themselves, fluctuations of intensity rise and fall, dividing and rejoining, according to their own dynamic, what kind of synthetic or reductive faculty is required for a series of fluctuations to be condensed into a smaller number of signs? A sign condenses all the traces of an intensity into one object. In an act of recognition – in Nietzsche's case, perhaps the recognition of a particular sensation, or landscape, or physical ailment – the functioning sign abbreviates a vast set of experiences into a single cognitive or impulsive act. Since such signs are by nature "comparable,"[88] this dynamic must pass from different, particular experiences at different places and times to a collection of similar experiences undergirding a general rule or law. Only through this passage could it give rise to the kind of criteria for selection capable of reducing the singularity and incomparability of intensity to something stereotypical – that is, a set of features which enable its comparison with, and equation to, other things.

Being a thinker concerned with regularity – how associations can be made between recognisably similar experiences, and indeed how two experiences can be cognisably similar at all – locates Nietzsche as a protagonist of a traditional metaphysical problem, gravitating around Hume and Kant as its prototypical theoreticians. Intensities themselves are repeatedly described as singular cases,[89] incommunicable and unexchangeable.[90] What kind of code could ever arise from these, and allow singularities to be compared with one another? Nietzsche is confronted with the problem of explaining the existence of comparable features (and, indeed, the existence of an organism sufficiently retentive to be capable of comparison at all) in terms of fluctuations which come and go – a quite different predicament to that of Kant, who made recourse to the transcendental.

The code in question arises as the product of "a long experimentation with the similar and the dissimilar, and thus with identity."[91] This experimentation

---

[88] Klossowski, P. (1997). p. 45
[89] Klossowski, P. (1997). p 79
[90] Klossowski, P. (1997). p. 77
[91] Klossowski, P. (1997). p. 45

concerns the relationship of a given organism to fluctuations of intensity, often modelled as excitations. As to this relationship, it is instructive to examine Freud's account of the development of the organism's powers to interpret these excitations (a domain in which the connections between Nietzsche and Freud are at their most profound, seeing as fluctuations of intensity do in many ways resemble excitations occurring within an organism). Freud's account conceives the initial state of an organism as that of an undifferentiated vesicle which relatively passively receives and transmits micro-aggressive stimulations originating outside it.[92] The outer surfaces of the organism will invariably be subjected to the most frequent and most severe stimulations, and will thus most rapidly be fashioned into a form "receptive" to these excitations, building an accumulated imperviousness to future aggressions. The organism prefers protection against stimuli to reception. Thus, the organism's nervous system is fundamentally defensive, dedicated to maximising its protection. The sensory apparatus is, for instance, protected by an expired outer cortical layer, retreating to the interior of the organism to which weakened stimulations are transmitted, via the nervous system, having been filtered through the protective layer. In aiming at its own receptivity as well as its own protection, the organism becomes progressively less susceptible to future modification.

Although it would be inappropriate to unthinkingly extract and crudely import this model into Nietzsche's writings from Freud's, not least in view of the host of assumptions made by Freud which are problematised actively in the theory of the vicious circle: that the inside and the outside are primordially discriminable, and that the outside is the predominant source of sensations which the organism experiences as an aggressive encroachment (although Freud also extends this model to excitations originating in the organism's interior)[93] – nonetheless, drawing upon Freud's account of the evolution of the sensory apparatus, conceived as an artifice for the processing of excitations – whether inner or outer – we can glean the thesis that the comparability of intensities made possible by signs results from the following two processes: firstly, its filtration through the apparatus which effectively subdues it, in the interest of self-preservation; secondly, its conduction along the same path carved out by other excitations. Summarily, repeated stimulation leads to a reduction of the degree of subsequent intensities, which are then processed according to the passage of previous ones. This, then, provides the foundation for the abbreviation of a fluctuating impulse. In associating with a fluctuation a particular sign in the code, we impose upon it

---

92 Freud, S. (2015). p. 20
93 Klossowski, P. (1997). p. 251

the same schema as other fluctuations – excitations – traversed, whether originating outside or inside the subject organism. Each sign in the code corresponds to a transmission along a familiar path – a path worn in by former excitations – and thus a trace, making possible the *comparability* of intensities with others. This is the first aspect of Klossowski's both Freudian and Nietzschean description of the abbreviation of signs.

The substitution of a sign drawn from the institutional code for a fluctuation *staticises*[94] this fluctuation:

> The impulses which confront and interpret each other through their fluctuations of intensity ... create forms out of these movements and gestures, and cannot be distinguished from this invention of signs, which stabilizes them through abbreviation. For in abbreviating them, these signs reduce the impulses, apparently suspending their fluctuation once and for all.[95]

This effect is the decisive point of divergence between the institutional or anthropic code of signs and the semiotic intrinsic to intensities. This principle can be summarised in the following form:

The code eliminates fluctuation once and for all. (Principle of Stasis)

By contrast, Nietzsche's semiotic, and his phantasm of vicious circularity, requires that "nothing ever succeeds in getting constituted in a single meaning, once and for all."[96] In which respects does exchanging something in fluctuation for a sign belonging to the code entail eliminating it? In Klossowski's text, the ubiquitous references to the "once and for all" can be consolidated into a more precise term: the permanence which is due to the suspension of fluctuation.

> The classic rule of morality ... makes humanity dependent on habits adopted *once and for all*. Instead, we must behave in accordance with the strict demands that ... arise in an unforeseeable manner ... Behaviour can never be limited by its regular repetition, nor can thinking limit itself ... In reality, any thought that experiences the uneasiness of this provisional state reveals its own lassitude. By contrast, any thought that allows itself to be called into question, whether by an internal or external event, reveals a certain capacity for starting over.[97]

This description of certain phenomena as "once and for all" applies to the code's abbreviating role in three respects: it establishes a kind of *index*, and converts

---

[94] Dries, M. (2008). pp. 1–19
[95] Klossowski, P. (1997). p. 48
[96] Klossowski, P. (1997). p. 64
[97] Klossowski, P. (1997). p. 4

fluctuations of intensity into something *spatial* and *extensive*. We analyse each in turn.

Indexation: Abbreviation by a sign of the code amounts to an act of indexation: a map which associates a specific location with a given fluctuation. How does the code of signs establish this index? In doing so, it must be able to select from a range of arbitrary and indefinite fluctuations and interpret them in a definite manner, so as to allocate a permanent signification – one allocated "once and for all." Hypertrophied desires for specific objects, organised into a routine, simulate the disquietude occurring at the level of fractious impulses, which in reality have no aim at all. These become the permanent significance of these impulses' movements, suitably reduced and contained within a coherent goal or wish. "What type of discourse can reconcile 'coherence' with the fact of the impulses? ... How could Nietzsche translate the arbitrary freedom of the unintelligible depth into a *persuasive* constraint?"[98] The index which eternalises signification must assign an exclusive specificity. "It is therefore necessary for this form to reproduce – under the constraint of the impulses and in a completely *desultory* manner – the discontinuity that intervenes between the coherence of the intellect and the incoherence of the impulses."[99] An intensity must be assigned one location which is not others, just as Nietzsche's abruptly separated aphorisms result from his varying degrees of lucidity and delirium, indexed by the code to specific series of expressions. Thus, for instance, his fleeting triumphs over illness and morbidity were converted into fragments of arguments for the identity of sickness and health.

The specificity of the result of this map is an integral feature of the index; were fluctuations to map to signs in anything other than a definite manner, they could never signify once and for all. As a result of this specificity, though, certain fluctuations have certain locations. In this regard, this specificity is the meaning of Klossowski's "once and for all" descriptions – having a definite location in time or space, and occurring as this rather than that, here rather than there, or now rather than then. Significations always admit a given location, defined at the very least by their relations to other significations: in the case of objects represented in space, their distances from other objects; in the case of written signs, the separation between words (or general units of syntax); in the case of speech, the position or status of the addressee. The code thus amounts to a mapping, assigning to a given fluctuation a definite, non-fluctuating position

---

98 Klossowski, P. (1997). p. 255
99 Klossowski, P. (1997). p. 255

in an edifice of signification, be it verbal, written or representational in some other way.

Given, however, that intensities are clearly not definite objects, this map cannot be regarded as a function on these impulses, in the way, for instance, that logical atomism attempts to iteratively define a language in terms of functions on elementary propositions, in turn defined by effectively functional correspondences (isomorphisms) to elementary sense-data. Fluctuations of intensity do not populate a limited domain; nor is there any specificity about when they do or do not fluctuate. Nonetheless, this inscrutability is eliminated by the code's indexation. (This act of indexation might, in a certain way, be regarded as the issuance of a *time-stamp*, for now – its properly temporal content is the subject of a separate chapter.) This indexation is one of the first chief aspects of the institutional code.

Spatiality: By assigning definite and specific locations to the signs which originate from fluctuations, the code arranges them in space.[100] Klossowski is explicit that the institutional code is at the origin of images (or representations, understood as images): "Every living being interprets according to a code of signs … Whence come *images:* representations of *what has taken place* or *what could have taken place.*"[101] Only because of the effects of the code do fluctuations form images. Visual experience is thus just such a representation produced as the intensities reach degrees of excitation. Defined in such a broad way, the code of signs includes representations such as Kantian intuitions, which, *a priori*, make possible relations between bodies in space such as exteriority and adjacency. In Nietzsche's Nachlass, the *Zeitatomenlehre* or Time-Atom Theory fragment offers a detailed explanation of the way in which spatiality emerges from fluctuations brought about by discontinuous time-points, which Klossowski does not see fit to analyse in detail. Most important for his purposes, however, is Nietzsche's evident commitment to the view that fluctuations are reduced and stabilised by language to the point where adjacency, direction, and other relations between bodies which constitute a primitive intuition of space can be conferred. Thus, intensities considered in themselves, are pre-spatial, and do not admit description in space, but are gathered, organised and presented together by the institutional code – disparate intensities or elements of intensities are brought alongside one another and thus spatialised.

---

100 Space in this context cannot be understood by comparing and contrasting it to time. The relation between these two categories is untypical in this context, not least since the institutional codification itself contains a determination of time, and so the spatialization it brings about can hardly be opposed to it.
101 Klossowski, P. (1997). p. 47

Extensity: The code relates intensity to extensity. Above, several definitions of intensity were supplied, in opposition to extensity:

(i)   as the unity of a sensation
(ii) as quality, unassimilable to space;
(iii) as confused;
(iv) as divisible only with qualitative change;
(v)   as subsuming a hierarchy.

Extensity is defined accordingly:

(vi)   as the plurality of a sensation, or its unity being possible only under synthesis;
(vii) as quantity, assimilable to space;
(viii) as distinct;
(ix)   as divisible without qualitative change
(x)   as subsuming no hierarchy.

These aspects of the code follow from the spatial character of signs, and from the specificity of the association of fluctuations with locations. If the code is able to furnish a space, then the signs of the code (as the range of the map) are assimilable to space. In Kantian metaphysics, for instance, a set of intensive sensations organised by the *a priori* (spatial) form of intuition can be interpreted as a codifying structure which leads to spatial intuitions – the signs related in a now-extensive spatial medium. Abbreviation does not, therefore, refer to a diminution of an already-extensive quantity, but rather the conversion of an intensity into an extensity, an abbreviation not by virtue of its *comparative* extension, but rather its having extension at all.

It is in these respects, then, that the institutional code appears to eliminate fluctuation once and for all, in an act of an abbreviation. Conceived as skepsis, Nietzsche's thought aggressively confronts the distortion, or falsification, of intensity effected by an agent's consciousness, on behalf of institutional significations. However, abbreviation (or reduction, suspension or staticisation) is not the only symptom of the distorting effect that Klossowski alleges takes place as a result of the code in the second chapter of his study. Among its chief aspects is, in addition, the reduction of intensities to intentional states: "Intensities take on a signification [for consciousness] only if they are first reduced, by the abbreviating system, to the intentional states of the agent."[102]

---

[102] Klossowski, P. (1997). p. 49

Given that an intention is directionally or vectorially structured, what topological effect needs to be exerted to transform a fluctuation into an intention? According to one of the originators of the modern conception of intentionality, Brentano, "every mental phenomenon is characterized by ... reference to a content, direction to an object,"[103] a definition which may be thought to entail a distinction between the intentional mental state and its referent. However, need we assume that this object be distinct from the reference or directedness towards it in the mental phenomenon? If so, giving a derivation of an intention from fluctuation would involve explaining how something unitary could produce the appearance of a duality. Avoiding any loss of generality, however, and simply assuming this directedness is sufficient as a definition of intentionality, the explanatory challenge remains as follows: How can reference emerge from sense, in Nietzsche's sense?

> By what measure can we say that the agent is '*conscious*' of not speaking, of remaining silent, of acting or not acting, of deciding or remaining undecided? Only in terms of a more or less *unequal exchange* between the impulses and the signs of the everyday code. But is not the agent unconscious of what these impulses are willing for themselves? Hence the inequality of the exchange, and the fact that the impulses lose out in the transaction: an *intention* is formed through the signs – minus their impulsive intensity. The intensity oscillates while thought as such is being formed, but once the declaration is produced, it is reduced to the inertia of signs.[104]

The crucial derivation of a notion of intentionality from fluctuation can be located in this passage. The intensity oscillates while thought is being formed: a fluctuation is replaced by an intention with a defined end. Whether this end is an object, desire, decision or "declaration," a direction and finality is imposed on the fluctuation. As a result, it takes on the inertia of signs – whether these signs are linguistic, and spoken or written, or non-linguistic. Aside from these signs, however, the intensity only ever oscillates. Thus far, the replacement of intensity by intention seems to be a simple restatement of the *abbreviation* effected by signs and the principle of stasis: intensity fluctuates, but in the regime of signs it becomes stable. There is, however, another aspect to intentionality: an "unequal exchange," or loss of content, not least because intensity is, as per the above recapitulation and summary, by nature indefinite and thus unamenable to definite exchange. There is always more in the foam of intensity than in its fabricated equivalent. Nietzsche himself claims that intention results from the

---

103 Brentano, F. (2009). p. 68
104 Klossowski, P. (1997). p. 37

selection of a subset of the components of an event.[105] The premonitory fluctuations which excite the desire for an object, which lead to the subject's interpretation of itself as existing in a certain state, which allow it to formulate a description of this or that object, or which ultimately produce an action which manifests an intention of whatever sort – all of these become mendacities, by virtue of the loss of content which occurs between the fluctuation and its moment of surfacing in consciousness.

From a structural perspective, can these results be reconciled with Klossowski's topological reflections on the nature of fluctuations of intensity? In dividing and separating from itself, before rejoining – the movements of fluctuation – the intensity takes on a microcosm of an intentional structure: although referring only to itself, it nonetheless sets up a rudimentary kind of reference by virtue of being separated from itself. This (the point of division and separation) is the only point in the fluctuation of intensity where there exists the kind of *difference* which could stir up a goal or desire at the level of representation. Intentionality, then, seems to be related to the splitting and self-repelling proclivity of intensity. It is not, however, until Klossowski's appropriation of Nietzsche's philosophy against the category of causality is fully developed that the reasons for the attack on intentionality can be pronounced fully. In the early stages of his text, and directly following the description of the semiotic of intensity, the remarks on intentionality remain prolegomena.

2.10 Signs and Genesis

In review, then, there is not only one semiotic in the ambit of Klossowski's study, but two: both (i) fluctuations of intensity and (ii) the institutional code of signs. The second differentiates itself from the first as a difference in degree and not of kind, hence the parasitism of which the code stands accused, emerging only as an *abbreviation or falsification* – and an abbreviation or falsification *of* intensity. But there is a further difference between the two, analysed extensively in the text, which is embedded in Nietzsche's typology of morals, and which is not derivable from these other characteristics. Not only in assessing the possibility of formulating his own hypotheses in the only available terms (the code of signs), but also as a means of interrogating the fluctuating and predominantly morbid states he was unable to avoid himself, Nietzsche established two oppositions: morbid vs. healthy signs or impulses and singular vs. gregarious ones.

---

[105] Klossowski, P. (1997). p. 51

The former opposition allowed Nietzsche to carry out a diagnosis of the affects, desires and traits of his own organism, with the latter providing, at first, the terms for this diagnosis. Whereas the singular states of the organism are its own incommunicable impulses, unassimilable to the institutional code and thus veritable fluctuations of intensity, gregarious states are impulses which aim at the conservation of the species, and of the individual as the species' servant. What is singular belongs authentically to the organism; what is gregarious belongs only to the species. The difference between the two semiotics thus corresponds to a moral opposition.

Nietzsche's oppositions are, by his own admission, ambiguous. The morbid and healthy types he repeatedly places into question (in as much as "health and sickness are not essentially different"[106]) and, as Klossowski notes, partially defines in terms of another opposition which appears and reappears in his writings, namely the opposition between singularity and gregariousness.[107] If declarations are first of all of a phylogenetic order, belonging to the species, it seems unproblematic to identify signs, representation and language with the species' encroachment on the individual, and the spontaneous fluctuation of impulses with singularity. But, for Nietzsche, this would amount to an untenable position. The impulses (instincts, reflexes, phantasms) are as much a product of the species as the code which abbreviates them, and, according to the above, differ from the latter by degree alone. Thus this seeming opposition quickly becomes more complicated:

> Every personal declaration is first of all of a phylogenetic order – by consequence, the species is present in the terms used to designate that which excludes the species in the experience characteristic of the singular state, or that which excludes from the species the subject who singularizes this experience.[108]

According to this passage, the institutional code consists of signs belonging to several orders, all of which originate from a genetic dynamism. In a typically Nietzschean gesture – an avowed part of his project since some of the earliest published texts – seeking the origin of a sign, and attempting to classify or diagnose it as an instance of a given type, requires tracing its evolution, or genealogical development:[109]

---

106 Klossowski, P. (1997). p. 81
107 Klossowski, P. (1997). p. 76
108 Klossowski, P. (1997). p. 79
109 Such a development can take several forms. Firstly, there is the phylogenetic development alluded to by Klossowski, who in this respect chose to follow Haeckel's appropriation of the

If the body concerns our most immediate forces as those which, in terms of their origin, are *the most distant*, then everything the body *says* – its well-being as well as its diseases – gives us the best information about our destiny. Nietzsche therefore wanted to go back toward what, in himself, was most distant in order to comprehend the most immediate.[110]

For the analytical interpreter, the distinction between morbid and healthy, gregarious and singular types is not of itself a resource which yields a conclusive elucidation of the relationship between the two semiotics. Indeed, this distinction between evaluations is ultimately itself explained in terms of the evolution and genealogy of a given individual's position relative to its "species." This dynamic, however, is in turn only clearly visible in the context of the theory of time which depends on the foundational semiotic of intensity. The moral typology, then, can hardly be regarded as the groundwork of Klossowski's project.

2.11 Conclusion: Thought and Representation

If fluctuations of intensity are the fundamental components of Nietzsche's semiotic, do they leave room for the traditional categories – for thought and representation, rather than impulse? In Nietzsche's semiotic, thought and representation belong to the institutional code of signs. All thoughts and all representations abbreviate and falsify fluctuations. Given the status of this code over against intensity, what follows as regards these two categories, which may be contrasted with the undulating corporeality of the impulses? How can a theory which prioritises impulsive life be reconciled with these categories – or is its credibility destroyed by its failure to do so?

Greek term φῦλον – the genesis of the species from generation to generation, a process normally embedded in the organism's phenotype. A phylogenetic property, or a sign of a "phylogenetic order" is thus, in this context, one which originates in the species' development. The reproductive instinct, manifested in the appraisal of a prospective partner as favourable to the ends of the species, is phylogenetic in this sense, and this aspect of the code is thus essentially hereditary. Secondly, ontogenesis is confined to an individual's own development, including the phenotype whose elements may or may not be genetically transmissible (that is, from generation to generation). As ontogenetic, the signs formed from the residues of Nietzsche's experiences, and the reactions they condition, are owed to the individuated organism. Thirdly, there is the epigenesis of the individual, in which the genetic traits emerge from the spontaneous confrontation between the individual and the species. Epigenetic signs are those defined by Malabou as those "founded at the point of contact" (Malabou, C. (2016). p. 36) between species and individual. They are not part of the type *transmitted to* the embryonic individual, but emerge spontaneously over the course of its development, unlike those of an ontogenesis.
110 Klossowski, P. (1997). p. 23

In accordance with the semiotic of intensity, the intellect is included among the impulses, insofar as they can be considered a totality: "The intellect is a constraining and selective *impulse*,"[111] just as the code filters out the greater part of an intensity. As Tremblay notes,

> The intellect substitutes itself for the primitive insignificance of primordial impulses, it would be the name of the 'selective' impulse which knew to create for itself the principle of reality, it being understood that the code is both its symptom and its principal solicitation.[112]

As Klossowski, too, notes in view of the following *Nachlass* extract, the concept which ensures the comprehensibility of experience to an intellect is itself within experience:

> The general problem of organization is the following: "How is experience even possible?" We have only one form of comprehension: the concept – the general case that contains the special case. In one case, the general, the typical seems to us to belong to experience – in this sense, everything that is "living" seems comprehensible to us only through an intellect.[113]

The intellect comprehends an excitation through the concept, being the general case that contains the special case. The code of signs is therefore required for the intellect to interpret experience, insofar as the code of signs enables comparison between cases, allowing an excitation to be judged an instance of something else. This definition is far from a mundane one – we can contrast it with, for instance, the Kantian definition according to which a concept is a representation *contained within* an infinity of possible representations,[114] thus capturing a commonality between a plurality of representations. Representations are contained "*under*" a concept, but not "*within*" a concept. With Nietzsche, though, the concept indeed contains various cases *within* itself. The distinction between these two conceptions is not that the relation of containment runs inversely to the relation of dependency; although in Nietzsche the concept's containment of other cases signals its dependency on and, in some sense, its origination from these cases, as opposed to its innateness, Kant does not admit only the existence of *a priori* concepts of the understanding, but a host of empirical ones in addition: the concept "red" no less than that of causality are contained within various rep-

---

111 Klossowski, P. (1997). p. 254
112 Tremblay, T. (2012). pp. 169–170
113 Klossowski, P. (1997). p. 257
114 Kant, I. (1929). B40

resentations. Rather, there is a more important contrast to be drawn between the Nietzschean and Kantian gloss of the concept. In Nietzsche, the concept arises as the result of the *incorporation* of experience: every experience being an excitation or fluctuation, and signs (including concepts or representations) their traces, the general is itself a direct object of experience: "The general, the typical seems to us to belong to experience."[115] If the particular case is a fluctuation in itself, originating either in the organism's interior or exterior to it, then what kind of act of thought integrates with other fluctuations whatever this fluctuation might be?

A process of assimilation governs the organism's digestion of excitations. Already formed unities, constituted as incorporated impulses, are compounds of special cases forming a general case. These impulses stimulate excitations, as well as reactions to other excitations, such as "complex actions of appreciation"[116] (implying in turn a kind of mechanics of actions and reactions on the part of the impulses). Conceptual representations are products of instinctual recognition formalised in the code of signs, corresponding to these impulsive excitations. By contrast, isolated, apparently singular cases are yet to be assimilated fully, awaiting integration into the depth of the impulses and "floating on the surface."[117] The non-conceptual representations of these singular cases are, rather, bestowed with the power of *resistance*.

Thus, the textual evidence presented in Klossowski's study suggests a fundamentally dualistic role to thought and representation in the context of his contributions to semiotics. On the one hand, there are impulsive unities, comprising assimilated or bound excitations, and their correspondingly *general conceptual* representations. On the other, there are impulsive pluralities or fragments, comprising excitations yet to be integrated, and their corresponding non-conceptual representations. Klossowski enshrines Nietzsche's thought, and aphoristic writing, with the merit of reflecting with a rare transparency an impulsive state of *resistance*, which will form the basis of his attacks on inherited systems of thought. But, in both cases, the *derivative* character of thought, relative to intensity, remains. Were the contrary the case, thought would no longer be an epiphenomenon, but would truly take on a power over the impulses – a position completely foreign to Nietzsche's own, which rather regards the impulses as fundamental entities.

---

115 Klossowski, P. (1997). p. 257
116 Klossowski, P. (1997). p. 257
117 Klossowski, P. (1997). p. 257

Insofar as something can still be invoked (recalled) as an isolated factum, this something has not yet been merged into the whole: the most recent experiences are still floating on the surface. Feelings of inclination, repugnance, etc., are symptoms of already-formed unities; our so-called "instincts" are similar formations. Thoughts are the most superficial things; appreciations that survive and impose themselves in an incomprehensible manner have more depth.[118]

---

[118] Klossowski, P. (1997). p. 257

3 The Sign of the Self

The fourth volume of Heidegger's lengthy exegesis of Nietzsche sets the latter, with his perspective on subjectivity, against the Cartesian *cogito*. It is known that Nietzsche disparages the subject as an article of faith posited over and above variable forces, which are described under the rubric of the will to power, just as he disparages substance as the misdirected application of this concept to subjects other than human subjects. Assuming the equivalence of the subject with the "human 'I'" or the self,[1] the self instead becomes a function of the will to power. Yet, despite his protest against the theocratic and hypostasising Cartesian worldview, Nietzsche was, for Heidegger, unable to escape Descartes' determination of Being as representation:[2] "Nietzsche agrees with Descartes on the very point on which he believes he must oppose him. Only his *way* of explaining the origin of Being and truth in thinking is different ... Without being sufficiently aware of it, Nietzsche agrees with Descartes that Being means 'representedness.'"[3] But whilst covertly Nietzsche remained, from Heidegger's *ontological* point of view, tributary to the tradition he professed to have overturned, from the point of view which contemplates *subjectivity*, Heidegger admits that Nietzsche's was a broadly anti-Cartesian one, and thus the point of departure from this tradition.

In Deleuze's work, the Nietzschean critique of subjectivity arises as the transformation, or inversion, of a unitary and monistic principle – will to power – by and into the subject equipped with a will. Thus Deleuze cites the *Genealogy of Morals:* "We split the will in two, involving a neutral subject endowed with free will to which we give the capacity to act and refrain from action."[4] These are figures which echo those regurgitated in this present study, such as the division and separation of intensity into the signs of the code. "Nietzsche constantly exposes 'the subject' as a fiction or grammatical function,"[5] as "little imaginary incubuses,"[6] such as, again for Deleuze, "Descartes' substance."[7]

Stambaugh, in her seminal scholarship on Nietzsche, assigns to the critique of the self a prominent position in the Nietzschean philosophy of time. The object

---

1 Heidegger, M. (1991c). p. 130
2 Heidegger, M. (1991c). pp. 124–131
3 Heidegger, M. (1991c). p. 129
4 Nietzsche, F. (2006). p. 113
5 Deleuze, G. (1986). p. 123
6 Nietzsche, F. (2006). p. 13
7 Deleuze, G. (2004). p. 123

of this critique again incepts with Descartes. "The indubitable attribute of thinking leads Descartes to the thinking thing, a substance characterized by duration. To the famous dictum '*cogito ergo sum*' Nietzsche remarks: 'He ought to have said: "*ergo est.*"'"[8] Locke, Berkeley, Hume, Kant and Hegel are implicated as accessories but, more radically, Klossowski will question how Descartes could have said anything at all of whatever "*ergo est.*"

These scholars thus acknowledge the attack on subjectivity as an important and explicit component of Nietzsche's thinking. However, Nietzsche was not, of course, the only thinker in and after his time to target the categories of subjectivity and selfhood (which are not always cognate, although they are treated as being so in Klossowski's study). Many and various others have implicitly adopted Nietzschean lines of argument, as a secondary inspiration if not their primary source. We can distinguish two such lines of these attacks. Firstly, Freud's work addresses the nuclear or atomistic conception of the self – ubiquitous metaphors in Nietzsche's notebooks – with its extended analysis of the unconscious: the unconscious encapsulates the causal dependency of the conscious mind on forces it does not contain. "I propose ... calling the entity which starts out from the system *Pcpt.* and begins by being *Pcs.* the 'ego,' and ... calling the other part of the mind, into which this entity extends and which behaves as if it were *Ucs.*, the 'id.'"[9]

In a telling footnote, Freud traces back his picture of this gradated distinction between the ego and the id to the physician G. Groddeck, who in turn, Freud states, "No doubt followed the example of Nietzsche, who habitually used this grammatical term for whatever in our nature is impersonal and, so to speak, subject to natural law."[10] Although fluid, Freud's separation of the ego and the id (which he diagrammises beneath these passages) derives from the passivity of the ego, and its dependency on "unknown and uncontrollable forces."[11] This distinction is not straightforwardly assimilable to the distinction between the conscious and the unconscious, since the ego is both conscious and unconscious, both the site of resistance to sensory excitations (Pcpt. Cs.) and also the driver of the exclusion of certain excitations into the unconscious sink of repressed material. It is clear, however, that Freud's differentiation of these elements of the subject occurs as a result of forces which are multilocular and on which these elements depend, and that these forces also dictate the var-

---

8 Stambaugh, J. (1972). p. 63
9 Smith, I. (2011). p. 3957
10 Smith, I. (2011). p. 3957
11 Smith, I. (2011). p. 3957

ious ways in which the conscious, the preconscious and the unconscious are separated.[12]

The phenomenological and structuralist tradition, no doubt indebted to Nietzsche, diverges from the psychoanalytical critique of the self: its foundation is not so much the self's dependency on internal psychic forces, but its inescapable relatedness to the world, and eventually to institutions, language and political power – whether or not these eventually manifest themselves by movements in the pre-individual psychic forces in which they are sedimented. The inability of the subject to think itself as it is and the corresponding loss of reflexivity originate in the fact that its conditions lie in contingent historical and societal facts, such as the education and judicial systems, policing, labour markets, psychiatric institutions, ethico-political standards etc. These, ironically, are precisely the forces Klossowski alleges inflict the sign of the self upon the otherwise ephemeral and indeterminate coruscations of sensory intensity.

As the work of these scholars indicates, the numerous depredations that the self has endured in modernity owe a good deal to Descartes' carving of mind from body. Announcements of the death of the self have proliferated following the attacks on Cartesian philosophy in the late 20th Century, with Nietzsche customarily cited as their augur. Is this citation of Nietzsche as the instigator of this critical tradition appropriate? To what extent are his inheritors faithful to this augury, given the content of his writings on the self – at least as far as Klossowski relates them? This section, rooted in the foundational semiotic described in the previous chapter, attempts to address these questions, and to provide some definition of Klossowski's own position.

Nietzsche and the Vicious Circle proposes a definition of the self which encourages interpretation both in semiological terms, and also as a component of the foundational notion of intensity. Nietzsche's criticisms of the self must be reformulated in light of this definition.

Klossowski takes the terms "self," "subject" and "I" to be cognate.[13] He provides several definitions of the self, directly or indirectly:

(1) "There is *one* sign ... that always corresponds to either the highest or lowest degree of intensity: namely, the *self*, the I, *the subject of all our propositions.*"[14]

---

12 Smith, I. (2011). p. 3954
13 Klossowski, P. (1997). p. 62
14 Klossowski, P. (1997). p. 62

(2) "But what then is the *identity* of the self? It seems to depend on the *irreversible history* of the body, a linkage of causes and effects."[15]
(3) "In relation to the code of everyday signs ... I can only will myself once and for all."[16]

The first and third of these definitions refer to the semiotic of intensity elaborated in the preceding chapter, referring to signs and codes of signs. The self refers to the outcome of the highest or lowest degree of intensity, or its strongest or weakest fluctuations, implying an unlikely kinship, a "coincidence"[17] or "resonance,"[18] between two extremes one would assume to be each-other's antitheses. This poses an immediate problem. How can this amount to a consistent position, given the nature of intensity already extrapolated from the text? How can one sign correspond to both the highest and lowest degrees of intensity?

In examining Nietzsche's semiotic, we distinguished two modes of signification: the institutional code, which imposes a fixity, a location, and a determinate designation on the fluctuations of intensity which gave rise to it; and the fluctuations themselves, which in fluctuating lack fixity and specificity, and designate nothing other than themselves.

At the highest degree of intensity there is an activation of a multitude of signs. As traces of previous fluctuations, these signs establish the self as a *history* of states. The self is nothing more, in this regard, than a set of such states. Its identity derives from them in a manner evocative of Locke's *Essay Concerning Human Understanding:* "as far as this consciousness can be extended backwards to any past thought, so far reaches the identity of that person; it is the same now as it was then."[19] In accordance with the everyday code, each state has a specific position, indexed and thus affixed to something external, giving rise to the extensional semiotic of correspondence described by Eco, and by Klossowski as a "correspondence between our own degrees of presence or absence, and the degrees of presence or absence of the outside."[20] The alignment between the first and the second definitions ordered above follows from this, insofar as the highest degree of intensity establishes the self as historical, with this activation of a multitude of signs. From the perspective of the institutional or everyday code,

---

15 Klossowski, P. (1997). p. 29
16 Klossowski, P. (1997). p. 64
17 Klossowski, P. (1997). p. 114
18 Klossowski, P. (1997). p. 113
19 Locke, J. (1999). p. 319
20 Klossowski, P. (1997). p. 63

therefore, the high degree of intensity corresponds to a greater activation of signs, and thus a personal history or selfhood born out of indexation.

From the perspective of pure intensity – that is, the dynamic of division, separation and rejoining proper to intensity alone, and prior to the imputations and filtrations of the institutional code – at the highest degree of intensity, there is no designation, and *a fortiori* no designation of self. At the lowest degree, by contrast, the characteristics of this dynamic are lost: the infinite deferral and phantasmic indefiniteness of signification, opposed to the characteristics of the everyday code, disappear. From the point of view of this semiotic, the self-referential intensity fades into reference back to the self. It seems, then, that there is a natural way of accounting for how the self can correspond to the highest and lowest degrees of intensity: which of these it corresponds to depends simply on which of the two semiotics is considered.

Yet these arguments, dispersed throughout the text, cannot lead to conclusions consistent with one another. If the institutional or everyday semiotic attributes a high degree of intensity to the sign of the self, and the unbastardised semiotic intrinsic to intensity attributes to it a low degree, the obverses must hold equally; the former semiotic must suppress the sign of the self at the trough of intensity and the latter must see it re-emerge it at the peak of intensity. In this case, these cannot count as credible explanations of the dual or Janus-faced nature of the sign of the self. Unless one of these two semiotics exercised sole control, and so long as they coexist to any degree at all, antinomy seems to be unavoidable. In Smith's terms, the "constant variation"[21] between the two seemingly opposed strata of "fluctuations of intensity, their rises and falls, their manic elations and depressive descents"[22] is imperilled. Whilst we must therefore follow his tenet that "what makes every individual a 'singular case' or an 'idiosyncrasy' is the unique constellation of impulses of which it is constituted,"[23] it is less obvious how to reconcile this with Klossowski's explicit pronouncements.

The difficulties implied by Klossowski's definition of the self do not end here. In fact, the definition (1) is subject to an additional antinomy. That a sign can correspond to an intensity's degree *at all* is not *prima facie* problematic, seeing as the *degree* of intensity *determines* the signs with which it coincides or joins up. Klossowski is clear that all of the characteristics of a sign are determined by quanta of intensity. But, in other places, Klossowski refers to the

---

[21] Smith, D. (2005). p.9
[22] Smith, D. (2005). p.9
[23] Smith, D. (2005). p. 9

self as a sign associated with a *specific* intensity, and not merely the degree of an arbitrary intensity, speaking of "that degree where the sign of the *self* in its tonality is devoid of intensity, and where all significations of this self are emptied."[24] This would imply that individual signs arise not so much from quanta of intensity but from different particular intensities, regardless of quantum. As much as the self corresponds to a degree of intensity, then, the self is also itself a sign, originating in a particular intensity. These two formulations consequently equivocate between the self as a *specific* degree of an *arbitrary* intensity and an *arbitrary* degree of a *specific* intensity. As a result, the tension between the two competing semiotics is reproduced in the sign of the self itself. How can these antinomies be resolved?

3.1 The Homonym of the Self

Klossowski produces a biologistic account of what he deems to be the illusion that the body is the homonym of the self. The self, the subject or the person originates in the development of the brain from the organism's nervous system. The body and the self (or its equivalents) are addressed as one and the same being, identified despite their differences, and despite the fugacity of the impulses which make up the body. This identification is the origin of our impression that the body's automatistic actions and reactions depend in some way on the prior decisions of our person.

The body is, originally and in fact, in no way dependent on the person. As evidence, Klossowski considers the pulsations which bring us into the waking state, in which a personal identity or unitary self appears, out of sleep, before submerging once again: between and even within moments of apparent concentration, we are periodically reabsorbed into a somnolent state as different impulses assert themselves and then withdraw – oscillations which carry us into and out of lucidity with a near unnoticeable frequency and amplitude. Asleep – in the "somnolent state" – there is no person or self, but as many personas and selves as there are arbitrarily constraining impulses. Freud, similarly, declares, "Experience goes to show that a psychical element is not as a rule conscious for a protracted length of time. On the contrary, a state of consciousness is characteristically very transitory; an idea that is conscious now is no longer so a moment later."[25] In Klossowski's dialectical staging, we thus "oscillate contin-

---

24 Klossowski, P. (1997). p. 114
25 Smith, I. (2011). p. 3948

ually between somnolence and insomnia, and what we call the *waking state* is merely the comparison of the two, their reciprocal reflection, like a play of mirrors,"[26] a universal narcolepsy.

In moments of intensification such as extremes of pain or excitement, in this sense no different from somnolence, there is no homonymy between the body and the self, since the self disappears or dissolves altogether. In such moments, the impulses which make up the body have no tendency except to dissolve and de-individuate the self. The body survives only as a haphazardly integrated Frankenstein of conflicting and incongruent instincts, each of whose chaotically selected aims points in directions alien and incoherent from the perspective of any other impulse. The extent to which, or duration in which, the impulses can productively misinterpret one another grounds their period of *entente*, namely the body's life-cycle. Impulses, fluctuations of intensity, are beyond conditionality (nothing can be said or known of their causes); the self is conditioned by these impulses. "As soon as the cerebral activity diminishes, the body alone remains present, but in reality it no longer belongs to a *person*."[27] This is Nietzsche's theory of fortuity. Although later invested with metaphysical significance by virtue of its relation to chance and the philosophy of the event – where this theory will be differentiated from a physicalistic or mechanistic determinism, governing the behaviour of the mind in relation to the body – Klossowski confines this theory initially to the impulses and the corporeal symptoms which derive from them.

It is in this sense that the magnification of intensity corresponds to the dissolution of the person. The self disappears in moments of intensification – intensification of specific impulses at the expense of others. Correlatively, given that there are multiple intensities (as multiple impulses) the *specifically* lowest degree of an *arbitrary* intensity corresponds to its emergence.

If the body's impulses bear analogy to the dynamic of division, separation and rejoining of intensity, so too does the homonymy between the body and the person to the code of signs. This homonymy is established by the brain, and by consciousness, by definition: "Consciousness itself *constitutes this code of signs* which inverts, falsifies and filters what is expressed through the body."[28] Nonetheless, for Klossowski, the brain is no less a part of the body, and this homonymy does not imply the existence of a *mind* as a distinct substance: rather, the body and the brain interact in the manner of a "competition

---

26 Klossowski, P. (1997). p. 27
27 Klossowski, P. (1997). p. 27
28 Klossowski, P. (1997). p. 26

between the *arbitrary* constraint imposed by the freedom of the impulses, and the *persuasive* constraint of the intellect – the latter being in turn defined as an impulse."[29] The impulse is no less a "force which is also the intellect."[30]

Viewed in respect of their effect on the impulses, the terms "brain," "intellect" and "consciousness" are synonymous: they are defined as the obverse of any impulse in general.[31] For any impulse, in whose nature there is apparently nothing attributable to the individual, the role of the brain is to restrain the agent's tendency to abandon itself to the impulse, or repel it from this impulse. In his Additional Note on Nietzsche's Semiotic, Klossowski rigorously argues that this abandonment, and therefore the de-individuating tendency of the impulses, cannot pre-exist the intellect of the agent. It is not that the agent independently identifies with a set of impulses, until the constraining influence of the intellect comes about; rather, it is only by virtue of the repulsion of the intellect that the individual agent can be under the influence of the impulse at all, or, in Klossowski's terms, can obey a coherence with such an impulse. Accordingly, "there is neither coherence nor incoherence in the activity of the impulses; yet, if we can nonetheless speak in these terms, it is thanks to this other *impulsive force* which is also *the intellect* ... the impulse seems to exist only *because of* the intellectual *repulsion* exerted by the agent to preserve the agent."[32] Intellectual activity is, in this regard, entirely parasitic and reactive, arising only as the obverse of impulsive intensity, but the impulsive tendency to cause the agent's fragmentation is a product only of the intellect's capacity to conceive the agent at all. But the intellect is also, for these reasons, no lesser an occupant of the plane of the impulses than they are themselves, and no less of a force. It is the obverse of any given impulse and therefore itself an impulse. As Smith demonstrates, "there is no struggle of reason against the drives, since what we call 'reason' is, in Nietzsche's view, nothing more than a certain 'system of relations between various passions,' a certain ordering of the drives."[33]

These propositions, as well as positing this obverse relation between impulse and intellect, form the theoretical support for the foregoing observation that *in moments of extreme intensification the self dissolves and disappears*, being no longer "homonymous" with the body. With these propositions, Klossowski asserts two coherences: both the attracting coherence of the agent *with some impulse*, and the agent's repelling coherence *with itself*, owing to the intel-

---

29 Klossowski, P. (1997). p. 255
30 Klossowski, P. (1997). p. 259
31 Klossowski, P. (1997). p. 259
32 Klossowski, P. (1997). p. 259
33 Smith, D. (2011). p. 10. The quote from Nietzsche comes from: KSA 13, 11[310] = WP 387.

lect. It is essential for these to be separated. The coherence of the agent with its impulses is the dissolution of the agent for itself; the coherence of the agent with itself, relative to which the impulses are incoherent, is its inversion by the intellect. The agent's incoherence is, therefore, its tendency to deindividuate and dissolve, and its coherence its ineluctably paranoiac degree of individuation. The self is indistinguishable from the reaction and suppression wrought against the intensification of impulsive forces. It is then tautological that the self, *conceived simply as the agent's coherence with itself*, must disappear at the maximum of these forces' intensity, since the agent's decoherence with itself, in favour of its coherence with the impulse, is the condition for every movement in which the latter is able to intensify.

3.2 Resolution

Recall that above the way the self is defined in *Nietzsche and the Vicious Circle* generated two problems. Firstly, from the perspective of intensity itself, the highest point of intensity seemed to imply the activation of a greater number of signs, naturally accommodating the definition of the self in terms of this high point of intensity. However, the lowest point of intensity seemed to imply the disappearance of such signs, clashing with the definition of the self in terms of the low point of intensity. Alternatively, from the perspective of the institutional code, the lowest point of intensity seemed to imply the subjugation of the fugacity of the impulses, naturally accommodating the definition of the self in terms of this low point of intensity. However, the highest point of intensity seemed to imply the re-emergence of impulsive fluctuations, clashing with the definition of the self in terms of the high point of intensity. The apparently inconsistent definition of the self (i) becomes no more consistent when interpreted in light of the two available semiotics. Whichever of the two semiotics is adopted, it seems that the definition of the self as both the highest and the lowest degree of intensity can only end in incoherence. And not only this, but secondly the self seems simultaneously to be explained as a specific degree, high or low, of any intensity whatsoever, but also as *any degree whatsoever* of a certain intensity or its trace, and thus a *particular* and privileged sign, distinguished from others.

How does our analysis of what Klossowski terms the homonym of the self resolve these concerns? The two semiotics can be translated into the terms of the homonymy or non-homonymy of the body and the self (or moral agent). The formation of the self is conditional on the impulses, as fluctuations of exogenous intensity which constitute the body. Since these intensities aim at de-individuation, their magnification suppresses the (endogenous) self; ostensibly, their diminution allows its emergence. However, with Klossowski's assertion of the dependency of these individuating and de-individuating forces on the intellect, this contrariness can be resolved. The intellect is the obverse of any impulse in general, as intensity. If it is only by virtue of the intellect, which conceives intensity as a threat to the agent's coherence, that the impulse can *deindividuate at all* (with its intensification), the impulse is *necessarily* intellectual: it creates its own obverse as a means to achieve the dissolution of the self – "at the *limit-point* where this impulse is turned *into a thought (of this impulse)* as a *repulsion* against the *adulterous coherence* – precisely so that it can appear at the level of the intellect, no longer as *a threat to the agent's coherence with itself*, but on the contrary as a legitimate coherence."[34] Now, unlike the oppositional vicissitudes suggested before – the intensities' tendency to de-individuate *versus* the intellect's conservation of the individual – there is here a coexistence of these two forces: "These centrifugal forces never flee the centre for ever, but approach it anew only in order to retreat from it yet again."[35] Each therefore implicates the other. The high point and the low point of pure intensity thus coincide, the high point of de-individuating impulsive intensity accompanied by its suppression to nothing by the intellect, insofar as the movements towards the persistence and the destruction of the agent are inseparable – an adumbration of the circular figure of return which is developed and analysed later in the study.

Klossowski's undeniably confusing and backhanded definition of the self will be misconstrued if taken to refer to discrete states of intensity. It must not be taken to imply that the self emerges from intensity at *isolated* extremities of its degree. The self may dissolve at the highest point of intensity, but with the excitation of the intellect its coherence with the self can be established at the very same time. The sign of the self corresponds to the highest degree of intensity as the obverse of the intensified impulses, and as the coherence with this impulse which results. On the other hand, the coherence of the self as self, of the agent as agent, requires the de-intensification of the impulses which aim at dissolving it into them. The sign of the self in this sense corresponds to the lowest degree of intensity, as the preservation of this self in the face of intensity. These two conclusions – that the two opposite extremes of intensity equivocally correspond to the self, in one state as the obverse of any given intensity, and in another as its coherence with the agent as the agent – explain Klossowski's elliptical, and somewhat unhelpful, definition (i).

---

34 Klossowski, P. (1997). p. 260
35 Klossowski, P. (1997). p. 216

Accordingly, by way of response to the second of the above two problems, we can glean from this argument that the self arises neither as a specific degree of an arbitrary intensity, nor the arbitrary degree of a specific intensity. The self cannot admit a specific degree since the high and low degrees of intensity coincide, nor can it belong to an arbitrary intensity, since the specific constraint of the intellect (as impulse, and thus intensity) is necessary for it. Equally, the self cannot admit an arbitrary degree of a specific intensity, since it corresponds to the highest or lowest points of intensity, and is thus distinguished by degree and not by kind. However, we must acknowledge that it seems at this point as if Klossowski's account *does* intend a distinction between intensities of different natures or kinds, whose degree produces the qualitatively different effects of the code, and those of the self, as a result of nothing other than this degree of intensity – once the intellect intervenes. Were this so, the agent would not be constituted by one and the same intensity at various stages of fluctuation. This is what, again, seems to be the meaning of the definition of the intellect in terms of the obverse of impulsive intensity. Does the fact that there are *multiple* coherences of the agent with impulses, brought about by the intellect's activity, not imply that there are multiple impulsive intensities, and therefore multiple intensities? Importantly, the existence of distinct impulses, or forces or drives, does not imply the existence of so many intensities, even if different impulses fluctuate to different degrees of intensity.

As evidence for this distinction, Klossowski overwhelmingly employs the term "intensity" in place of its plural form, despite that in a few places the latter does appear: he speaks of "intensities of the impulses"[36] "other intensities"[37] and "impulses ... respective intensities,"[38] but never in a way which suggests a one-to-one correspondence between distinct impulses and intensities. Smith's prefatory claim that "Klossowski frequently employs the French term *tonalité* to describe these states of the soul's fluctuating intensities,"[39] which is found in the introduction to the English translation, does not therefore assert that intensity is separable into states *qua* instances of intensity with distinct characteristics, nor that intensity is a general term subsuming particulars, but quite correctly equates the "diverse tones, timbres and amplitudes"[40] of intensity with states of the figurative soul, or corporeal states of the agent, like the resonances of a string.

---

36 Klossowski, P. (1997). p. 134
37 Klossowski, P. (1997). p. 216
38 Klossowski, P. (1997). p. 46
39 Klossowski, P. (1997). p. x
40 Klossowski, P. (1997). p. x

3.3 Two Images of the Unconscious

Despite conceiving itself as a break with the philosophy of the self, psychoanalysis, according to Klossowski, only partially succeeds in expunging the notions of consciousness and unconsciousness which in fact reinforce this category's predominance. The critique apparent with the discovery of the unconscious effectively reinforces the centrality of the subject, agent or person, by reinstating its entanglement with the mind *beneath the level of consciousness*. It is this entanglement of the notions of the unconscious and of personality which Klossowski attributes to convention, or to institutions.

Klossowski's assault on the psychoanalytical framing of the unconsciousness-consciousness dyad occurs in an opaque proof which follows his extended citation of Zarathustra. What proposition is targeted by this assault? This proposition is stated long after the argument's conclusion: "The ruse consists in making us believe in the coexistence of a *consciousness* and an *unconsciousness*; for if the latter survives in us, our consciousness would merely be a *capacity* to enter into an exchange with the exteriority of the code."[41]

It is this assumption that the conscious and unconscious, Cs. and Ucs., coexist which the following argument denies:

P1) The coexistence of the conscious and the unconscious requires the unity of the person, ego or subject.
Def.) The unity of the person, ego or subject is the constancy of an active set of signs or designations.
C1) The coexistence of the conscious and the unconscious requires the constancy of an active set of signs or designations.
P2) The activity or inactivity of all signs or designations is an exclusive function of the prevailing excitations (which is to say that excitations are required and sufficient for the activation of signs).
C2) If there are excitations, there are signs; if there are no excitations, there are no active signs.
P3) Excitations are inconstant.
C3) Either everything in us is unconscious, or everything in us is conscious.
C4) The conscious and the unconscious cannot coexist. [42]

The justification for premise 1 is the following. Were consciousness and unconsciousness to coexist, the difference between them would be chiefly one of volition, in that the unconscious would be simply the region of the otherwise con-

---
41 Klossowski, P. (1997). p. 40
42 Klossowski, P. (1997). p. 39

scious psyche whose forces and content are not expressed. One of them is "carried out on some material which remains unknown, whereas the latter (the *Pcs.,*) is in addition brought into connection with word-presentations."[43] To summon unpredictable outbursts, such as the multiple personalities Nietzsche assumed and proclaimed after his mental disintegration in Turin, or Klossowski's examples of dreams or slips of the tongue,[44] as instances of material penetrating to the surface of consciousness which ordinarily lies dormant in the unconscious – repressed material, in Freud's terms – is to conceive of the unconscious as a latent reservoir of contents forcibly submerged, but always ready to escape. What is conscious is willed, whereas what is unconscious is not willed, though otherwise no different. In Freud's image of the iceberg, the volume of the submerged parts therefore corresponds simply to the quantity of pre-conscious material not allowed to reach the surface of the ocean, and its depth how vigorously this material is repressed. Thus, Klossowski states, "consciousness would merely be a *capacity* to enter into an exchange with the exteriority of the code."[45]

Following these remarks, if we assume the only difference between the unconscious and conscious states is this difference of volition, or repressive mechanism, it is possible that all excitations which remain in the unconscious could be conscious, were it not for this mechanism. Just as, for Kant, the sheer *possibility* of self-attributing a manifold constitutes a transcendental subjective unity, the coexistence of these two states requires that unconscious states be perfectly *capable* of passing in and out of consciousness. In this context, then, unconsciousness does not denote the fluctuations of intensity which are unfathomable from the perspective of the conscious mind (for, according to this argument, this coexistence can never arise). Rather, it would denote something fundamentally unified with the conscious mind: the two would constitute a unity, or continuity, between impulsive states and their signifying crystallisations. Although Freud conceives of this relationship in terms of an iceberg structure, equipped with a temporal dimension, the relationship between the two is more properly visualised as tetrahedral: a continuous stack of unconscious material lying beneath a conscious tip, and whose base and highest vertex are capable of continuous deformation as more or less repressed content is brought to consciousness from moment to moment. The unity of the base is a clear property of such a figure. In conclusion, "The notions of *consciousness* and *unconsciousness*, which are derived from what is responsible or irresponsible, always presuppose the

---

[43] Smith, I. (2011). p. 3954
[44] Klossowski, P. (1997). pp. 39–40
[45] Klossowski, P. (1997). p. 40

unity of the person of the ego, of the subject."⁴⁶ This is the ground for the first premise.

Secondly, the definition of the unity of the ego or self in terms of a set of signs imposed by the code is a rudimentary consequence of the semiotics of the second chapter. Indeed, such a statement recapitulates the Lockean view previously outlined in passing, wherein any self-ascription of identity is equated to a mnemic consciousness, of all the states which are so ascribed. P2), the crucial premise in this deduction, is equally a corollary of these semiotic considerations. With the fluctuation of an intensity or an excitation, a certain number of signs are activated, depending on the intensity's degree. The term "signs" is employed in as general a sense as possible, designating "groups of events that are being lived through or thought at a given moment, whether near or far,"⁴⁷ and, as such, inclusive of memories, desires, premonitions and base instincts as well as short-lived perceptual content or abrupt sensations. But what causes these signs to be obscured is only "the afflux of another excitation, at another moment, which absorbs all of the *available designations* – while the rest of our 'general' apparatus is put into 'abeyance'."⁴⁸ Thus, in a given state of excitation, *all* signs are included, whether or not all of these reach the very surface of consciousness on which the sharpest perceptions are deposited. Klossowski's references to occlusion are motivated by his inability to refer to inactivity or disappearance, since he is committed to the thesis that even signs which have disappeared are active in the prevailing excitation, if camouflaged by it. Signs which are occluded and hidden from view from excitation to excitation are not for all that inactive. This is characteristic of the Nietzschean life-world: all of the lessons from dozens of years of dedicated studies, the energising triumph over countless bouts of debilitating illness, the pulsating traces of rejection and betrayal by Rée and de Salomé, the concentration attained by virtue of his previous decisions to pursue social and intellectual isolation, his desolation of Wagnerian ideology and the fitness improved by moving to a cooler climate – all of these were at work as active signs, if hidden, in Nietzsche's final efforts as a philosophical writer – a connectivity consecrated in the temporality he enacted in Turin, the subject of the penultimate chapter. Thus, Klossowski must assert that the state of these active or inactive signs depends solely on fluctuations of intensity and excitations: *all* signs are implicated in *any* excitation, and *none* are implicated without some excitation, as per C2) and, finally, C3). Tremblay concisely cir-

---

46 Klossowski, P. (1997). p. 38
47 Klossowski, P. (1997). p. 39
48 Klossowski, P. (1997). p. 39

cumscribes this result in the chapter of his *Anamnèses* dedicated to the Klossowski-Nietzsche nexus:

> One possible trick would be to presume the existence of a dualism which would oppose unconsciousness to consciousness, where consciousness would sustain the principle of reality which manages the disorderly unconsciousness of the depth. Now, if the unconscious disorder (or, more thematically, Chaos) arose only at the cost of becoming conscious, it would be, Klossowski writes, the same operation in accordance with a different usage, of the same code, an operation which already took place in the *suppôt* before the separation directs the prevalence of the intellect in a dualistic opposition, consciousness and unconsciousness.[49]

Since consciousness is *defined as* the institutional code, all conscious states are the results of the filtration and inversion of intensities transmitted through the brain. The distinction between conscious states and unconscious states is, in this respect, a mere reflection of the difference between the vastness of intensity and the shallowness of the signs activated in the code. As a result, the unconscious remains nothing more than whatever is forgotten when excitations pass through consciousness.

3.4 Cohesion and Fortuity

So far, these arguments have addressed the relation of the self to the semiotics of intensity, and have attempted to elaborate the various ways in which Klossowski defines this category, as well as resolving the difficulties which result. But Klossowski's fundamental thesis on the self is not a direct result of this definition, nor deducible from these elaborations: The cohesion of the self is fortuitous. Bracketing the effects of the intellect or cerebrum, and the relation of consciousness to the unconscious, the self is only coherent in as much as it is fortuitous – as fortuitous as the vicissitudes of the impulses. In the text, fortuity comes to occupy the role of a law governing fluctuations of intensity and, in obscure fashion, relates to variety of related notions such as contingency, facticity, randomness, chaos or chance, in remarks such as the following:

---

49 Tremblay, T. (2012). p. 171

Intensity is subject to a moving chaos without beginning or end.[50]

Chance is but one thing at each of the moments (the individual, singular and hence fortuitous existences) of which it is composed.[51]

All that remains, then, is for me to re-will myself ... as a fortuitous moment whose very fortuity implies the integral return of the whole series.[52]

Now in a universe dominated by the inorganic, organic life is itself a fortuitous case – hence a possible '*error*' in the cosmic economy. It is within this economy that interpretation, *grounded in the fear of error*, becomes susceptible to *error*. Even if the origin of organic life lies in *purely random* combinations, it can no longer behave *randomly* once it comes into existence.[53]

What is the nature of this random or fortuitous behaviour? What does Klossowski, as a consequence, mean when he ascribes fortuity to the self's cohesion? How can this behaviour lead to the asymmetry inherent in organic life, which aims at its own law-like conservation, despite being brought about by destruction and chaos in the inorganic world? In this latter remark, the combinatorial conception of fortuity, offered by Klossowski as an account of abiogenesis, and subsequent phylogenesis, immediately evokes a philosophy rooted in thermodynamic concepts.

Regardless of whether or not Nietzsche was aware of developments in thermodynamics which are integral aspects of its modern formulation, such as the work of Boltzmann and Gibbs, the thermodynamic backdrop to his reflections on chance and probability, taken up at length in *Nietzsche and the Vicious Circle*, bears striking analogies to certain elements of this theory, in contrast to the philosophy of mechanism he regarded as prominent in the physical sciences of his time – and which is noted in later chapters as "the order of the day."[54] This philosophy is subjected to a barrage of denouncements, along with a panoply of physicists including Boyle, Dühring and Kelvin in the later works, and is the point of departure for his increasingly metaphysical theories developed in the 1880s.[55] It is, however, rarely given a precise definition in his work. How are we to understand mechanism, and therefore Nietzsche's understanding of chance? The doctrine of mechanism is in Klossowski given various affiliations, including atomist commitments, principles of conservation, and conceptions

---

50 Klossowski, P. (1997). p. 62
51 Klossowski, P. (1997). p. 72
52 Klossowski, P. (1997). p. 58
53 Klossowski, P. (1997). p. 45
54 Klossowski, P. (1997). p. 101
55 Babich, B. (1999). pp. 187–203

of motion, it principally refers to nomological or automatistic behaviours:[56] "*Critique of the Mechanistic Theory:* Let us here dismiss the two popular concepts 'necessity' and 'law.'"[57]

The mechanistic-deterministic worldview Nietzsche targeted was broadly that the universe progressively explores an infinite, endless sequence of states, each related to the next by determinative physical laws. Each state consists of an arrangement of particles whose interactions, under the cardinal forces of nature, give rise to its successor. The research programme which consists in, and imparts consistency to, these laws and descriptions of such states qualifies as a dynamical theory. In terms of any given state, any other state is calculable by appeal to these dynamical laws, according to the Laplacian prognosis, and insofar as they are conceived as mechanisms, each state is mechanistically determined. *No* notion of chance belongs to these aspects of such a theory, other than incidentally.

By contrast, at the level of statistical mechanics, random behaviour is suggested in a way which presents salient resources for developing the inchoate Nietzschean conceptions of probability. Statistical mechanics can be characterised by a distinction between two kinds of states occupied by the universe or its subsystems. Dynamical states are microscopic commitments about the system, only mediately observable, and describable in terms of a *space* of coordinates, or assignments to each particle of critical variables (position and velocity) which determine its trajectory. By contrast, the thermodynamic characteristics of the system are macroscopic, perhaps phenomenological, observables: temperatures, pressures and volumes which are measurable, independent of measurement of the coordinates of the constituent molecules, i. e. microscopic features. This distinction between two kinds of states – microstates and macrostates – is generative of the predictive and explanatory power of thermodynamics, on the basis of Boltzmann's observation that the relationship between these states is not in general one-to-one.[58] There are ordinarily *many* microscopic arrangements corresponding to a given macroscopic distribution – infinitely many, if arrangements sit along a continuum. A macroscopic description contains correlatively less information than a microscopic one.

The probabilistic implications of this backdrop arise in the following manner. Due in large part to the work of Boltzmann, the entropy of a distribution is defined in terms of the number of microstates corresponding to a given macro-

---

[56] Klossowski, P. (1997). p. 54
[57] Klossowski, P. (1997). p. 108
[58] Boltzmann, L. (2015).

3.4 Cohesion and Fortuity — 65

state – more formally, as the phase-space volume occupied by the microstates in phase space. Assuming, by an *a priori* principle of indifference, that every microstate, every microscopic arrangement of particles obeying the relevant dynamical laws, has an equal probability of obtaining, the probability of occurrence of a given macrostate will be *proportional to* the number of microstates corresponding to it, or their phase-space volume. For a given macrostate, then, *entropy* involves a measure of *probability*.

The central postulate underpinning this statistical notion of probability is the *a priori* equal distribution of probability over a range of microstates. What is the basis for this hypothesis? On the one hand, it might be justified by appeal to the epistemic constraints on the observer – the accessibility of macrostates only to observation, and the lack of information about which of the permissible microstate(s) are in fact occupied. Given scant data, the principle of indifference might dictate we construct a correlatively disperse distribution. As Albert notes, however, this involves the conversion of an *a priori* critical proposition about our more or less limited epistemological *access* to phenomena into an empirical, predictive one, problematising the employment of statistical mechanics in deriving laws about the behaviour of actual systems, such as their tendency to approach maximally dispersed or disordered distributions, with sufficient time. Strangely, it is ignorance which then produces entropy.[59] On the other hand, it is customary to appeal to the following provision in order to rectify these problems: the ergodic hypothesis. Ergodicity is the assumption that systems explore for a given fraction of their time microstates with an equivalent fractional volume of phase space, subject to an energetic constraint.

> Now in a universe dominated by the inorganic, organic life is itself a fortuitous case – hence a possible '*error*' in the cosmic economy. It is within this economy that interpretation, *grounded in the fear of error*, becomes susceptible to *error*. Even if the origin of organic life lies in *purely random* combinations, it can no longer behave *randomly* once it comes into existence.[60]

Now, abandoning the description of the universe's progression in terms of microphysical dynamics, and reconceiving structures as Nietzsche does, with organic life and apparent order and consistency appearing only as fortuitous cases, and as the errors which result from random combinations, appears to conform to the image of ergodicity, whereby any constituent of the universe "wanders aimlessly, randomly, every which way, in no particular direction, favouring no particular

---

59 Albert, D. (2000). p. 64
60 Klossowski, P. (1997). p. 45

region."[61] From a thermodynamic or energetic perspective, the formation of concentrated regions of negentropy which lead to organised matter and life are the result of ergodic microphysical behaviour. Conversely, if we are to conceive the combinations of particles referred to here as microscopic arrangements whose behaviour can be described only probabilistically, but which produce relatively stable macroscopic distributions, then an analogy seems to follow between these arrangements and the randomness which predates the organic, and between the distributions and organic life. Is this, then, the foundation for fortuity – the randomness inherent in ergodic statistical fluctuations? Does ergodicity provide an interpretative cue for Nietzsche's philosophy of chance? The ergodic conception of a random walk through phase space would, in such an event, amount to one interpretation of Klossowski's allusion to random combinations, buttressed by Nietzsche's investigations into the quantities treated by thermodynamics.

This combinatorial or statistical interpretation of Nietzsche's remarks on the nature of fortuity and chance is allied with a particular vision of the metaphysics of eternal return, in a way which casts much more light on this interpretation. In part in response to the development of statistical mechanical theorems, the recurrence theorem of Poincaré and Zermelo concerns the behaviour of the phase space inhabited by the aforementioned microstates and their dynamical evolutions, rendered by Brown, Myrvold and Uffink as follows:

> Almost all points in the phase space define orbits which return arbitrarily closely to the initial point. More specifically, consider an arbitrary measurable set g in the -algebra $\mathcal{A}$ and some arbitrary finite real number . The subset g̃ of g that contains all the points x in g such that $T_t x \notin g$, for any finite t <, has measure zero: (g̃) = 0.[62]

Heuristically, a dynamical system considered over a sufficiently extended – thus unempirical – timescale returns to its previously attained conditions, with arbitrary closeness, so long as it is constrained to explore a finite region of phase space.[63] This phase space, representing microscopic distributions of particles, evokes the kind of behaviour typically associated with Nietzsche's vision of eternal return: closed sets of qualitatively identical states arranged in a sequence, repeating endlessly in time, an infinitely capacious container, not unlike the "circulating decimal of many figures" overlaid by Mill onto Laplacian determinism:

---

61 Albert, D. (2000). p. 59; see also De Oliveira, C. and Werlang, T. (2006). pp. 189–201
62 Brown, H., Myrvold, W. and Uffink, J. (2009). p. 181
63 Albert, D. (2000). p. 74

> If any particular state of the entire universe could ever recur a second time, all subsequent states would return too, and history would, like a circulating decimal of many figures, periodically repeat itself ... the whole series of events in the history of the universe, past and future, is not the less capable, in its own nature, of being constructed *a priori* by any one whom we can suppose acquainted with the original distribution of all natural agents, and with the whole of their properties, that is, the laws of succession existing between them and their effects: saving the far more than human powers of combination and calculation which would be required, even in one possessing the data, for the actual performance of the task.[64]

The justification for interpreting this cyclical vision to be representative of Nietzsche's position, an interpretation accepted by what is probably a uniform scholarly consensus, is often wedded to beliefs about the particular scientific theories that, it is claimed, Nietzsche supported. Ansell-Pearson, for instance, in his review of *Nietzsche and the Vicious Circle*, invokes the Poincaré recurrence theorem as a potential resource for enriching Nietzsche's position, and which he paints as lamentable omission from Klossowski's text. In addition, G. Whitlock assembles a series of remarks in which Nietzsche appears to side with the cyclical vision, on the basis of comparable remarks in the work of the physicist and astronomer Boscovich.

> The world of forces never attains equilibrium, never has a moment of rest, its force and its movement are equally great at all times.[65]
>
> The *cycle* is not *something that has become*, it is fundamental principle, just as quantitative force is fundamental principle, without exceptions and violations. All becoming is within the cycle and its quantitative force.[66]
>
> Nothing infinities found actually existing; the only thing possible is a series of finite things produced indefinitely.[67]

Thus, one interpretation of the kind of fortuity latent in the passages cited at the beginning of this section is this statistical-combinatorial kind. This interpretation draws upon the nascent thermal physics of Nietzsche's day. To be compatible with determinism, the only entry of fortuity into the theory is as *probability*, either due to *epistemic restrictions* (our inability to measure every one of the micro-

---

64 Mill, J. (2011). pp. 329–330
65 Babich, B. (1999). p. 195
66 Babich, B. (1999). p. 195
67 Boscovich, R. (1922). This conception of cyclical return did not, therefore, originate with Nietzsche, if it is to be found in his work at all – indeed, it will be argued that neither is it accurate to construe his position with respect to the notion of return in terms of cycles of this kind.

states underlying a phenomenon) or due to *ergodicity* (the tendency of the system to explore microstates in proportion to their phase space volume).

However, there are of course many points of dissimilarity between the random arrival of organic matter from the inorganic on the one hand, and ergodic phase-space trajectories on the other, among them the fact that ordered and steeply negentropic organic matter is a probabilistically unfavourable cosmological outcome. Subject to broad assumptions about the macroscopic properties of a system taken in isolation, such as its energy and volume, these highly ordered, low entropy states become problematic when taken in the face of a law which suggests that entropy-extremising states are, by contrast, overwhelmingly more likely to arise. In the philosophical literature which debates these states, the insertion of a supplementary set of boundary conditions into the theory, for instance the "past hypothesis"[68] – that the measurable universe incepted after an initial microstate of extraordinarily low entropy – is often asserted to be needed to account for them.[69] This fact in particular exposes the limitations of a purely combinatorial conception of fortuity.

In this regard, and given the difficulties with interpreting fortuity in a statistical manner, consider the following thesis: *"Chance is but one thing at each of the moments* (the individual, singular and hence fortuitous existences) of which it is composed."[70]

This remark poses a dramatically different perspective on the Nietzschean notion of fortuity, and one which does not square readily with the initially obvious analogies between this notion and the prevailing physics, including the statistical-combinatorial reading. Roughly equating chance with fortuity, fortuity is here not only surmised as a necessary condition for the singularity of the individual's – the self's – existence. More importantly, fortuity, now synonymous with chance, is construed univocally. In order to comprehend the proposition that chance is one thing for any and all selves, we can consider its negation. Were chance *not* one thing at each of the moments, it would be specific to each, different in respect of them. Every separate state would be fortuitous in a different way. In scholastic terms, fortuity would be an equivocal notion. The essential contrast being drawn is between something which is different in every fortuitous case, which therefore need not be fortuitous in the same sense as another may be, and something fortuitous in the same sense as is every other fortuity. For instance, contingency is one construal of chance and for-

---

68 Callender, C. (2016).
69 Earman, J. (2006).
70 Klossowski, P. (1997). p. 72

tuity which is equivocal: a group of contingent events need not be contingent for the same reasons, nor in the same sense. Contingency, understood as the indifference of physical laws to the occurrence or non-occurrence of these events, or, from a logical point of view, the dependency of a sentential truth-function on the assignments of truth values to its sub-sentences, has a different meaning depending on the proposition thought to be contingent. Mundane physical observations and empirical refutations of sentences deeply embedded in the hard core of a scientific research programme are contingent in different ways. Thus, if fortuity and chance are re-interpreted as contingency, chance would differ similarly from contingent event to contingent event, and therefore equivocate. Klossowski's univocal notion of chance, the fortuity which is one thing at each moment in which the self appears, does not differ in such a way. Indeed, as a direct consequence, he claims that, "as soon as the individual exists it cannot fail to re-will all the prior and subsequent events of its own existence."[71] Just as chance is univocal, it is a unitary feature of the individual's existence. Chance, like fortuity, being a term which to Nietzsche denotes the conditions under which an individual is formed, is as a result bound to all other individual states: the fortuitous conditions on it apply to all states equally, as opposed to merely one. What, then, is this notion of chance, which is so distinct from the combinatorial or deterministic conceptions of mechanism, as well as from the notion of contingency which varies from event to event?

Initially, the theory of the fortuitous case is articulated in moral terms, as a line of escape from gregarious or institutional morality.

1. "My endeavour to oppose decadence and the increasing weakness of personality. I sought a new centre.
2. Impossibility of this endeavour recognized.
3. Thereupon I advanced further down the road of dissolution – where I found new sources of strength for individuals."[72]

Superficially, fortuity in this passage means the dissolution of the individual by and into the impulses. But if Nietzsche's theory of the fortuitous case is a theory of the self, and of the sense in which the self is fortuitous, fortuity surely cannot designate the self's opposition to itself in dissolution. If the fortuitous cohesion of the impulses is the self, and the fortuity of the self were to refer to its dissolution, fortuity would be patently antinomical. Moreover, as already deduced,

---

71 Klossowski, P. (1997). p. 72
72 Klossowski, P. (1997). p. 219

the intellect and its creation of the self is the obverse of the de-individuating force: only by virtue of the intellect's *restraining* force on the impulses is the self constituted – as the tension between a coherence with the impulse and itself as an agent – and only by virtue of the impulses which aim to undo it. Klossowski himself is unbending as regards the arbitrariness that is an implication of this interpretation of fortuity: "What would happen to human behaviour ... if at every moment individuals *understood each-other* by the fact that they were not 'willing' *this* when they were nonetheless designating it? ... Nietzsche clearly foresaw that such a lucidity ... would institute such a new conformity that he turned away from it in derision."[73] This incongruous lucidity would be the result of fortuity, were the latter defined as self-dissolution.

> We have to be destroyers! ... I perceived that the state of dissolution, in which individual natures can perfect themselves as never before – is an image and isolated example [*cas singulier*] of existence in general. Theory of the *fortuitous case*, the soul, a being that selects and nourishes itself, strong, crafty, and creative – continually (this creative force normally passes by unseen! it is conceived solely as 'passive') I recognized *active force*, created out of the fortuitous! – the fortuitous case itself is only the mutual collision of creative impulses.[74]

Nonetheless, fortuity obeys a central relation to the impulses. In this passage, the destruction, dissolution and de-individuation wrought by the impulses culminates in the *making and re-making* of the individual self, in the undoing of the self as a means to self-perfection. The self "selects and nourishes itself," sacrificing parts of itself to itself in creating a new self. As alluded to at the beginning of the passage, the self is ordinarily assimilated to a centre; all impulses, no matter how compulsive their fluctuations, refer back to it. The oscillations away from conservation and equilibrium disturb this self, pulling it in directions as various as are the impulses' movements. But the vicissitudes of one's moods and outbursts, however intense, are centripetal – moods always attributable to the agent and its intentional states (whether intended or not). The "centre" described in these passages is, therefore, constituted in the always-possible referral of a fluctuation back to a self – just as, in the Kantian critical tradition, all representations can be (i) attributed to the self which (ii) is the same for all representations so attributed, yet (iii) distinct from any of these and (iv) conscious of them,[75] according to the doctrine of the unity of apperception. With Nietzsche, however, all of these conditions are modified: (i) representations are attributable

---

[73] Klossowski, P. (1997). p. 53
[74] Klossowski, P. (1997). p. 220
[75] Kant, I. (1929). A116/B131–132, B134–135

to the self only after the impulses which produce them undergo filtration through the code; (ii) there are as many subjects as there are impulses, since the self, subject, agent or intellect is simply the obverse of any impulse whatever, and therefore arises as what Klossowski baptises a "coherence" between the self and the impulse; (iii) as such an obverse, these selves are not distinct from said impulses; and (iv) consciousness may or may not accompany the impulsive movements.[76] The continual seeking of a "new centre" follows naturally from these modified conditions. The self reflects only the impulses, no longer as one and the same self, nor the self as agent, but as the obverse of a fluctuation. This new centre, or the condition of searching for it, is the fortuitous self. Indeed, if this search is continual, and a permanent centre unfindable, as Klossowski claims,[77] then the fortuitous self is also in this sense provisional and dispersed. The *centrifugality* of fortuity is the exchange of one self for another, as obverses of different impulses, one or other of which intensify at different moments, in opposition to the centripetal forces of the intellect. As a result, the body creates as many selves as it undergoes different fluctuations; each self aims to "create another"[78] body – to maintain itself in spite of this overpowering decentrement.

In this regard, there are three central propositions which express Klossowski's exposition of fortuity, as an attribute of the self or ego:

> The centrifugal forces never flee the centre for ever, but approach it anew only in order to retreat from it yet again.[79]

> If these oscillations overwhelm him, it is because each corresponds to an individuality *other* than the one he believes himself to be, from the point of view of the unfindable centre.[80]

> As a result, an identity is essentially fortuitous.[81]

We endlessly oscillate between various centres, or selves, and multiple individualities emerge as a result. These are the fundamental parts of the doctrine of fortuity.

---

76 Klossowski, P. (1997). p. 26
77 Klossowski, P. (1997). p. 216
78 Klossowski, P. (1997). p. 29
79 Klossowski, P. (1997). p. 216
80 Klossowski, P. (1997). p. 216
81 Klossowski, P. (1997). p. 216

3.5 Fluctuation and Discontinuity

Both the earlier and later stages of Klossowski's study posit strong connections between the agent, self or ego and the notion of discontinuity. Ordinarily, discontinuity is understood in terms of the existence of lacunae or breaks in a series. In the mathematical context of functions, this amounts to the proviso that to sufficiently small changes in the input correspond arbitrarily small changes in the output. By what right does Klossowski appropriate these terms? What is the series in which the self appears, or the function or mapping which may or may not be continuous, depending on the nature of the contents it relates?

The term is used in two ways in the text, initially denoting a characteristic of the agent's vague experiences, but secondly an interruption occurring between intensity and consciousness. Firstly, then, discontinuity is lived, obfuscated by the "unity of the person of the ego,"[82] overlaying periodic interruptions with an illusory steadiness and consistency. Secondly, however, discontinuity is located "between silence and declarations in the agent"[83] or "between the coherence of the intellect and the incoherence of the impulses."[84] Whereas lived experience, as well as sequences of declarations, can form series of occurrences, the coherences and incoherences of the agent with signs and intensities suggest a kind of function: the signs which populate experienced are produced depending on fluctuations of intensity, but by virtue of the work of the code, become specifically indexed and localised. The code can be described as a map in the basic sense that it translates such fluctuations into these specifically indexed and localised signs.

Since the impulses are silent or mute – signifying nothing other than themselves – there is an affinity between the discontinuity which holds between silence and declaration and that which separates the intellect from the impulses. On the one hand, a series of declarations is discontinuous in that its terms are separated by breaks, such as the spaces between written words or pauses between utterances. However, this cannot be the sole ground of the interruption occurring "between silence and declarations." The silence referred to by Klossowski is not the simple absence of a declaration, such as is latent in a pause in a speech or a space between two inscriptions, but the intrinsic muteness of intensity. This silence could prevail whether or not the subject was speaking or ruminating, or whether or not at a chosen point in a given string anything

---

[82] Klossowski, P. (1997). p. 38
[83] Klossowski, P. (1997). p. 37
[84] Klossowski, P. (1997). p. 255

at all was actually inscribed. Even in apparent silences, the agent remains conscious as long as the code is active and signs are available. Thus, on the other hand, we are led to an alternative interpretation of this statement: discontinuity lies between the coherent declarations and the incoherent fluctuations which produce them. It separates subterranean fluctuations, which are pre-linguistic, from properly formed discourse or meaningful utterances.

In order to elucidate this thesis concerning the discontinuity between these two fields, we can consider its antithesis. Were the relationship between them continuous, each variation of intensity, however minute, would in some manner be reflected in a modification at the level of the code. Moreover, any modification could endlessly be subdivided and a change in intensity corresponding to it found nonetheless. In this way, one is tempted to assume that the representation of an object we believe may satiate or nourish us, and the conscious avowal of our desire for it, or the gradual intensification and increase in magnitude of a conscious sensation, each derive from appropriately granular shifts in our impulsive condition. But this is not the way declarations are born of impulses. Although Klossowski makes reference to intensity as if to something divisible, as well as to its degree, he nowhere admits its continuous variability. At no point in the text is there the indication that an intensity is a signifying element – or mode of existence or event – which can be broken into isolated intervals, and the contribution of each to a certain conscious state reckoned independently. Yet only if one admits (fallaciously) the legitimacy of such a procedure can one infer the continuity of its effect on the conscious mind of the agent; for continuity requires that a sufficiently small shift in intensity can in principle be located such that for *any* effect, arbitrarily chosen, the former accounts for the latter.

However, what is noteworthy here is not only the fact that continuity cannot be proved to feature in the relationship between impulse and sign, but also that continuity is a property inapplicable *in principle* to this relationship, since declarative outbursts and self-ascriptions are always *spontaneous*, in the above sense. One cannot always locate a *specific* determinative fluctuation for them. This amounts to denying that, for any given declaration or representation – any sign belonging to the conscious agent – one can point to its source in an underlying fluctuation. Such outbursts or images always develop suddenly, and although they derive from intensity, they in no way culminate *immediately* from them, in the manner of a causal dependency. "The evaluations lay below the surface a long time what comes out is the effect,"[85] which is not as such contiguous

---

[85] Klossowski, P. (1997). p. 256

with the evaluations Nietzsche classifies as evaluative. Consciousness as a semiotic depends only discontinuously on intensity, as a result.

By way of a more concrete demonstration of this difference, we can consider the judgements Nietzsche attached to the fluctuations which disturbed him. For any consciously perceptible difference in a sensation, or any appreciable change in Nietzsche's diagnosis of his own state, there would have to be corresponding to any such difference or change a difference or change in fluctuations of intensity which could explain it. "The designations of the everyday code ... intervene in accordance with changing excitations, upon which they impose their own linkages in order to conceal the total discontinuity of our state."[86] Changes in Nietzsche's own bodily state, in his underlying functions, were rooted in the discordant impulses that formed a relatively stable and individuated organism, underlying the code's designations. But changes in Nietzsche's constitution were transmitted sporadically into consciousness. Sometimes his work and habits continued uninterrupted in spite of tectonic movements; other times enormous changes in his own perceptions of his physical state, in his self-diagnoses and in his reckoning of his own recovery prospects, arose from the merest intensive shifts.[87] Accordingly, because of the lack of proportion and delay between their own movement and their transmission to consciousness, these intensities were "given names only through the interpretation of those who receive his messages."[88]

What are the consequences of this thesis which concerns discontinuity in the context of the self and its fortuity? The attack on the self derives from the multiplicity of the self, whether by virtue of the self being distributed over the unconscious as well as the conscious mind, or by virtue of its relationships with political, moral or social phenomena. For illustrative purposes, a noteworthy contrast can be drawn between the discontinuity and the Kantian philosophy of the self, where unity is centralised. The Kantian interpretation of the self, which can be contrasted with these theses *apropos* discontinuity, crystallises in the doctrine of the unity of apperception, characterised above by several conditions: "It must be the case that each of my representations is such that I can attribute it to my self, a subject which is the same for all of my self-attributions, which is distinct from its representations, and which can be conscious of its representations."[89]

---

[86] Klossowski, P. (1997). p. 38
[87] Klossowski, P. (1997). pp. 16–22
[88] Klossowski, P. (1997). p. 232
[89] Kant, I. (1929). A116, B131–132, B134–135

3.5 Fluctuation and Discontinuity

Every representation is attributable to the self – not necessarily, but possibly, attributed. Kant's phrasing is notably ambiguous, in that the self to which any representation is possibly attributable is not obviously equivalent to the identical or "same" "subject" to which all representations that are attributed are attributed, any more than a possible act is a completed one. The proposition that each representation can be attributed to the self, being the same for all self-attributions, is distinct from the proposition that each representation can be attributed to the self, being the same for all *possible* self-attributions. In this vein, commentators such as Van Cleve and Howell have distinguished between two interpretations of the doctrine of the unity of apperception, each of which cast into different relief the attack on the self's unity with which it contrasts.[90] Interpreted strongly, the doctrine entails that a single act of attribution – a simultaneity or co-consciousness – is required for all relevant representations. Any representation must be accompanied by the same unifying, subjective act of thought as any other. The self that they are attributable to is the same for all attributions: for any set of possible attributions, these possible attributions refer to one and the same entity. Each can be attributed to the self, the same for any possible attribution, whether so attributed or not. But interpreted less strongly, the doctrine entails only that an act of attribution is required for any one representation – but not necessarily any and all representations. For any representation, it is possible to attribute it to the self, but only for the actually attributed representations is this self an identical subject. The identity of the self is not, therefore, indifferent to which representations are or are not attributed to it.

There are competing interpretations to consider in the context of Kant's instructive doctrine, with materially different implications, as can be seen here. One of these interpretations proceeds from a set of representations to their possible attribution to a single self; the other assumes the attribution of such a set to some unified self and deduces its necessary conditions. Notwithstanding the competition between these two interpretations, however, what they share is the following admission: whether a relevant set of representations, a manifold, are attributable or attributed to the self, this self is the same for all these possible or actual attributions, by virtue of the prefixture of the "I think" attaching the subject and the proposition. Either there exists one subject to which all these actual attributions are made, or there exists one subject to which all possible attributions are made.

Thus, Kant interrogates the relation of receptivity, or intuition, to the understanding, or thought. Four terms are posited as a result: receptivity, as the faculty

---

90 Van Cleve, J. (1999); Howell, R. (1992); see also Pereboom, D. (2014).

for receiving representations; intuition as the manifold through which objects are given; the understanding, conceived as the faculty for producing representations; and thought, the spontaneous act of synthesis. The principle of the unity of apperception discussed above implies that, insofar as representations, of intuition or otherwise, are attributed or attributable to a subject, this subject is one – by virtue of the synthetic "power of associating perceptions."[91]

It is at this point that the Nietzschean semiotic becomes particularly relevant. Firstly, indeed, the fact that Klossowski *defines* consciousness as the code of signs enabling representation, itself a kind of sign, prohibits the distinction of the conscious subject from representation: the two effectively coalesce. Moreover, there is no in-principle-associability of distinct perceptions. All perceptions and representations, as signs, arise due to fluctuations of intensity, from without. The subject, as the obverse of a given impulse, a conservative force, has nothing in this sense in common with other impulses. If the impulses are several and disparate, then it follows that no obverse of some impulse is unified with any other. The signs produced by their fluctuation do not *a priori* belong to an identical or unified subject, and still less can one use this as a basis to derive its transcendental conditions.

Conveyed in accordance with the Kantian conceptual architecture, at the level of receptive representation there is no spontaneity of understanding or thought. "If the receptivity of our mind to receive representations, insofar as it is affected in some way, is to be called sensibility, then the mind's power of producing representations from itself, the spontaneity of cognition, is the understanding."[92]

Whereas Kant's Transcendental Deduction attempts to demonstrate the necessary applicability of the categories of the understanding, which are themselves derived in the Metaphysical Deduction, to the manifold of intuition, in Klossowski the most comparable relations – of intensities which lie at the origin of sensation to the signs which (mis)represent them – contain a discontinuity. The synthesis of the elements of a manifold in a unified subjective act, delineated by Kant as a condition of experience, cannot occur if there is a discontinuity between the elements and their synthesis. This synthesis requires the subjection of the manifold "to universal rules of a thoroughgoing connection in their reproduction."[93] Thus a collection of possibly disparate elements of the manifold are connected determinately, in "thoroughgoing" fashion, by thought: in thought,

---

[91] Kant, I. (1929). A122
[92] Kant, I. (1929). A50/B74
[93] Kant, I. (1929). A122

given one of two elements subject to a determinate or thoroughgoing connection, the other necessarily follows. In essence, we can consider any two perceptions one of which follows upon the other as adjacent as we please, and nonetheless a sufficiently minute fluctuation of intensity can be located which produces them, one directly after another. Empirical perceptions, organised from the manifold into a determinately connected series of events, would be free of interruptions or sudden changes. But these are exactly the changes that characterised the Nietzschean experience: sudden bursts of philosophical fecundity and similarly unexpected bouts of invalidity, the reactivation of memories and the premonition of destinies all came from without, unconnected to anything empirical preceding them. The discontinuity described by Klossowski discontinuity entails that there are no arbitrarily small changes capable of being isolated at the level of representation, such as could be related to sufficiently small changes at the level of intensity in order to for the Kantian commitment to be borne out. Not only are the declarations which attribute representations or signs to the self absolutely separate. The small shifts in intensity which produce enormously different and unpredictable upsurges in conscious sensations, memories, emotions and resonances – the landscape of Nietzsche's symptomatology – involve a discontinuity irreconcileable with the requirements of Kantian subjectivity.

This discontinuity between the self constituted in conscious states and its origin in intensive fluctuations is the foundation for the conspiratorial element of Nietzsche's thought, examined at length and in almost every chapter of the text, as its dramatic and theatrical centrepiece: "As Nietzsche's thought unfolded, it abandoned the strictly speculative realm in order to adopt, if not simulate, the preliminary elements of a conspiracy."[94] The dependency of conscious states on a series beyond, behind or beneath them, the impossibility of identifying a particular underlying state responsible for their augmentation and diminution, or for the sudden upspringing of phenomena represented in them, amounts to the powerlessness of the self in the face of the inscrutable machinations of intensity. Not only are they passive; their origin appears to obey a different kind of law entirely, unconscious and outside of empirical parameters – thus the "hidden reason"[95] responsible for the genesis of the self. This incongruity between the fluctuation and its effect in consciousness generates, from a temporal perspective, a reflected anachronism between the two: "The singular case rediscovers, in an 'anachronistic' manner, an ancient way of existing – whose reawakening in itself presupposes that *present* conditions do not correspond to the

---

[94] Klossowski, P. (1997). p. xv
[95] Klossowski, P. (1997). p. 32

impulsive state which is in some manner being affirmed through it."[96] The comparatively ancient origin of the fluctuation which now manifests itself in a conscious state (with the activation of a sign) renders it an anachronism. Like all subterranean incoherences, it refuses incorporation into the coherent mass of codified intensities. The irony proper to the Nietzschean discourse derives from the discordance between the institutional regime of signs, each attributable to the self, and the thought of this discontinuity, which undoes this regime, yet in whose service the latter is employed. Ultimately, because of the obstinacy of this discordance, and by way of a compromise between the incoherent intensity and coherent self, this thought could be communicated only as a drama, with Nietzsche its living incarnation during his mental collapse.

As a logical consequence of the incongruity between the institutional code on the one hand and intensity on the other, the self is confronted by two forces it straddles and triages. The impulses are intrinsically incapable of being represented, yet the self is confronted by signs which are representations. The self is constituted by the interaction between the intensity of these impulses and the intellect: the intensity aims at dissolution, and obversely the intellect at conservation, producing the fragile solidarity between impulses constitutive of the self. In siding with intensity, the self tends towards self-destruction, and with the phantasms, producing the phantasmic coherence of the agent with an impulse. In siding with the intellect, the self refers to itself, and claims states, moods, emotions, thoughts and desires, according to the institutional code, producing the coherence of the agent with itself. In acting or incarnating these phantasms, the self attains the relief of finding an "equivalent" to the incoherent or unconscionable impulse, without succumbing to the invasive tendencies of the external world, imposed on us through the code, dramatising "what it 'means' for our declaration,"[97] and achieving a manufactured harmony between the two. Analogously, by falling back on language (by referring to itself, or describing its underlying state) it balances the protection offered by the code's stability against the dissolving impulses with the apparent freedom to describe itself at its whims. The self is nothing more than a series of such bargains.

---

96 Klossowski, P. (1997). p. 80
97 Klossowski, P. (1997). p. 260

3.6 Conclusion: Discontinuity and Selfhood

In a precious instance of alignment between Klossowski's argumentation and the consensus of scholars, both locate strongly critical tendencies in Nietzsche's analysis of subjectivity. Here, however, the essential points of contrast drawn between the philosopher and the tradition he opposes are far from identical in these cases. Nietzsche's attacks on the categories of the self or ego do not especially concern Cartesian subjectivity, or the distinction between the conscious and unconscious mind of psychoanalysis, but rather follow from his theory of signs: the self is the sign of extreme degrees of intensity, as either the reflexive coherence of the self with itself, or as its obverse coherence with impulses. As a result, Klossowski advances an entirely different conception of the relation of the unconscious to consciousness, and the relation of the body to the self. But aside from his relation to the tradition, the role played by the self in the architecture of his study is dominated by the property of fortuity – and, in spite of Nietzsche's extensive superficial flirtations with thermodynamic formulations of such a notion, it is ultimately to be interpreted in terms of the discontinuity between impulse and sign, or mute intensity and the institutional code.

4 Possibility and Fortuity in the Vicious Circle

In spite of its quietist persuasion, the progression of Klossowski's study of Nietzsche broadly fits the Cartesian paradigm of construction atop a sedentary foundation. Its grounding, laid out after the introduction, is the semiotic of intensity: degrees of intensity are the source of experience, manifested in specific signs. The resultant architecture is the study's content: the vicious circle, variously encountered and elaborated. Yet, as yet, this present essay has neglected the latter almost entirely. The second chapter attempts to deduce the key characteristics of the semiotic, asserting several contrasts with that of the institutional code which allows for reference and representation, but asserting also affinities with the triadism of Peirce, Eco and Wittgenstein. The third attempts to interpret the critical Nietzschean discourse of the self in light of intensity, which lead to Klossowski's talk of the fortuity of the self. At this point, however, this talk begins to trace out a theory of possibility exhibited in the vicious circle. We must now address these theses directly.

4.1 Definition of the Circle

The vicious circle is a notion given a rigorous definition, albeit effaced and buried in Klossowski's fourth chapter, and despite its seemingly moralistic tenor. In the "Attempt at a Scientific Explanation of the Eternal Return," he declares:

> If a fluctuation of intensity can take on a signification only in the trace it leaves – that is, in the meaning of a sign – then the sign of the Circle is at once the trace (in the mind), the meaning, and the intensity itself. In this sign (*circulus vitiosus Deus*), everything becomes merged with the movement itself, which by turns resuscitates and abandons the trace, empty, to itself.[1]

The Circle is, as intensity, the trace of itself. (Definition)

The vicious circle is an intensity which is its own trace. As the trace of itself alone, it is not that of a previous or ensuing fluctuation. Any sign being the trace of a fluctuation, it is as a result its own sign. Any sign which is not an intensity and thus its own trace is consequently the trace of another – either as the trace of a trace, or the trace of something other than a trace, thus an intensity. Ordinarily, outside of the privileged moment of the vicious circle's enactment,

---

1 Klossowski, P. (1997). p. 114

all fluctuations belong to pure intensities, and the signs which are activated as a result are their traces. Signs, as traces, refer to something *other than themselves*. Whether or not these signs' immediate referents refer in turn to others, the chain of referents terminates in an ultimate link. Most importantly, the reference to something (mediate or immediate) confers upon a sign its actuality: it represents a state, and is the actualisation of something particular. With the vicious circle, in which intensity traces its own trace, there is no such reference, nor such actuality. In Klossowski, the term "intensity" is thus used to designate impulsive movements which are never actual, and never specific. Accordingly, a fluctuation in which the circle emerges is an empty trace of itself, and thus void of content.

In the circle, the sign, intensity and trace adopt an irreducibly multiple form; multiplicity is its essential consequence. The sign has no particular object, relating to an intensity neither directly nor mediately. It is therefore pure iterability: only ever a trace of itself, without termination. The circle's capacity to act as its own trace means that its identity is its own reference to itself, identified by the fact that its reference is constant wherever and however such a sign might arise, since it points simply to itself. Such a trace cannot be one, despite this criterion of identity; it cannot specify a determinate location, and it is multiple, just as there are different possible occurrences of this intensity. Unlike signs which form a finite chain, terminating upon an ultimate element, the multiplicity of the sign of the circle is irreducible in nature, "a multiple alterity already inscribed within an individual,"[2] and therefore a multiplicity which is not exhausted at the level of the individual, an apparent unit.

This multiplicity, for Klossowski, takes a serial form: "I deactualize myself in order to will myself in *all the other selves whose entire series must be passed through* so that ... I once again become what I am."[3] The sign of the circle – at once trace, intensity and sign – here conceived of as a subjective state, or as an affection of the individual, thus suggests passage through a series. This series, however, appears at first to be precisely the kind of interpretation inveighed against in the previous chapter: a series of states, deterministically conditioned, one after the other, bringing about a definite outcome – in this case, said outcome being reattainment of the circle's revelation. Not only this, but such an interpretation is quite explicitly suffused with notions of individuality which, at this stage in the study, have already been carefully refined. Interpreted simplistically, the "other selves" forming such a series would be regarded as nothing

---

2 Klossowski, P. (1997). p. 69
3 Klossowski, P. (1997). p. 58

other than the retentive individual's concrete history from birth to death, insofar as memory succeeds in preserving this history. But this cannot be an adequate interpretation of this serial property. Firstly, although the vicious circle, being as it is a movement of necessity, avowedly exhibits law-like behaviour, it derives from the theory of fortuity which is incompatible with this species of determinism. Secondly, the series formed by the circle's multiplicity is to be distinguished from the individual's history: it is, by contrast, that of "innumerable others,"[4] since a "single individual, as the product of an entire evolution, could never *reactualize* all the conditions and random events that led to his own consciousness."[5] Rather, these "other individualities ... those that have prepared for the present life, and those that the latter is preparing for others, remain totally unsuspected by consciousness."[6] A different conception of individuality than that of theinitial approach, cast in terms of the history of the individual – the approach refuted in previous chapters – is at stake here. What, then, are these other individualities, and other existences which their series comprise? Without an explanation, the definition of the circle in terms of an intensity which is its own trace, or in terms of a recursive multiplicity with no specific extension, risks appearing to be nothing other than a meaningless abstraction.

The first noteworthy characteristic of these serial individualities is that they reflect the indeterminacy of fluctuation. Fluctuations vary by nature, being perpetually a movement or becoming. Since an intensity always involves a complex of impulses, any fluctuation excites combinations of these competing impulses to differing degrees, which compete with each other for dominance over the organism. Alterity is therefore inscribed in the nature of fluctuations which traverse multiple states, never something singular and determinate. These metamorphoses[7] thus inscribe plurality into the individual. Klossowski's arguments, however, apply not only to a series of individual states, but to a series of individualities *per se*, and therefore to a series of series. This important distinction in Klossowski's analysis between series and series of series is supported by a unique method of formalisation developed by Ingrid Orfali in her *Fiction érogène à partir de Klossowski*. Seeking a more effective way to represent the various forces at work in the images and scenarios depicted in Klossowski's work, and to analyse the "engines"[8] of the subject in each scene, Orfali appeals not so much to series of images, but series of series:

---

4 Klossowski, P. (1997). p. 58
5 Klossowski, P. (1997). p. 94
6 Klossowski, P. (1997). p. 70
7 Klossowski, P. (1997). p. 69
8 Orfali, I. (1983). p. 151

> Having defined the different types of driving forces involved ... and having evoked some characteristics relating to their usage, let us ... propose the following formulations of them: let us designate by lower case letters the sequences constituting an erogenous scenario, each letter representing a particular sequence [a, b, c, d, e].[9]

Aside from the excitation of fluctuations which may generate a series pertaining to one individual, there must be some intensive force which generates a series of these in turn, and therefore generates other individualities. Equivalently, there must be a kind of complexity.

Secondly, on top of their intrinsic variability, fluctuations of intensity relate not only externally, that is, in a relation which fastens upon two otherwise independent parts, but internally, fluctuation *within* fluctuation.[10] Fluctuations thus inter-mix. The disparate resonances that are excited by a single intensification, such as fantasies which arouse numerous emotions, or perceptions which elicit recollections or premonitions, attest to this inter-mixing, and to the containment of fluctuations within one another: the intensification of one is an intensification of the other, like waves battling to superpose. As evidence of this, Klossowski adduces Nietzsche's reflections on disingenuously *simple*, rudimentary impulses such as hunger: hunger appears to be a unified and singular impulse, which, with knowledge of the "means to suppress it"[11] picks out a determinate object – anticipated nourishment. The ostensible simplicity of the impulse follows from its seemingly *exclusive* fixation upon its object, food, as means of suppressing a certain feeling. But we can imagine the impulse quite apart from this epistemic element. "A series of movements can take place in the organism whose aim is to suppress hunger: the *stimulation* of this mechanism is *felt at the same time* as the hunger."[12] In this case, the impulse is merely correlated with knowledge and action – and only for this reason do we associate the two, impute a causal relationship, and believe in the impulse's simplicity. The impulse does not, however, have an exclusive or singular content, but the confused content of a mixture. What we call hunger, in other words, is complex, and the fact that it impels us towards a relatively defined course of action is no mark of simplicity, but the fact that its stimulation occurs "at the same time." Fluctuations are, then, subject to a fundamental indeterminacy, on the basis of the *co-intensification* of multiple intensities. The resultant *inter-mixture* generates a series of individual series of states, or a series of individualities – not a determinate one.

---

9 Orfali, I. (1983). p. 151
10 Klossowski, P. (1997). p. 62
11 Klossowski, P. (1997). p. 34
12 Klossowski, P. (1997). p. 34

4.2 Receptivity and Displacement

With the merging of the intensity and its trace which defines the vicious circle, the individual becomes displaced: its only content is the ability to receive the sign of the circle as another individual (at another place or time). Descartes' *Second Meditation* provides useful material for comparison with this aspect of the kind of individuality multiplied by the vicious circle:

> But here I shall rather direct my attention to the thoughts that ... came to my mind beforehand, whenever I considered what I was. The first was that I have a face, hands, arms, and this whole mechanism of limbs, such as we see even in corpses; this I referred to as the body. Next, that I took nourishment, moved, perceived with my senses, and thought: these actions indeed I attributed to the soul. What this soul was, however, either I never considered, or I imagined it as something very rarefied and subtle, like a wind, or fire, or thin air, infused into my coarser parts.[13]

For Descartes, the individual is at first divided between the thoughts of the body's inert members and the unseen force which allows them to move, and which consists in actions (such as taking nourishment and moving), thought, and perception. In this passage, aside from the epistemic complications which will follow and lead to Descartes' dualism, and among many other insights, the individual is presented as a state of thought which consists in a set of combinations of *determinate particulars immediately accessed:* perceptions, feelings, sensations and reflections. We can right away draw a contrast with the vicious circle, in which immediate access is replaced by infinite semiosis, and determinate particularity by recursion. How and why do these replacements occur?

Whereas the actualised self, a sign in the institutional code and accordingly distinct from intensity, has specific content that persists with the variation of time and location, the deactualised subject of the vicious circle has no location and does not persist, since it is only ever a trace of another existence, which is in turn a trace, *ad infinitum*. This is the reappearance of the infinite semiosis which featured in the second chapter, and the recursion of signs implicit in it, following from the fact that the chain of signs does not terminate in an ultimate sign. However, in this discussion, infinite semiosis was a result of the definition of the sign as a trace, and therefore the re-excitation of a prior intensity, and the fact that the signification of the sign is dependent on degrees of fluctuations:

---

[13] Descartes, R. (2008). p. 17

> If a sign retains its meaning, it is because the degree of intensity coincides with it.[14]
>
> It signifies only through a new afflux of intensity, which in a certain manner joins up with its first trace.[15]

In this context, by contrast, not only are signs dependent on fluctuations. Further, fluctuations of intensity themselves are their own traces. Thus, it is not simply that signs are traces of intensities which come and go, perpetually (infinitely) modifying and revising their meaning. The chain of signs now exhibits a recursive structure, since the intensity itself is not independent of the sign: the sign is a trace of intensity and thus the trace of itself. There is, therefore, a recursive dynamic internal to mediation itself, and if signs are construed as media of determination, recursivity must hold of semiosis by the same token.

As a consequence, the signs that populate the individual's conscious experience, such as represented visual experience, become nothing other than a realisation of a commitment to receive such a representation made previously, and the commitment to realise a similar state of affairs in another context – a purely receptive capacity. The determinate particulars which Descartes describes as immediately accessible are no longer the constituents of individual experience:

> The same revelation could have occurred at any other moment of the circular movement. Indeed it must be thus: for in order to receive this revelation, I am *nothing* except this capacity to receive this revelation at *all the other moments* of the circular movement: nowhere in particular for me alone, but always in the movement in the whole.[16]

Once the individual recognises the structure of the vicious circle, to receive a particular experience is to receive it in any of an infinity of its recursions. The individual is a receptacle, and its sensory contents are just commitments to receive this same content at another point in the circle. But in order to comprehend more precisely how this strange receptivity can displace the individual from the immediate particulars of its experience, as we claimed above it did, we must turn to the Nietzschean notion of interpretation.

---

14 Klossowski, P. (1997). p. 61
15 Klossowski, P. (1997). p. 61
16 Klossowski, P. (1997). pp. 59–60

4.3 Economy of Interpretation

In the chapter "The Euphoria of Turin," Klossowski garners further resources for evaluating this multiplication of the individual driven by the circle. The intensive state in which the vicious circle appears most resoundingly is defined by an "interpretative availability,"[17] the accessibility of possibilities by impulsive interpretation. Interpretation enters the semiotic and temporal theories of the study at its very foundations. From first principles, impulses or drives themselves are interpretations of events. Klossowski states that our needs interpret the world:[18] perceptual experience of the external world no less than the internal, instinctual "wind, or fire"[19] of Descartes is a manifestation of impulses. Comparable to Husserlian intentionality and Heideggerian φαίνεσθαι, perceptions are intrinsically interpretive; they are no mere indifferent presentations which may or not be *supplemented* by judgements about what they are. Perception equates to interpretation, to interpretation-as: "In appearing, a being appears *as* something meaningful in the broadest sense ... The 'as'-character bespeaks the arrival of meaning amongst beings."[20] Since impulses, as interpretive, exhibit this taking-as structure, perceptions are themselves interpretations.

Further, relations among impulses lead to competitions between interpretations: the same event means different things to different impulses. From the perspective of his desire for intellectual partnership and exchange, Nietzsche's attempt at a liaison with Lou Salomé had ended in humiliation; from the perspective of his desire for isolation, alienation and distance from the conditions of bourgeois society and servitude, its failure was a liberating and perhaps deliberate act of self-sabotage, propelling him towards an enhanced creative output. But since there is a distinction between the representation of an event given in the code of signs and, on the other hand, the impulses which interpret them and bestow them with meaning, an infinity of aspects of any event stand to be revealed by the possible fluctuation of an impulse, notwithstanding the stability wrought on them by the code. Impulses are in this sense perspectival. Correlatively, it may only be "late that one musters the courage for what one really *knows*,"[21] that is, long after a certain excitation is received that the meaning of it becomes determined in a certain way, just as two versions of the premonitory dream are related in "The Consultation of the Paternal Shadow." Nietzsche at-

---

17 Klossowski, P. (1997). p. 251
18 Klossowski, P. (1997). p. 218
19 Descartes, R. (2008). p. 17
20 Sheehan, T. (1975). p. 89
21 Klossowski, P. (1997). p. 125

tests to this difference, consecrated between what is *hitherto* and *recent* in his own revelation: "That hitherto I had been a thorough-going nihilist, I admitted to myself only recently."[22] The multiplication of possibility which becomes explicit in the vicious circle comes about in this way – that is, from an infinity of admissible interpretations.

In order to reinforce and develop these considerations, two short passages, set apart widely in the text, must be underscored, being mainstays of the vicious circle conceived in terms of this economy of interpretation.

First passage:
1) "The 'death of God' (the God who guarantees the identity of the responsible self) opens up the soul to all its possible identities."
2) "This subject is no longer able to will itself as it has been up to now, but wills *all* prior possibilities."[23]

These propositions connect possibility to the exclusivity of identity, maintained by personal history (the self as it has been up to now), and the witness of this history (God). Identity is the singular and bounded history of the person.

Second passage:
1) "A single individual, as a product of an entire evolution, could never *reactualize* all the conditions and random events that led to his own consciousness."
2) "It is only in admitting his own fortuitousness that an individual will be open to the totality of fortuitous cases, and thus ... the necessity of returning in the Circle."[24]

These propositions oppose possibility to actuality, conceived as the set of conditions for the production of consciousness, and posit fortuity as the condition for possibility.

Both of these two passages, each a pair of propositions, make material additions to the account of the vicious circle developed thus far. They assert a distinction between actuality and possibility, albeit each in a different way. In the second, possibility is distinguished from the actuality *per se*, whereas in the first it is distinguished from actuality *qua* history of the individual. In order to com-

---

22 Klossowski, P. (1997). p. 125
23 Klossowski, P. (1997). p. 57
24 Klossowski, P. (1997). p. 94

prehend this distinction (in its two forms), we must once again refer back to the semiotic theory of the initial chapters: the distinction between actuality and possibility rests on the distinction between fluctuations of intensity and the everyday code of signs, and the latter's corresponding representations. In his exposition of Nietzsche's semiotic, Klossowski demonstrated one of the primary marks of the code: its suspension of fluctuations once and for all. This suspension derived from the permanence of an index, which assigns to an intensity a given location, associates it with a sign or representation and suppresses its fluctuation. The theory of the death of God posits God as just such an index: as the horizon of meaning, the fixity of history and the exclusivity of interpretation, all of which disappear with the proclamation of the death of the deity. Transmuted into the terms of interpretation, the suspension of fluctuation once and for all, according to the second passage, or the death of God according to the first, equate to the following: Only one interpretation of a fluctuation is permissible, and no fluctuation can modify such an interpretation. Outside the confines of this semiotic, however, that of intensity is marked by the collapse of "once and for all" interpretation. The phantasm of vicious circularity which replaces it requires that *nothing is ever constituted in a single meaning, once and for all.*[25]

The imprecise styling of the phrase "once and for all" can be more formally rendered in terms of indexicality: a signification is once and for all insofar as it can be regarded as an indexical. This term originates in the Peircean theory of signs, which divides signs into a triad of *types:* icons, indexes and symbols. According to Silverstein's account of Peirce, an indexical is defined as a type of sign such that the "occurrence of the sign vehicle token bears a connection of understood spatio-temporal contiguity to the occurrence of the entity signalled,"[26] or "the property of a sign vehicle signalling contextual 'existence' of an entity."[27] The specific sign or sign vehicle is connected to a context which it signals: "The presence of some entity is perceived to be signalled in the context of communication incorporating the sign-vehicle."[28] The distinguishing feature of such indexical signs is their status as shifters, in Silverstein's terms: indices whose reference is a function of a set of situational variables, themselves not analysable in terms of purely semantic constituents. Aside from the grammatical and logical features of a proposition by virtue of which it refers to some state of affairs, there are, in addition, relations to this proposition's context. Whereas several tokens of the former instantiate the same type, tokens of the latter, such as "you"

---

25 Klossowski, P. (1997). p. 64
26 Silverstein, M. (1976). p. 27
27 Silverstein, M. (1976). p. 29
28 Silverstein, M. (1976). p. 27

and "yesterday," may not. Importantly, then, as fixed as may be a signification or reference due to the semantic properties which determine it (in part), the signification of indexicals varies from event to event.

Notwithstanding the variation from context to context of the meaning of a sign or token, the relation of each sign or token to its specifically determining context does not, by contrast, vary. Each sign is tethered to its context in a way which is both determinate and permanent. The connection of the token to the variable on which it depends is fixed once and for all; the variability of the context does not extend to the function (else, indeed, it could not be a function). In Silverstein's terms, these indexicals are functions of contexts and semantic features are isofunctions.[29] As a result, they maintain the permanence and specificity of their signification. As much as I can declare that my work is done, for instance, and completed, and as much as this proposition may derive its sense from extra-semantic features – the possessive pronoun, which depends upon the identity of the speaker, and the past participle, whose tense invokes a specific *time* – for given features (a given identity, and a given time) this proposition has a determinate and singular content. The fact that the truth or falsity of this statement depends on who is referred to with the term "my" as well as the meaning of "work" and *when* the statement is uttered – whether before or after completion – does not preclude the permanence of the meaning of the statement. As long as these terms are defined, the meaning is fixed. Otherwise, the description of its meaning as a function would be spurious: given an exhaustive specification of the variables on which it depends, the purported function would not determine any meaning at all. Indeed, in this regard, it is noteworthy that Silverstein defines the indexical in terms of a spatio-temporal contiguity between the signified entity and the occurrence of the sign. This contiguity bestows their connection, and the sign is in this sense in contact with the context it picks out, and by virtue of which it is determined.

Since the connection of a given sign to a given context does not vary, but only the contexts and signs themselves, this notion of indexicality can be substituted for signification that occurs once and for all. *That which is once and for all is the indexical.* Indexical signification is not independent of its context or situation, and context and situation can be as variable as the events which are signified, but the contiguity of the two ensures the two are permanently linked, and a determinate, specific and singular signification is established.

Consider, then, how this notion of indexicality might assist in elucidating the notion of possibility which flows from Klossowski's discussion of interpreta-

---

29 Silverstein, M. (1976). p. 25

tion. As is evident from Nietzsche's writing alone, any event of signification whatsoever is an interpretative event. Interpretation, in turn and as has been shown by reference back to Klossowski's semiotic, vitiates permanent and determinate indexicality, as signification once and for all. Altogether, it is as a clear consequence of the semiotic of intensity that possibility becomes distinguished from actuality, and multiplies as a result. The following sequence of propositions summarises this reasoning:

- No interpretation is once and for all. (Axiom)
- All events are given a signification only by interpretation. (Axiom)
- Signification is the signification of an event. (Definition)
- No signification is once and for all. (Thesis)
- Actuality is once and for all. (Definition)
- Possibility is never once and for all. (Definition)
- Signification is the signification of possibility. (Conclusion)

Here, then, the denizens of the Klossowskian-Nietzschean life-world are possibilities and not actualities. At the beginning of this chapter, we laid out the semiotic definition of the vicious circle – the coincidence between the intensity and its own trace – and assembled the textual evidence for the close relationship this enjoys with multiplicity, and its self-referential or recursive structure. Questioning this relationship to multiplicity has led us to the additional evidence for these characteristics offered by the Nietzschean theory of interpretation, and its repudiation of indexicality, and permanent signification. It is precisely owing to this failure of indexicality, and the repulsion of the once and for all of signification, that possibility multiplies. The statement, "My work is done," loses the permanent signification which is attributed to it by the indexical perspective – the perspective which accords to it a definite meaning, provided definite semantic and extra-semantic features. One's work may or may not be done at a given time, depending on what one means, but whether it is or not, its status is always as variable as the conception of exactly what one's task is, and exactly what one has achieved, and what remains to be achieved. Attempting to strip out this variability by, for instance, removing the tense of its participle "done" and specifying the context which elucidates the reference of "my work" etc. does not remove this variability.

The vicious circle, then, involves the multiplication of the self by dint of possibility: the self wills itself in series of series. These series, however, must be carefully understood, lest they once again expose Klossowski's argument to appropriation by the discourse of mechanism. What exactly are these series? Turning to one avenue of interpretation, residues of a statistical-combinatorial metaphysics clearly remain in the insistence on the necessity of the realisation of a totality of possibilities. Such pronouncements evoke the work of Poincaré and Zermelo concerning the dynamics of recurrence.[30] In the context of Klossowski's discussion of the metaphysical and physical grounds of Nietzsche's cosmology, these affinities threaten to obscure the content of the doctrine, despite the various analogies which they appear to support. Firstly, the notion of a series following upon another series which the self multiplies as it explores conjures the image of causal linkages between events, which is to say that the moments making up one series appear as if deterministically related to each other, and each series so related to the others which precede or follow it (whether or not such a distinction can be maintained in the context of the vicious circle). In particular, this appears as the natural meaning of the fact that such series succeed one another as they are alleged to.[31] If Klossowski's work is as incompatible with this train of thought as has been argued, then the conception of possibility which supports it must accordingly be quite separate. The infinity of aspects generated by impulsive interpretation cannot be distinct events which flow into one another. What, then, is Klossowski's alternative?

To account for this, we must distinguish two views of the totality of possibilities the individual is forced by the vicious circle to confront. According to one, possibilities are simply events consistent with the universe's physical laws, whether known or unknown. The totality of them that the individual "re-wills"[32] as opposed to his or her personal history would then be successive chains of causally related events. As successive, they are actualised progressively, in a horizontal series. This position is a clearly affiliated with statistical-combinatorial conceptions of return.

However, this particular construal of the totality of possibilities does not cohere with Klossowski's usage. There are several ways in which these two must be winnowed. Firstly, possibility is to be regarded as a consequence of fortuity. As per the second extract above, it is only in admitting its fortuity that the individual is open to the totality of possibilities – fortuity which must be distinguished from the statistical-combinatorial or ergodic explanations which failed to reconcile with this perspective in the previous chapter. Secondly, the statistical perspective is resolutely deterministic, and suggests chains of events which repeat because their recurrence is nomologically mandated. The contention of this pre-

---

[30] In the late 19th Century, Poincaré discussed a theorem later applied to Zermelo to the theory of heat such that, with sufficient time, a dynamical system indifferently explores all orbits compatible with the finite region of phase space in which it is constrained.
[31] Klossowski, P. (1997). p. 57
[32] Klossowski, P. (1997). p. 58

sent study is, by contrast, that indeterminacy is an elementary consequence of the definition of the circle.

4.4 The Vicious Circle and Necessity

Despite connoting both indeterminacy and indeterminism, the vicious circle is repeatedly described as more than simply a momentary or arbitrary experience, although clearly an exceptional one which required the contrivance of particular circumstances, such as Nietzsche's *Stimmung* or tonality of feeling, as well as one which generates ethical criteria designed to ensure the survival of "singular cases"[33] in opposition to "gregarious needs."[34] In fact, the circle is repeatedly described as a law[35] and as something which involves a degree of necessity. What does it mean, then, to assert that the individual experiences the necessity of exploring these series, which show up as destinies in the vicious circle? The vicious circle is a sign which is at once intensity and its trace. The intensification latent in the vicious circle entails the deactualisation of the individual as an isolated case, in favour of its serialisation. Whatever is signified is itself only by indefinitely referring to itself, repeating itself and returning to itself. This thesis, however, does not entail the thesis that the circle "brings about, as necessity, the successive realizations of all possible identities,"[36] "all possible acts,"[37] and "all possible individuations."[38] What does the vicious circle's revelation of a recursive structure belonging to intensity have to do with these results?

The final chapters of Klossowski's study which intermittently address these issues contain, in several places, a doubly iterated modality.[39] The law of the circle, revealed to Nietzsche, is summarised in the following formula:

P) "Every identity must pass through a series of individualities in order for the fortuitousness of a particular identity to render them all necessary."[40]

---

[33] Klossowski, P. (1997). p. 120
[34] Klossowski, P. (1997). p. xiii
[35] Klossowski, P. (1997). p. 67
[36] Klossowski, P. (1997). p. 57
[37] Klossowski, P. (1997). p. 71
[38] Klossowski, P. (1997). p. 221
[39] Being the occurrence of one or more than one modality within the scope of another.
[40] Klossowski, P. (1997). pp. 216–217

Necessity is iterated over the fortuity of particular identity, construed as a modality, and over the necessity of the series which this fortuity entails. The formula encases operators with an unusual combination of scopes. The necessity of passing through a series follows from the implication that the series is necessary, by dint of the fortuity of an identity. We therefore have a state of affairs whose fortuity implies the necessity of another state of affairs, which implication itself implies a necessary state. Symbolically,

$$\Box \forall x \exists y_1 \exists y_2 \ldots \exists y_n((\mathrm{O}Q_0 x \rightarrow \Box(Q_1 y_1 Q_2 y_2 \ldots Q_n y_n)) \rightarrow (Q'xy_1 Q'xy_2 \ldots Q'xy_n)))$$

where the quasi-modal operator O has been used to indicate the fortuity of a state of affairs, as distinct from possibility, and where the one- and two-place predicates Q and Q' respectively (i) qualify the y_i as individualities and (ii) state that x passes through each of the y_i.

What is the nature of the logical connection between the elements of the first argument of this function – how does the fortuitousness of a particular identity relate to the series it necessitates? *Prima facie*, fortuity might seem to be nothing more than a contrast between the particular identity which is fortuitous and some set of other identities. An individual identity is fortuitous, in its occurrence or presence, with respect to others, just as one's escape of a number of unwelcome possible fates, in favour of a more welcome one, might be also. The particularity, specificity or non-seriality of the identity collapses into a necessary series. However, Klossowski is attuned to Nietzsche's distinction between individuality and identity in this passage, and has in mind something more specific. Firstly, individuality is in this passage such that a series of individualities, or purportedly specific primitive states, correspond to a single identity. Identity can accordingly be understood as an individual's history, which strictly speaking amounts to a series of individuals. Identity encloses a series:

"The incessant metamorphosis: in a brief interval of time you must pass through a series of individual states."[41] (Pluralisation Thesis)

Thus, there is a "multiple alterity already inscribed within an individual"[42] in that a series of purportedly individual states replaces an individual purported state. This tallies with the remarks cited above, in order to exhibit the definition of the vicious circle: we cannot conceive an individual state independent of the series to which it belongs. Insofar as each state is, conceived in accordance with

---

41 Klossowski, P. (1997). p. 69
42 Klossowski, P. (1997). p. 69

the Nietzschean semiotic, ultimately a sign excited by fluctuations of intensity, such a state is impermanent. It is neither marked by an indexical, nor a signification "once and for all." Viewed in relation to these original terms, the series of individual states corresponds to the *multiple possibilities* generated when an event is given competing interpretations. The *identity* equated to the series corresponds in turn to this multitude of interpretations.

These remarks do not add materially to Klossowski's theory of possibility as described thus far. The identity posited to contain numerous individuals is equivalent to the series of series above, just as is the notion of a series of states equivalent to that of multiple interpretative possibilities. However, with the ambiguity inherent in the scope of the final universal quantifier in the formula P), a second consideration arises. What does the fortuitousness of a particular identity render necessary? The entirety of something is necessitated owing to fortuity – but is this entirety the entirety of *individuals* or rather of *identities*? In passing through a series of individualities, an identity might well allow fortuity to make the totality of such individualities necessary in series; but it might equally well do so for the totality of identities. In the former case, however, the fortuity of an identity, and therefore the fortuity of the series of individualities, would imply the necessity of the series of individualities. The fortuity of the series would necessitate its elements. Yet it cannot be so: not only does this involve the platitudinous consequence that a series requires elements, or that a specific characteristic of this series does so. It mystifies the connection between fortuity and this necessity. Why should the fortuitousness of a series relate to the necessity of its terms, and what should the passage through these terms in P) have to do with this relation?

Klossowski clearly inclines towards the alternative construal of P), with the statement that the vicious circle "brings about, as necessity, the successive realizations of all possible identities."[43] Here, identities, not intra-identical individualities, are necessary. One fortuitous identity implies the necessity of other identities. This holds only if the identity is a series of individual states, and the other identities other series. Fortuity variously refers to (i) the occasional cohesion of the self – understood in contrast to the deindividuating tendency of unconscious impulsive forces – (ii) the non-homonymy of the relation between the body and this self, and (iii) the discontinuity of the intellect with the impulses. Summarily, the specific and localised signs which rise to the thin surface of consciousness are fortuitous with respect to the indeterminacy, the fluctuation and the vastness of the impulses. These signs are individual states, whether perceptions or messages from sensations, which are transmitted to the intellect.

---

43 Klossowski, P. (1997). p. 57

Now, a series of these states, as a more or less cohesive identity, is *equally fortuitous*. Not only is the general discontinuity of an arbitrary state – one element in the series – itself fortuitous, and not only is fortuity the result of a definite state's emergence from indefinite intensity; in the vicious circle, any actual state is deactualised by the dynamic of interpretation, and submitted to the whims of its re-emergence. Accordingly, any series of states, and any identity, becomes fortuitous. In the circle, any state can be deactualised and reinterpreted. But, in addition, the series itself – as a set of distinct terms admitting a specific order and relationships – can be deactualised and reinterpreted. Thus, *any particular identity is as fortuitous as individuality*.

These two aspects of the dynamic of interpretation exhibited by the circle must therefore be separated. Individual states are fortuitous roughly because the individual is fortuitous. But with the insertion of the notion of interpretation into the Nietzschean discourse, any series of events, connecting in whatever way, becomes the object of interpretation. Any series is defined by the number and type of its terms, putting aside their content, and by the relationships between them, such as their order. One event precedes or follows another, and groups of events can obey causal relationships, or principles of association, whereas others may be purely incidental. All these features become functions of interpretation. As it remains for the following chapters of this study to address, not only do the causal necessities "fall away"[44] but the very order of the events is subject to revision as a result, and in a way which entails fundamental revisions of the conceptions of temporality and causality which can be upheld in the face of the vicious circle's intensity.

Moreover, from the fortuity of a particular identity follows that of *all* identities implicit in the circle. Once the particular identity is deactualised and subjected to the indeterminacy of multiple interpretations, all identities which are possible, by virtue of this deactualisation and reinterpretation, are necessary. Assuming this proposition follows from the thesis that *any particular identity is as fortuitous as individuality*, this identity must have a serial form. Only as a result of the dynamic of interpretation, deactualisation and reinterpretation, productive of series, can these identities become necessary. Summarily: In order to transition from an actual given identity to all possible identities, a series is required. Without this series, not only would there be no identity, but further, neither deactualisation nor reinterpretation could then occur – and only in respect of the series of multiple identities into which the pre-existing identity dissolves: its possibilisation.

---

44 Klossowski, P. (1997). p. 183

From another point of view, if an identity is to be understood as the unity of countless different states, each the obverse of a different impulse, then it can only be consistent with the vicious circle, in which no state is determinate, and is only the trace of its pre- and post-existence – that is, its own repetition – if all of these states occur in the recursive series to be explored. Only by resurfacing after traversing the totality of possibilities, or the space of all other individualities, could this identity be itself. If an individual state, which contains a multiplicity of signs, can signify only if each sign is its own trace, and therefore repeats itself, and if an identity is a unity of all such signs, this identity must recur in order to occur at all. For this reason, connections between the vicious circle and the being of becoming have become ubiquitous citations in Nietzsche scholarship:[45] being what one is requires one become it, passing through whatever series are necessary, as opposed to maintaining this one moment against its tendency to decay into the next. The generation of a *circle* of series – the vicious circle – derives from the necessary reinterpretation of any individual state which occurs from series to series, and from the dictum that an individual state can re-actualise itself only after an exploration of a multitude of others.

The modalities in the sentence P) are therefore the justification for the nomological component of the vicious circle and, as a result, the law-like nature of the movement it specifies. The two modalities implicit in the sentence are the necessity of the series of *identities* on the one hand, and of the passage through a series of *individualities* on the other. Every identity is fortuitous as a rule, and as a rule makes all identities necessary, by exploring various individualities. This incessant movement, as a prerequisite for the pluralisation of identity, is the content of the law of the vicious circle.

There is a further subjectivity to note in respect of the scope of the penultimate quantifier in P). Fortuity does not apply merely to a given individual state, but by virtue of this theory of interpretation, to series and thus identity itself. At first, the fact that every identity is the subject of the passage through a series suggests a set of *numerable or countable elements* (each set being such an identity). The reference in proposition P) to "every" identity would then equate to "each" identity. P) would therefore be "valid on condition that what is *a priori* possible be thinkable in terms of a numerical totality,"[46] if formulated in the terms developed in Meillassoux's work; it would posit a *numerical* conception of totality. Indeed, this conception of totality is latent in the mechanical conception of the vicious circle. If we conceive fortuity as a feature of any system following some

---

45 Heidegger, M. (1991b). pp. 198–208; Deleuze, G. (1986). p. 23; Moore, A. (2012). p. 402
46 Meillassoux, Q. (2008). p. 166

random path through phase space – ergodically – in a gesture which we have found impossible to reconcile to the text of Klossowski and Nietzsche, then any path is then possible so long as it is consistent with the laws governing the phase space (as argued previously). In turn, a system can then be regarded as a phase space with a collection of subsets which define trajectories, and with some measure which allows for the definition of probabilities, and mappings which formalise the phenomenon of time-evolution. These are respectively recognisable in the quadruple $\langle \Gamma, \mathcal{A}, \mu, \mathcal{T}_u \rangle$. We therefore have a range of possible paths in the phase space, representing possibilities, or possible individual states, together with a probability measure, which as a function of a given path defines the extent of the path's fortuity. This formalism thus provides an ostensible analogue to the dynamic of the vicious circle, incorporating a gloss of the notions of fortuity and possibility. In order for this analogy to be valid, however, one must

> assume that a set of possible worlds ... is actually conceivable, if not intuitable, within which we can then carry out our extension of probabilistic reasoning from objects that are *internal* to our universe ... to the universe *as such*. Thus, probabilistic reasoning is conceivable on condition that it be possible to conceive a totality of cases within which one can then calculate frequencies by determining the ratio of the number of favourable cases to the number of possible cases.[47]

Just as a measure must be specified in order to derive a notion of probability from the image of a universe of states randomly wandering between one another, one inevitably appeals to assumptions about the totality of possibilities explored in the vicious circle in order for it to be converted into these terms. It is at least feasible, in fact, to choose an axiomatic – such as Cantor's transfinite – in which possibility fails to structure itself as a numerical totality. Even this in principle feasibility of an alternative serves to undermine the contrary assumption which is essential to the mechanical view of possibility. Possibility, understood in its entirety, is *not* a countable set of concrete elements, but an open one; the totality of possibilities is one of all possibilities and identities, and not of each and every one. It is illegitimate to reify possibilities as individual states, and to proceed to assimilate these states to a set of countable, distinct elements – a result which must be borne in mind when examining this prominent motif in *Nietzsche and the Vicious Circle*. As signified by the circle in its emergence from intensity, the notion of possibility "is a sign for everything that has happened,

---

47 Meillassoux, Q. (2008). p. 169

for everything that is happening, and for everything that will ever happen in the world."⁴⁸

4.5 Conclusion: Actuality and Representation

Accompanying this latter formula ("a sign for everything that has happened ...") upon its second appearance in the text's fourth chapter is an elliptical appendix – yet one which is crucial in completing any interpretation of the possibilisation at the heart of the circle. In Klossowski, the sign of the vicious circle, the coincidence of intensity with the trace of itself, stands for everything that can ever happen, that has ever happened, and that could ever happen – "and, indeed, in thought itself."⁴⁹ This remark materially enriches his notion of possibility. So far, we have discussed how the text refers to the deactualising movement in which the circle intensifies, and the economy of interpretation which follows as a consequence. These cause the multiplication of possibility, insofar as the individual state loses its permanent location, a location which would ordinarily be a function of indexical signs – the once and for all. All possibilities become necessary. As Castanet writes, "the disappearance of the 'once and for all' that perpetually characterises the unique identity" is "essential ... to note ... the revelation opens up the series of possibles."⁵⁰ These results are now familiar. But with the statement that these possibilities include those of "thought itself" – over against those which are merely physically possible, and consistent with whichever laws are taken to be determinative – an expanded domain of possibilities is invoked. Initially, the attribution of the same circular movement to thought as to intensity can be inferred from the identification of thought with the activity of the intellect, and of intensity with that of impulsive movements. The intellect is the obverse of a given impulse, inserted into the dynamic of fluctuation. It follows that there must be a similar obverse relationship between it and the impulsive intensity. Correlatively, if the circle describes the behaviour of intensity – from deactualisation to the suppression of indexicality – then it must describe that of the intellect and of thought as well. Such is, moreover, the impression evoked by the image of the waves of pure intensity, which produce significations, and in turn *thoughts*, as they rise to a crest: in the circle, "the intensity signifies itself ... and this is what we call thought."⁵¹ However, in various passages in the

---

48 Klossowski, P. (1997). p. 58
49 Klossowski, P. (1997). p. 66
50 Castanet, H. (2014). p. 106
51 Klossowski, P. (1997). p. 62

text, thought becomes detached from the intellect's purely preservatory role, and takes on various independent aspects.

> To prevent discourse from *being reduced to the level of a fallacious coherence*, it must be compelled toward a type of thought that does not refer back to itself (i. e., to the intellect), in a kind of edifice of subsequent thoughts, but is pushed to a limit where thought puts a *stop to itself*.[52]

Thought and the intellect seem to be distinguished by the following oddity: Thoughts are intrinsically limited, whereas the intellect refers to itself in an unlimited series of signs or statements, or "edifice of subsequent thoughts." "Insofar as thought turns out to be efficacious, it is not as an utterance of the intellect but as the *premeditation* of an action."[53]

Thought, again in contrast to the intellect, becomes active – no longer simply opposing the disorganising tendencies of the impulses as does the intellect.

> In the latter case, what thought retains from the intellect is only the representation of a possible event – a (premeditated) action in a double sense. Since thought is the act of the intellect, this *act of premeditating* – which is no longer a *new* intellectual act but an act that *suspends* the intellect – seeks to produce (itself in) a *fact*. It can no longer even be referred to as a thought but as a fact that *happens* to thought, as an event that brings thought back to its own origin. There is something resistant in thought that drives it forward – toward its point of departure.[54]

Despite being an act of the intellect and accordingly representational in nature, thought has – or manifests – the power to act. Thought is, once again, thoroughly conditional on the fluctuations which give rise to it. But its distinguishing trait relative to the intellect is its ability to be brought "back to its own origin" – thought itself embodies this dependency, and gravitates towards the event which produced it. (For now, the temporal implications of this gravitation is put aside, as a subject for the following chapters). "Nietzsche, following this process to its source, thus discovers that of which thought is only a shadow: the *strength to resist*."[55] If, according to this statement, thought is a shadow of the strength to resist, what is it that the strength to resist must resist? Thought must resist the incorporation of fluctuations into the code of signs. Fluctuations, stimulations or excitations which are readily assimilated to existing regimes of

---

52 Klossowski, P. (1997). p. 256
53 Klossowski, P. (1997). p. 256
54 Klossowski, P. (1997). p. 256
55 Klossowski, P. (1997). p. 256

signification do not become objects of thought such as these. These are readily absorbed, their singularity blunted, and appropriated by the tropes of the code. Those which resist incorporation are digested protractedly through the intellect, under the guise of thought.

> How then is the intellect constituted so that the agent is capable of producing only representations? Representations are nothing but the reactualization of a prior event, or the reactualizing preparation for a future event. But in truth, the event in turn is only a moment in a *continuum* which the agent isolates in relation to itself in its representations, sometimes as a *result*, sometimes as a *beginning*. As soon as the agent reflects on it, it is itself only the result or beginning of something else.
>
> Every meditation that happens to us is only the trace of something prior, a 'pre-meditation' incorporated into ourselves – namely, a *premeditation* of *the now- 'useless' acts* that have constituted us, so much so that our representations only *reactualize* the prior events of our own organization. This would be the origin of the intellect's representations and its products, of our thoughts that keep us from *pre-meditating* anew. But perhaps there is a different origin to the organization that is *particular* to each of us: something in that organization has *resisted* certain external actions. Something in us was therefore able to *resist until now*, though not at the level of the intellect's coherence. Would this not be a new *pre-meditation of acts to come* ... ?[56]

If the domain of thought, then, is the entirety of acts undergoing incorporation – the transition through the intellect from the impulses – then *all representable content is included* in this domain. Several steps lead to this conclusion. Firstly, representations only reactualise prior events. This reactualisation occurs on condition of what Klossowski refers to as the event's resistance, again employing the Nietzschean category of forces. Events that the organism is able to easily absorb, such as the millions of excitations mobilised in common nutritive, secretive or excrementitious processes, do not reach the level of thought, and remain in the organism's depth. If thought thus only reproduces already received excitations, perhaps in preparation for future ones, its role in relation to these excitations is that of a conduit for the digestion of experience. Events that resist this assimilation eventually surface at the level of the intellect, whilst those offering weaker resistance are incorporated unthinkingly. If this facility is a necessary condition for the production of representations, then all representations are simply events undergoing this process of incorporation. Even the representations which conjure fantasies, or are conjured by them, reproduce a corporeal excitation.

---

56 Klossowski, P. (1997). p. 267

In these remarkable passages in Klossowski's text, therefore, there occurs a stark revision of the distinction between possibility and actuality. Actualities are the "useless acts that have constituted us," the elements of the single series of the individual's history referred to previously. From this series, here described as a continuum, we continually extract events which appear to have caused other events, or which appear, to consciousness for example, to have been caused by them. There is, however, another class of events: possible actions, which have not yet been actualised, and are new in this sense. According to this line of reasoning, the distinction between possibility and actuality is described in terms of the distinction between new and old. However, it has another aspect. These possible actions also remain internal to the organism: they are "in that organization" that is the organism. This gives rise in turn to a further distinction: parallel to that of possibility and actuality, representations of actual prior events are distinct from *other* events which have been incorporated into the organism, but have not emerged at the level of thought. These are the elements of the individual which are singular, and are not due to the species.

The important contention to be extracted from Klossowski's account is that, posed in these terms, there is ultimately no categorical difference between possibility and actuality, such as would be involved by the proposition that actualities are real, and exist, but possibilities do not. Both arise from intensities, and their difference involves nothing more fundamental than degrees of incorporation. Possibilities correspond to singular excitations embedded within the individual as a distinctive characteristic. If we conceive the scope of this possibility to include all representable content, it is in fact closely related to actuality. We are accustomed to the belief that reality is exterior to us, and that the interiority we take to be our thought is of a different order. Yet, once not only this exteriority, but also this thought, are expressed in terms of the fluctuations which generate them, this distinction can be only a relative one.

In summary, Klossowski's stance is opposed firmly to a traditional notion of possibility. The latter effectively construes possibility as the semantic content of sentences with certain features, such as counterfactuals, or sentences whose negations are consistent with some set of privileged sentences – physical, logical, mathematical or other laws. These sentences need not pick out a state of affairs in the world, but a possible world, if at all. A hierarchy or ordering is therefore established, of states of affairs which hold of the world and thereby express realities, and those which need not hold of the world, and which express mere possibilities. Modality is therefore a property of sentences, determined by the variation of their values with those of the arguments of which they are functions. Further according to this account, possibilities determine sentences whose values vary over conceivable, thinkable or representable states of affairs more than do those whose content is nomic. Classically, the truth values of sentences deducible from laws of nature or of logic are independent of empirical particulars, just as the sentence, "A killer is a killer," is not true by virtue of the nature or existence of real killers, while the truth of the sentence, "This man here is a killer," depends on its denotation. Sentences which depend in this fashion express possibilities. Summarily, from this point of view, possibility is chiefly an attribute of sentences through which it is expressed, and originates in the variation of the truth of these sentences from circumstance to circumstance.

The principal corollary of such accounts is the opposition of possibility to reality. Realities are states of affairs on which sentences depend for their truth or falsity, if these sentences relate to possible states of affairs. (Statements of law, of course, are independent of particular such states.) In this way, possibilities determine the variable meanings the proposition can take on from circumstance to circumstance, but realities determine the truth value proposition in the end. However, with Klossowski's work, this opposition disappears. Possibilities are not realities that lack existence, or situations which although consistent with all relevant logical laws do not (perchance) obtain. They are rather the deepening and enrichment of reality itself,[57] the "multiple alterity inscribed within an individual"[58] reality. As the vicious circle leads to the possibilisation of the individual agent – its detachment from a specific actuality, and shattering into plurality, giving off the appearance of indeterminacy – reality is not evacuated of content but rather intensified. Possibilities are internal to any given reality, which takes on a serial form: there are no states which are not series of possibilities. The vicious circle instils in the individual the receptive power commensurate with this series: being no longer a reality which may or may not pass to and from other realities, but a series of possibilities which are to be received and lived by the individual undergoing the circular movement. Reality is not the fulfilment of possibility, possibility as a vestigial trace of reality – that is, each possibility equivalent to a reality, with its existence removed. The multiplication of possibility is rather reality's consummation and enrichment. And there is not a one-to-one relation of every possibility to a reality, but a relation of each reality to a series of possibilities. Nor are possibilities each distinct realities whose existence is voided abstractly; neither exists at the expense of the other, but both together.

It is clear that, by taking possibility as the clandestine or, in his terms, conspiratorial undergirding of what is real, Klossowski attributes to the latter, to re-

---

57 Klossowski, P. (1997). p. 70
58 Klossowski, P. (1997). p. 69

ality itself, the status of an epiphenomenon or effect. What is experienced as an everyday reality corresponds to a series, but this series is only revealed at the appropriate peak of intensity, where the vicious circle is implied, with the identity of the circle and its trace. Ordinarily, by contrast, the latent possibilities are hidden, and only a singular and specific reality exposes itself. How then is our experience configured so that we become aware of the series of possibilities in so few situations? What accounts for our intuition that reality excludes possibilities, and how was it that the character of a miraculous revelation was required in Nietzsche's own experience for this series to emerge? As a guide, we can first consider the opposite state to the one asserted by Klossowski: a lesser degree of intensity, where only specific realities appear, and possibility remains a pale imitation. At this lesser level of intensity, reality takes on the appearance of a singular and fixed state – fixed, once and for all. A series of such realities is taken to constitute an individual history. Such cases produce the impression that possibilities arise as nothing over and above weakened appearances, devoid of the vivacity of intensity, and as alternatives to the richer and clearer realities. How could a series of possibilities ever surface out of such a situation, with an increase in the degree of intensity?

First of all, the singular and specific nature of a reality in this context must be understood as presupposing the continuity of these real states. Any specific state, as a reality, is a member of a series of prior states of which it is the outcome. This is the unique series of events making up the individual, which is not itself a member of a further series, but one series of realities. In such a case, no possibilities are real. Each member of the series is deterministically related to the next, and states are expressible as functions of each-other known as laws. These are the "linkages of causes and effects" which constitute "the irreversible history of the body" and thus "the *identity* of the self."[59] But if the individual consists in this series of states, and these states can be only realities, then there is no point in any such series which a possibility could occupy, nor one intervening between two of its points. The series must contain exclusively real states, each merging into the next. In this sense, the series which makes up the individual must be continuous. But no such continuity applies to the individual, given the dynamic of intensity. Its fluctuations generate a cohesion of an individual which is relative, and do so fortuitously, carrying it away soon after. The discontinuous relations between the states thought to constitute such a series, and the individual corresponding to it, prevent the exclusion of latent possible

---

[59] Klossowski, P. (1997). p. 29

states internal to a given life, no less real than those which supposedly exclude them.

Secondly, the exclusion of possibility from reality, and the rejection of the individual's multiplication (occurring as the vicious circle intensifies) typically depend on the thesis that reality admits of a distinctive richness or clarity, or, in the Humean terms alluded to above, a distinctive vivacity and force which cannot be recovered by any attempt to translate experience into combinations of possibilities. This tenet presupposes that realities are realities because they are specific and determinate. Possibilities are, consequently, secondary: conceived as faded relics with features borrowed from past events, and grafted incongruously onto real experience, their sharpness eroded by time, or as vague and nascent projections of an event to come, they are distinguished from realities, whose specificity in space and time grounds their qualitative determinacy. Since today seems sharper and clearer than yesterday, and yesterday sharper and clearer than tomorrow, we are inclined to distinguish a unique interpretation which confronts us from all other possibilities, granting reality to this one alone. But in the experience of the vicious circle conveyed by Nietzsche, it was not so much this sharpness which was suppressed as it was its coexistence with all the other elements in the circle: the contents of the circle were irreducibly serial. In the circle, this series comprises a single identity, rather than each of its terms. The oscillation between specific visual representations, auditory effects such as long submerged melodies and rhythms resurfacing from without, lingering or anticipatory tactile sensations, or some other resonating affects, replaced the particularity of what Klossowski calls the everyday:[60] that is, a specific *inherence*, which all experiences must share in order to inhere in a single individual, as opposed to a series of possibilities. Whether conceived as a specific space or landscape, or a moment in which the subject is co-conscious of these diverse experiences, or otherwise, only if this inherence is assumed can possibility be excluded. Most importantly, such an experience as is described here is *entirely consistent* with the force, vivacity, sharpness or any other expression of definition accorded to the experience, which is mistakenly invoked to dispel possibility. However sharp or clear any or all of these experiences may be, and however forceful or vivacious they are, there is no common ground for all of these sensations – no here or now, separate from them, which they all share. Vivacity and determinateness do not inhibit multiplicity. For possibility to be unreal, rather, the circular oscillation experienced by Nietzsche – the exploration of different experiences, the circulation of different or partial bodies – would have been ex-

---

60 Klossowski, P. (1997). p. 251

plicable as inherences in one agent. This, however, is as a scenario a patent falsification of the experience undergone by the Nietzschean soul in Turin, an experience which serves as a staging for the metaphysical theories of possibility he both enacted and attempted to transcribe.

5 Temporality of the Vicious Circle

In the introductory statements to *Nietzsche and the Vicious Circle*, Klossowski claims to have composed a work "that will exhibit an unusual ignorance,"[1] promising to pass over in silence a vast quantity of salient scholarly output. Despite the evident singularity of the text, this may surprise the reader acquainted with the details of Klossowski's life. Conversant with the work on Nietzsche by Jaspers, Bataille, Löwith, and Heidegger, the latter of whose volumes he translated for French audiences, and presenting at a series of conferences and seminars, Klossowski was not oblivious to the prevailing interpretations of Nietzsche, despite operating outside the academy, as a private researcher.[2] This promise could not, therefore, have been the fatuous promise to exercise the kind of ignorance that would be aimed at preserving one's creativity "undisturbed" by the encroachment of actual *study*. One hardly gains independence by refusing to pay attention to one's peers, even if it proves inappropriate or impossible to draw upon them explicitly in the text being composed. To what stratagem, then, did this avowal of ignorance refer? In the time between his study and this study of a study, the output concerning many of the themes discussed in *Nietzsche and the Vicious Circle* has engorged – albeit in a highly selective fashion, and with only a subset of the Nietzschean opus enjoying the dissections of the academic scholars. The vicious circle which is the object of his study, whilst given a precise definition in light of his semiotics, unavoidably evokes the doctrine of Eternal Return. This doctrine has dominated the reception of Nietzsche's metaphysics, of time and causality in particular. Accordingly, two chapters of the text are dedicated to exploring the doctrine from both a foundational and biographical standpoint.

This "unusual ignorance" does not therefore seem to entail a departure from all of the themes of traditional and modern Nietzsche studies. It does not denote an attention to different problems, but rather the deployment of a variety of unusual conceptual resources, rarely cited and occasionally hallucinatory passages from Nietzsche's notebooks and letters, and only occasional references to other scholars, despite the evident depth of attention the author granted them over the decades it took to develop his work. There can be no doubt that the ignorance he professes is a facet of his vision of the vicious circle's temporality, which draws upon a number of these passages, places a weighty emphasis on the Sils-Maria experience in 1881, and contains a number of startling propositions which do not

---

[1] Klossowski, P. (1997). p. xiv
[2] Ansell-Pearson, K. (2000). p. 251; Klossowski, P. (1997). p. vii-ix

seem to exist anywhere outside this text. In this way, Klossowski's own contentions about this temporality become singular and "incomparable."[3] This essay now attempts to address these contentions.

The two or three chapters that most openly concern themselves with time and causality are the quasi-narrative chapter "The Experience of the Eternal Return" and the "Attempt at a Scientific Explanation of the Eternal Return," together with the return to a blend of theory-fiction in "The Euphoria of Turin." The first describes in the first- and third-person what the second attempts to explain or justify by its appeal to thermodynamic and cosmological resources and conjectures. Read attentively, however, even the remarks apparently directed at the self or individual, the unconscious, possibility, fortuity and chaos, and semiosis, possess latent if repressed temporal significance. This temporal undergirding, which is only avowed in a few brief passages, in fact imbues the entirety of the book with a conspiratorial tone (the conspiracy of the eternal return).[4] The notion of a conspiracy accordingly undergirds Klossowski's analysis of the shaping of Nietzsche's thought, appearing and re-appearing throughout: "As Nietzsche's thought unfolded, it abandoned the strictly speculative realm in order to adopt, if not simulate, the preliminary elements of a conspiracy."[5] "The plan for a conspiracy appears under the sign of the vicious circle."[6] "If there is a representation of a conspiracy in Nietzsche's thought, it is one that, in this regard, is no longer content to simply level a judgement against existence. Thought must itself have the same *effectiveness* as what happens *outside of it* and *without it*. This type of thought, in the long run, must therefore *come to pass as an event*."[7] The camouflaged revelation of return in the vicious circle permeated Nietzsche's whole thought – even the elements of it which contemplated philosophical categories with apparently little in common with the vicious circle. The various guises in which the doctrine appears – critiques of various categories including self, possibility and agency – become participants which uphold the conspiracy of the vicious circle.

The first chapters of *Nietzsche and the Vicious Circle*, containing semiotic allusions which are the groundwork for the study, can be easily reconceived in terms of time-structured notions. Klossowski's fundamental contention is that we cannot understand experience as Nietzsche relates it without conceiving it in terms of signs, and the conditions under which signs adopt various meanings.

---

3 Ansell-Pearson, K. (2000). p. 248
4 Klossowski, P. (1973). pp. 91–121
5 Klossowski, P. (1997). p. xv
6 Klossowski, P. (1997). p. 80
7 Klossowski, P. (1997). p. 169

These conditions lie in the impulses, revealing themselves through fluctuations of intensity. Such fluctuations are impermanent and indeterminate. The meaning which results from their propagation is infinitely deferred, as in the vicious circle they develop into series of possibilities. Just as they divide, separate and rejoin themselves in one movement, creating the impression of a distinction between a sign and its referent, or cause and effect, in the vicious circle the illusion of past and future collapses into one event. Insofar as we understand signs as events – events of signification – then the characteristics of signs pass over to events and, if events occur in time, or are time, so too to any theory of temporality.

This chapter describes several strata which define the Nietzschean theory of temporality inspired by the vicious circle. The first deals with Nietzsche's inversion of time, which once again parallels the inversion of the semiotic of intensity. This inversion derives from the following tenet: The order of events in time must be distinguished from the process which orders them. The second addresses the collapse of the distinction between future and past, or between the proxy concepts of forgetting and memory, which is asserted in "The Experience of the Eternal Return." Thirdly, and as a consequence of this second stratum, Klossowski attacks what he takes to be philosophical dogma: the existence of a permanent and consistent order of events in the series which comprise an identity. He does so by drawing on the rich biographical and autobiographical underpinnings of this in Nietzsche's later texts, before finally returning to a familiar feature of the account of the second chapter, namely the critique of intentionality, with its essential relation to the causal structures which human subjects, on the basis of the chimera of agency, subsequently project onto the empirical. Precisely the conception of reason dismissed by Spinoza as the epitome of an absurdity – by way of attestation to the extraordinary nature of these four lines of thought – that is, to overturn and invert nature, or "turn nature upside down,"[8] is at stake in the theses that there is no distinction between memory and forgetting, that there is no fixed order to events in time, that the opposition between cause and effect can be inverted or reversed.

---

8 Della Rocca, M. (2008). pp. 81–82

5.1 The Inversion of Temporality

> We believe in the external world as the cause of its action on us – but in fact it is precisely this action, which takes place unconsciously, that we have transformed into the external world: our work is whatever the world makes us confront, which will henceforth react upon us. Time is necessary for it to be achieved: but this time is so short.[9]

From the semiotic at the beginning of Klossowski's project to its ramifications through the metaphysics of possibility and chaos, the notion of *inversion* abounds as an organising principle. The axiomatic distinction between the everyday or institutional code of signs, whose ligatures ensnare our impulsive life, and the mute and inscrutable intensities underlying them, is based on a mechanism of repression, or inversion, of one by the other. The institutional code inverts fluctuations of intensity: our impulses, which have no meaning or aim, and signify nothing specific, are imbued with an artificial signification by the code of institutions. In linguistic terms, inversion can only be described as the transformation of the indeterminate into the determinate, or the indefinite to the specific, or the nonlocalised to the localised. Only late in the text, however, does this inversion's properly *temporal* meaning become clear.

The assumption scrutinised in Klossowski's remark above is the following thesis: in any series of events, each event is the cause of its action on its successor. Simplistically, if we grasp a charged object and then receive an electric shock, we believe the grasp to have caused this shock. On a smaller scale, the incidences of stimuli on the extremities of the nervous system precede sensations, whose provenance is ascribed to an external object. The receptive function of the sensory apparatus therefore fulfils its purpose as an intermediary between two otherwise unrelated events. It transmits the impact of one event to another. But, in order to explain this thesis and its denial, an additional framework must be posited. In his shifting portrayal of "The Experience of the Eternal Return," Klossowski relinquishes his prior semiological terminology, utilising instead the descriptive mechanistic language of events, albeit belying deflationary purposes in so doing:

> By embracing in a single glance the necessity of the Return as a universal law, I deactualize my present self in order to will myself in *all the other selves whose entire series must be passed through* so that, in accordance with the circular movement, I once again become what I am at the moment I discover the law of the Eternal Return.[10]

---

9 Klossowski, P. (1997). p. 251
10 Klossowski, P. (1997). p. 57

In addition, later on, the falsifying tendency of the code of signs and similar linguistic strictures is exposed, this time in temporal terms.

> Nietzsche's obsessive thought had always been that events ... have a completely different aspect from those they have taken on, from the beginning of time, in the sphere of language.[11]

These passages make clear that, as the study develops, time and events replace semiosis and signs as the processes and elements whose relationships with fluctuations are in question. *Events relate temporally to fluctuations as signs do linguistically.* The event is, therefore, the theoretical counterpart of signification from the viewpoint of time. The features accorded to the institutional code – such as stasis, indexation, specificity or determinateness – manifest themselves from this viewpoint in analogous ways. This is the sense in which *Nietzsche and the Vicious Circle* has a clear structure. Events, for Klossowski, show up in series of terms or elements. This initially suggests a commitment to combinations of distinct events successively represented – and thus representation, succession and a host of other categories which must be considered to have been placed into question in this context. Given that the decisive expressions of the eternal return are posed in terms of series, such organisations are clearly pre-eminent aspects of the extraordinary dynamic of the vicious circle. These stand opposed to the quotidian, diminished fluctuations assimilable to the static code: in the vicious circle, intensity's extremum, series of series emerge as a necessary constraint on individual identity; in the dynamic of the circle, series remain as the form of individual identity, construed as a history made of serial elements. If amenable to presentation as a series of elements, such as *ABCDE*, events must be representational and accordingly static: each has a specific and determinate location in the series, which does not vary over time, guaranteed either by an objective measure or by its relations with other elements. By fixing a given temporal location for every fluctuation, they effect an indexation of events, in the form of an assignment of a definite position in the series. It is possible, therefore, to organise events into series simultaneously representable by adjacent graphemes. These series will become the foci of the critique levelled at a defined conception of causality – the conception that, in a series of events whose order underpins the causal relations between the terms, the cause precedes the effect just as does the corresponding element in the series its relatum.

If the temporal equivalent of the signifying regime of the code is the series of events, the linguistic notion of a trace, indispensable to Klossowski's theory of

---

11 Klossowski, P. (1997). p. 251

signs, ought also to possess a distinctive temporal correlate. The sign is a trace of a prior fluctuation. What, then, is an event, given that this is the temporal equivalent of a sign? Is an event then anything other than the trace of a prior fluctuation, in its temporal as opposed to linguistic manifestation – that is, considered with respect to time as opposed to language? Klossowski seeks to demonstrate that precisely the same relations hold in the latter as opposed to the former environment: not only does a circular structure generate the infinite semiosis of the signs conjured by fluctuations; it is no less relevant a structure to the topology of the vicious circle, the eternal return.

In light of these similarities between events and signs, let us first revert to the tenets Klossowski began the study by targeting, as regards causality. In a series of causally related phenomena, the ordination of the events in series is absolute. With an apparently idealistic and Kantian manoeuvre, however, Nietzsche asserts a certain "reversal of time,"[12] positing the failure of these conditions. The external event is not the cause of the series of events which succeed it; the sensory excitation, thought to follow the external event, is in fact its origin. The external world follows from the stimulus. Such a stimulus or excitation is thus itself active, creating its own reflected origination. Seen in this light, it is often long after the superficial characteristics of an event have been transmitted and incorporated that their signification becomes apparent, such as words which are only heard once their sounds have already ceased to propagate. Accordingly, Nietzsche claims that it is only late that one summons the strength for what one really knows,[13] testifying to the delay between the knowledge, or rudimentary absorption of a stimulus, and the formation of conditions sufficient for a conscious signification. For instance, both in the case of a reflex response to and that of a deliberated action, a delay can intervene between stimulus and response, contrary to our intuition that both operate on a continuous basis, with each stimulus being received and responded to more or less immediately. However, the order in which the stimuli occur may be quite different to the order of the reactions they provoke: in many cases responses occur after a delay, after other representations: a sudden reaction to a deeply embedded stimulus crops up and prompts a re-evaluation of the intervening events, placing in question not so much the fact that we react to the past, or how we do so, but *when*.

However, there are reasons to believe this explanation is lacking in at least one important respect. Initially, it is presented in terms of the distinction between latent knowledge, unconsciously assimilated, and the conditions equal

---

[12] Della Rocca, M. (2008). p. 251
[13] KSA 12, 9[123] = WP 25

to it, and so still upholds and mirrors the distinction between an occurrence which precedes and causes a certain response, even if this response is protracted. The fact that a delay may separate the conscious signification of an event from its original moment of reception does not prevent the former occurring after the latter. So long as a distinction of this kind is upheld, and so long as cause and effect are interpreted in terms of an event and its consequences, a commitment to a definite conception of causality and time is maintained: cause precedes effect, and events are absolutely ordered. All the interpretable characteristics of any one event – its entire content – is given at once, once and for all, and this content is permanent, regardless of when the appearance of any of its specific features eventually surface in the organism. The event occurs at one time, and this time will always be this time, possessing all the features presented within it, whenever and however subsets of them reappear in faded remnants. Just as premonitions may have adumbrated this event previously, recollections of it may persist afterwards, but none of these characteristics are new, and the origin is fixed through time.

More precisely, there are two aspects to such a view which Klossowski and Nietzsche aim to undo:

I) The *permanence* of the presentation of the event with respect to time. Despite that, from moment to moment, different presentations are given, it remains the case that at one particular moment a certain presentation is given. The presentation of the event is simultaneous with a given moment (Permanence Thesis).
II) The *completeness* of the presentation of the event with respect to all those characteristics which can be veridically attributed to it (Completeness Thesis). All characteristics of the event, whenever they are anticipated or recalled, occur with the presentation of the event.

In order to formulate the position formed by the conjunction of these propositions, several definitions must be made. I) and II) appeal to the following notions. Firstly, they posit an event, which admits of characteristics, qua phenomenal or sensory content. Secondly, they posit its "presentation," which is its correlation with a state of the subject, and derivatively its temporal location and therefore its value – whether a rank in a series or a quantitative measure. Events have a certain content, and happen at certain times. Insofar as their presentation is *permanent*, they are correlated with a certain moment. It is always the case that, for a particular time value, a defined event with determinate characteristics occurred, regardless of whether this time value is the event's coming after a certain set of events, but preceding another, or its distance in time from a certain point in time – the period or duration in between the two. Insofar as their presentation is also *complete*, there is a single presentation of the event for all its characteristics. Its *complete* presentation has one time value.

Nietzsche's attempt to describe the inversion of causally related events in time addresses these aspects in the following way. Once the distinction between events and their temporal location is vitiated by the difference between fluctuations of intensity and their significations, whose residues constitute events' contents, so too is their permanence and completeness. As conveyed by Klossowski, Nietzsche first of all refutes the conditions of completeness, since there is no ordinal distinction between the fluctuation which produces the presentation's contents – the characteristics attributed to it – and their original presentation. Although the completeness thesis maintains not only that the presentation of the event, with a given characteristic, occurs prior to its reappearance, but also that there are facts independent of these fluctuations as to the temporal ordination of the presentations, with Nietzsche the presentation depends entirely on the fluctuations. The elements of the event which are brought out with the fluctuation were not characteristics presented before, independent of this fluctuation. It is in this sense that summoning up the courage for what one really knows only late in time captures just a limited part of the essential content of the Nietzschean position: The betrayal at the hands of Salomé and Rée occurred long after their departure from Nietzsche in 1882, only once it stirred up in its victim – or beneficiary – the quest for committed solitary work which gripped his final years. Only the powerlessness visited on him by his distance from her catalysed the hallucinatory appraisals of Cosima Wagner as a Dionysian goddess, in a staging which otherwise, such as in her *presence*, would have been impossible. As regards the thesis of permanence – a characteristic which mirrors that of indexicality in the context of permanent significations – similar consequences hold, as we now proceed to demonstrate.

5.2 Permanence and Relationism

A relationalist view of time interprets time as sets of relations between events, or, epistemically, as an abstraction from change. Time in general is deflated and reduced to its constituents. Time values, by contrast, are features ascribable to events. To ascribe a time value to an event is to order it relative to others, possibly allowing determinations of temporal distance. But whereas temporal absolutism prescribes that these properties are conferred only by virtue of a time over and above sets of relations of events, relationism must ascribe time values in some other way. Adopting a reductive or deflationary interpretative strategy with respect to a reified time, however, implies one which no less contemplates the explication of *temporal particulars*. Time is not a sea of identical temporal particulars $\{t_1, t_2, t_3,...\}$, by virtue of which temporal locations can be predicated, in a derivative way, of events in time $P_{e_i t_i}$. Time is itself a term which determined relations between events, manifestations of an absolute order. Rather, events generate, not particulars, but *relations*: $R_{abc...}$ Facts about the time at which a given event occurred *cannot* be rendered in the form

Event e_i occurred at time t_i.

where the latter is a variable which can be specified independently of any relational features. Rather, such facts which appear to index events to absolute times as t_i must be read as implicitly appealing to set of relational characteristics obscured by the employment of the variable.

Now, Nietzsche repeatedly endorsed a relational metaphysics of time, following Leibniz:[14]

> The continual transitions do not permit us to speak of the "individual", etc.; the "number" of beings is itself in flux. We wouldn't speak of time at all and would know nothing of motion if we didn't, in a crude way, believe we saw something "at rest" alongside things in motion.[15]

But if the Nietzschean perspective on time, which has commonalities with a number of modern theories, is endorsed, then the thesis of permanence – that, at a particular moment, a certain presentation is given – becomes even less defensible. First of all, as has been stated already, the moment is not a particular independent of the presentation – in this case, the event. Second of all, conceived relationally, any time or moment is just a set of events related in a certain way, an abstraction of change, and time *values* ascribed to these events is equally an abstraction. The idea of permanence, whose content is the unchangeable or unchanging nature of the correlation of the presentation and the moment, seems to presuppose these time values, or terms with an equivalent function. Time values act as labels, by featuring in multi-place predicates or relations which attach them to other terms, conceived as events, such as $P_{e_i t_i}$. The convenience of attaching such labels is that they facilitate comparisons, assigning some time to one event which may have occurred long ago and another to what is observed presently, these labels permanentise the status of the first event, and allow it to be fixed in an order relative to any others with similar labels. But without the particularised time which seems to accompany absolutism, how can such

---

14 Ansell-Pearson, K. (2000). p. 8
15 KSA 11 , 36[23] = WP 520

labels be generated, and how can their functions be explained? If time is abstracted from relations between events, we cannot avoid asking exactly which events, and how many events, must be so related in order for particular events to admit of absolute temporal locations or labels. Equivalently, this question concerns the arity of the corresponding relation (being the number of places of the terms it relates).[16] If t_i is nothing more than a surreptitious expression of sets of events arranged in a certain way, it is problematic as to how one can make sense of presentations being permanently correlated with given moments.

This perspective can be posed more transparently in the terms of Klossowski's semiotic and view of temporality. With the reduction of an intensity to zero, its significations vanish altogether, and the assignment of a temporal value which is not itself variable to the events they once formed or will form becomes impossible. If time values arise from relations between events, and these events are functions solely of intensity, arising and falling away with its fluctuations, then the time values of events, just like their order, derive also from fluctuations. What allows me to ascribe a time value to a previous event or presentation, and compare this with something present (in order, for instance, to determine the measure of time elapsed between the two) is its afflux in a fluctuation. The repeated afflux of fluctuations, which produce related sets of events, is thus the circuitous replacement for permanent moments in the Nietzschean framework.

Klossowski's inversion of time thus objects to the ordering of events inherent in the causal schema, targeting the above two theses – the theses of permanence and completeness. The first objection derives principally from the fact that these events depend solely on fluctuations. The second derives from the fact that the kinds of temporal values, which allow locations in time to be construed in such a manner as would be needed for the events occupying them to be permanent, can be understood neither relationally nor absolutely. Although these considerations clearly presuppose a deflationary antagonism with respect to absolutist conceptions of time, or conceptions couched in terms of time's independence of events, several passages in Klossowski themselves display several of the idiosyncrasies of this approach. In later sections of "The Origin of Four Criteria," he posits a distinction between two kinds of times, each of which possesses a structure which does not at first seem to be a simple abstraction from its content. What kind of theory of time, advanced by Nietzsche, could be consistent with the rejoinder directed at permanence and completeness, given its assumptions –

---

16 Grenon, P. (2006).

whether construed as an attack on the possibility of temporal locations, or on orders or distances in time?

5.3 Palingenesis and Kenogenesis in the Circle

In order to adequately understand the distinction between the two temporal structures which appear to commit Nietzsche to the kind of "reified time" he denounces – a distinction, indeed, which parallels the rupture in the conceptions of time the vicious circle is designed to bring about – we must examine several passages in the chapter "The Origin of Four Criteria." These passages on the one hand allude to the present epochal time of common or everyday events. The fluctuation of the singular impulse is incongruous with this time, and thus anachronistic. On the other hand, we have the time of this fluctuation itself. The distinction to be interrogated therefore contrasts present, common or everyday time with the anachronism of the singular impulse. In the context of the chapter, the distinction parallels a distinction between more general singular and gregarious traits and tendencies, as part of Klossowski's symptomatising or typological approach to the conditions governing the individual. "For Nietzsche, the singular case rediscovers, in an 'anachronistic' manner, an ancient way of existing – whose reawakening in itself presupposes that present conditions do not correspond to the impulsive state which is in some manner being affirmed through it."[17]

If "present conditions do not correspond to the impulsive state which is in some manner being lived through it,"[18] what separates these two sets of conditions or states? Initially, there is an affinity between this distinction and that of intensity and the signs of the institutional code. In this sense, Klossowski's allusions to "present conditions" refer to this code – the significations which are imposed by the species, as opposed to the singular meaning generated by fluctuations. But in the ensuing exegesis, this correspondence is modified and revised:

> The species is present in the terms used to designate that which excludes the species in the experience characteristic of the singular state ... language will have to circumscribe the singular muteness, and what it contains that is unintelligible to the species, with respect to the intelligibility required by gregarious institutions.[19]

---

17 Klossowski, P. (1997). p. 80
18 Klossowski, P. (1997). p. 80
19 Klossowski, P. (1997). pp. 79–80

The singular state of intensity repudiates the species' terms, and thus can only be circumscribed by them, being beyond or beneath their domain of judicious usage. Once again, the intensity of the state, singular because of its lack of any equivalence to representation, refuses theorisation by the terms and propositions of the code of signs. It can be addressed only by circumscription – and hence by terms such as "meaningless," "unintelligible" or "incoherent."

This first characteristic establishes the analogy between the semiotic distinctions developed at the beginning of Klossowski's study and the current temporal framing. But is there not also here a fundamental transformation of the relationship between these two regimes of signification? The apparent exclusion of the signs of the code by those of the impulses and those of the impulses by the signs of the code is now no longer described in terms of universal or inalienable semiotic features. It is here that it becomes instead a purely relative distinction, dependent on the differing *temporal* structures presented by the two, because the foregoing principle (that the singular impulses are somehow opposed to the institutional code) "is not to say that what forms the unintelligible depth of the singular case has always been so for the whole of the species."[20] Here, the incapacity to represent the intensities which are beyond or beneath language is equated to *forgetting*. In this equation, not only is experience once again assimilated to signification; the distinction between representation and intensity, and the semiotic of the institutional code and that of the impulses, allegorises the distinction between memory and forgetting. The intractability of the impulses is a result of their disharmony with *present conditions*, not a difference of essence. *The time of the impulsive state is asynchronous, or out of joint, with that of the present.*[21] But in what does this asynchrony, which manifests the semiotic's proper relation to time, consist? By virtue of which of these two times' characteristics are they distinct?

5.4 Asynchrony

Just as argued above, Klossowski's remarks in this context suggest a potentially problematic commitment, not to two periods of time distinguished within a reified time, but two different temporal structures. Accordingly, asynchrony is not the asynchrony of two times in a system of time, but the asynchrony of two systematisations of time – two flatly different conceptions of time. The previous ex-

---

20 Klossowski, P. (1997). p. 80
21 Deleuze, G. (1984). p. vii

periences now forgotten which constitute the singularity of the organism's depth are not simply different events to those which are now present, any more than two events occurring at different times are asynchronous or out of joint. In order for there to be a fundamental *anachronism* between the two, of the kind Klossowski posits, a more radical synchrony must be broken by them: they must exhibit two entirely different temporal structures. Such is, in addition, the direct implication of the forgotten experience's sudden reversal of what counts as anachronistic in the vicious circle, which, as we will see, follows directly from Klossowski's argument.

The structure of the present conditions, to be contrasted with those of the initially anachronistic time, can be elaborated in the following way.

a. In the present time, each moment in time is determinately located. Just as, in the semiotic of the code, indistinct fluctuations become localised, and just as, in the above reasoning, the thesis of permanence was attacked due to its dubious assignment of locations in time, the time of present conditions is in turn evaluated in this chapter. Here, however, this location is determinable in one of two chief ways, unexplored in the text until this point. With the first, the location is measured by its distance from another point in time. Extensive measures of duration, as temporal quantity, intervene between any two moments capable of being distinguished. Thus, I can, by some measurement or other, determine the quantity of time between the emission and reception of a photon at two ends of a tower, or between my birth and Nietzsche's death. My birth, or the photon's emission, thus has a location relative to the event separated from it in time. The passage of time does not, according to this position, preclude the possibility of representing non-simultaneous states, and in so doing detecting the duration elapsed between them. In turn, this quantity or duration characterises time as an extensive property.

Alternatively, this location can be determined not so much by the cardinality of these extensive measures, but ordinally. An event's temporal location is simply its rank in a series of other events. There is no notion of distances in time between these locations, nor any essential notion of duration. Consequently, time cannot be understood as independent of the events which occur in time: temporal locations are not precedent to but derivative from occurrences in a given order. But whichever of the two of these principal determinations of temporal location are admitted – in the terms of McTaggart, respectively A-serial or B-serial definitions – it suffices as the underpinning of the notion of the present time, in terms of determinacy of location. This can be contrasted with the anachronistic time of the singular impulse.

b. It is in principle possible to assign a determinate location to the *origin* of any given event. First of all, if the time which is opposed to the anachronism is composed by extensive durations of qualitative content, which form events of certain lengths (thus taking up certain "amounts" of time), then these contents, by virtue of their distances relative to other contents, or by virtue of their order in the series of such contents, have a determinate place in time. Either way, for a particular content – a certain event, sensed or lived by the agent – it can be assigned a definite place. Whether or not this content is repeated in other temporal locations, one occurrence of it is the original one: if it occurs only once, such is this one occurrence; if it occurs more than once, then either the first in the order of the series, or the one which is displaced from this point the least of all, is the original event.

c. *Successive* events fill the present time. Events follow one upon the other, either by virtue of continuous qualitative differences in an otherwise homogeneous medium, or in an uninterrupted series, independent of any medium. The singularity of Nietzsche's predominant phantasm (distribution of impulses), and the inability to quell its agitation which fuelled his philosophical and artistic productivity, must be understood as an interruption not only to the circumstances surrounding him in general, but to successive phenomena and events which befell him (or which, perhaps, he befell).

d. The progression or movement which generates duration – summarily, temporal flux – is a linear one. If the flux of time can be distinguished from the events which are its contents, then it accrues ceaselessly, independent of the latter. If, as in the case of the B-series, this distinction cannot be maintained, owing to the fact that the only meaning of progression in such a series is the increase or decrease in rank or order as one traverses the series, as opposed to a movement, this linearity is recovered by the direction of ascent or descent implicit in the series' ordination.

All of these are break points between the time of the present conditions and the anachronism of the singular case: the determinacy of their location in time, the determinacy of their origin, their succession and their linearity. These aspects correspond to those of the institutional code: its significations are determinately located, with definite beginning and end points, which constitute the specious continuity of lived experience, and seem to linearly accrue experiences to the history of the individual, as state after state is lived through.

To the contrary, the anachronism of the singular case, or forgotten previous experiences, presents a different combination of attributes:

a. The anachronistic previous experience does *not* occupy a determinate temporal location. The fact that this experience is a previous experience is inadequately conceived if regarded as a feature of another determinate time of a lesser value than the previous time. Its having been forgotten is equally inadequately conceived if regarded as an experience initially retained by memory, but lost as it passively decays. These conceptions are rather the results of the temporal structure of Klossowski's present conditions. We have that, properly conceived, the previous experience which forms the depth of the current singular case, reflects the multiplication inherent in the vicious circle's intensity. At the peak of intensity in which the circle emerges, the agent glimpses the liquidity of the series of individualities and identities due for return, de-actualising its present conditions, just as described in the previous chapter. The agent is no longer an individual state, but a series of series. This relation, a feature of the earlier arguments of *Nietzsche and the Vicious Circle*, is equally explicit in "The Origin of Four Criteria":

> Depending on the strength of its intensity, however, this singular state, though anachronistic in relation to the institutional level of gregariousness, can bring about a de-actualization of that institution itself ... To the extent that he isolates its periodicity in history, the plan for a conspiracy appears under the sign of the vicious circle.[22]

The previous experiences referred to in this context thus mirror those arising in the circle: not a particular individuality since shod by an imperfect memory, but a suddenly differentiated serial existence. As opposed to having a determinate location which becomes further and further past, or more and more "previous," as the intervening duration extends, or intervening events accumulate, this kind of event was never present at all. No moment was ever correlated with it. Only in its contrariety to present conditions, and only in the deactualisation of such conditions induced by its intensity does it arise – just as, in "The Experience of the Eternal Return" elaborated in the last chapter, the dynamic of deactualisation and interpretation undoes the present individual, and replaces it with a combination of past and future identities. It has no presence, and therefore no correlation to a specific time. Nietzsche himself encapsulates this intractability of the singular case to any kind of presence in the formula: "My constitutive elements are dispersed in past time and the future."[23] The dispersion of the content of what is present into a series, and its uncoupling from any particularity, usurp the determinacy of temporal location definitive of Klossowski's "present conditions."

b. Nor is there any specifiable origin to this previous experience. Not only does it have no *location* in time which could ever count as its origin, but the notion of a beginning has no application to the singular case. It exists only as differentiated from present conditions, only as anachronistic: "the representation of

---

22 Klossowski, P. (1997). p. 80
23 Klossowski, P. (1997). p. 185

a prior life and an after-life no longer concerns a beyond, or an individual self that would reach this beyond, but rather the same life lived and experienced through its individual differences."[24] In this vein, Nietzsche declares, "*I am already dead as my father, whereas as my mother I am still living and becoming old.*"[25] Being his father, and being his mother, were two interpretations he imposed on his origin, Nietzsche as either his father, as the permanentising of identities, or his mother as his own self-creation. But neither of these is a determinate origin. As mother of himself, Nietzsche gave birth to himself as many times as he felt himself metamorphose; as his dead father, he experienced his own consumption and loss of origin altogether.

c. The suddenness predicated by Klossowski of the eruption of this anachronistic singularity stands in opposition to the succession of present phenomena. The signs and representations which follow one upon the other are a continuous series of events, but the singular case exists as a result of a periodic resurgence. The intensities[26] sufficiently powerful to generate the resonances of an anachronism are discontinuous. It is not that a period of empty time elapses between each intensity, but that there is nothing apart from the fluctuation of these intensities which span a range of significations before once again falling away.

d. Finally, the dynamic obeyed by the singular state displays nothing of the linear behaviour of the present temporality. It is a periodic and circular movement, described consistently in terms of a wave which rises and falls repetitively. It is by no means regular in its periodicity, seeing as it could only be regular if it could be shown to oscillate over continuous time, with it shown also that the end of each identical cycle were to lead directly into the next – just as there is no telling how long waters observed from above may remain still before the fluttering of the next disturbance.

There are, therefore, four chief points of divergence between the time of the present conditions, corresponding to the institutional code, and the anachronistic singular intensity. The temporal distinctions between these positions mirror the semiotic differences of previous chapters. Does this commit Nietzsche and Klossowski to exactly the kind of hypostasising manoeuvre they disparaged with their antipathy to independent temporal structures, as we suspected previously? Does not the fact that the dynamic of the singular case is "periodic and circular," or the fact that it constitutes series of series as opposed to individual

---

[24] Klossowski, P. (1997). p. 72
[25] Klossowski, P. (1997). p. 172
[26] Klossowski, P. (1997). p. 252

states, amount to as pronounced a commitment to independent or non-abstracted time as the objects of these disparagements themselves admit? On the contrary, the irregularity of this periodic movement, and the discontinuity of cycles with one another, as well as the "suddenness" which leads to the production of series upon series and the deactualisation of the individual, attest to precisely the dependency of this temporality on fluctuation, harmonising adequately with the Nietzschean critique. These characteristics are direct ramifications of the semiotic of intensity, temporally manifested.

5.5 Asynchronous Time: Forgetting

In this distinction we have drawn between two temporal structures, like in many aspects of the argumentation of Klossowski's study, forgetting is an indispensable conceptual progenitor. But what is the specific import of forgetting in this context? The distinctions made here by Klossowski, which reformulate and underpin the semiotic distinctions on which his study rests, are distinctions between temporal structures as opposed to merely different events, but the claim that the singular state's anachronism specifically pertains to *forgetting* is a distinct one. In order to assess whether this constellation of temporal features delimiting the singular case can be veridically be termed "forgetting" we must examine precisely what is meant by this term. In order, moreover, to accurately state the connection between forgetting and these temporal and semiotic structures, we must reconsider the dynamic of the vicious circle which lies at its extreme, since it is in the first discussions of the vicious circle that forgetting appears:

> It is inscribed in the very essence of the circular movement, which I necessarily forget from one state to the next (so that I can reach another state and be thrown outside myself, even at the risk of everything coming to a stop).[27]

What role does forgetting play in the circular movement? We have already established that the moment of the vicious circle deactualises the agent as an individual with a history, in favour of series of series. Now, the necessity of forgetting refers to the knowledge of these series which is thus necessarily eschewed by the agent, escaping the moment of the revelation in favour of continuing to explore the series of individual states which constitutes its most familiar identity. The circle dictates that the individual re-explore its past – at least, as this past

---

[27] Klossowski, P. (1997). p. 59

appears in the series which is revealed in the moment of return. Inevitably, this re-exploration passes through states other than the privileged and isolated case of the singular subject of the circle, which thus forgets the movement which controls it. The "risk of everything coming to a stop" is the attendant risk of depressed or reduced movement once the revelatory moment, with its propulsive movement, is left, and the agent conceives itself as simply the individual with a fixed history, obeying all the characteristics of the time of present conditions. Accordingly,

> This revelation did not come to me as a reminiscence – nor as an experience of *déjà vu*. Everything would stop *for me* if I *remembered* a previous identical revelation ... It was therefore necessary for me to forget this revelation in order for it *to be true!*[28]

As is evident from this additional comment, the doctrine of the vicious circle, as the radicle of the Nietzschean theory of temporality, is thoroughly predicated on forgetting; the latter is its "source as well as the indispensable condition"[29] for its revelation and ramification. But, initially, if the vicious circle is to count as a revelation, it must have arisen suddenly, in contrast to one's previous state; one acquires knowledge one lacked before. If this revelation is to recur going forward (an incontrovertible corollary of the doctrine), such knowledge must disappear, in order to reappear as suddenly as it does in this revelation.

Although a logical consequence of the revelatory character of the circle, such a condition is in one regard the natural result of considering the nature of fluctuations. Their dynamic is one of rise and fall, and with it the arrival and departure, presencing and withdrawal of perception and sensation. Every welling up of intensity produces a rising fluctuation together with its significations, inevitably followed by a state of forgetting: the intensity diminishes, the fluctuation subsides and this empirical content is lost by the agent. When Klossowski tells us, then, that forgetting is a necessary condition for the truth and fulfilment of the vicious circle, this is a suggestion that may at first appear unmotivated. Moreover, given that the vicious circle is revealed at a particular moment, and that there are other moments, is it not redundant to adduce the necessity of forgetting for the circle's fulfilment? The fact that I will instantly disappear from the moment in which the circle is revealed as another moment appears seems sufficient for this conclusion, with no need at all of appeal to forgetting. It follows from temporality itself – provided that the revelation is not the moment of death – that time passes in this way, and that no moment persists be-

---

[28] Klossowski, P. (1997). p. 59
[29] Klossowski, P. (1997). p. 56

yond what instantaneity might allow. Why, then, aggrandise the role of forgetting to the extent that Klossowski insists in doing? Is there any content to this notion of forgetting beyond the platitudinous fact that fluctuations come and go, that time passes moment to moment?

Inviting as this conclusion may be, the looser notion of forgetting – that is, the notion at work in the suggestion that it is a trivial consequence of fluctuation and becoming – can be clearly contrasted with the prior, stronger notion. The foregoing reasoning, with its weaker notion, holds only if it is the *content* of the revelation that is the basis for its distinction from other moments. For forgetting to be redundant, the change in content from the revelatory moment to any other non-revelatory moment must itself account for the difference between the two. It is clear, however, that it is not only this that drives the agent away from the revelatory moment:

> Already, *I am no longer in the moment when the abrupt revelation of the Eternal Return reached me*; for this revelation to have meaning, I would have to lose consciousness of myself, and the circular movement of the return would have to be merged with my unconscious, until the movement brings me back to the moment when the necessity of passing through the entire series of possibilities was revealed to me.[30]

The moment of the revelation has a propulsive tendency: the agent is instantly ejected from the moment of revelation at the moment of revelation. This moment is, as before, distinguished by the agent's acquisition of knowledge of the vicious circle's form: the coincidence of the relevant intensity with its own trace, and the multiplication of the intensity which results. The serial realisation of all possible identities, from series of individualities to series of other individualities, is the denotation of the circle. The supplementary term "moment" in this way picks out a single state from each series, each one a multiplication of the others. Thus, in knowing that the present moment has been lived through before and will subsequently be lived through – in short, as the moment multiplies – the agent attains consciousness of the distinct individual states in the series parallel to, and thus prior and subsequent to it. The agent is confronted with the incoherent tension of being other than it now is. The repulsion effected by the moment of the revelation then derives from the inability of an agent to be simultaneously itself and other.

Consequently, the stronger notion of forgetting, which is the prerequisite for the dynamic of return, is the forgetting of a temporal *structure*, namely the law of the vicious circle, and is no trivial corollary of the nature of fluctuation or the

---

30 Klossowski, P. (1997). p. 58

brute passage of time. At the moment of the revelation of this structure, the agent conceives a certain set of relations between the events which comprise it, and forgets this conception in order for it to hold. Forgetting of the looser kind, which occurs with the diminution of intensities, namely the reflux of a fluctuation, is by contrast the forgetting of specific content: a particular experience atrophies and disappears.

This interpretation of forgetting, distinguished here from the looser kind, must be the operative one in the arguments and narratives in which the vicious circle is introduced, dispelling as it does any sense that these arguments and narratives simply recapitulate mundane characteristics of fluctuations of intensity. In the passages first cited here, however, forgetting was the foundation not only for the vicious circle, but also for the distinction of two conceptions of time: the time of present or everyday conditions upheld by gregarious normative forces, in Klossowski's styling, and the authentic time of fluctuations, embodied in the ethically problematic singular case. These two conceptions provide further resources which elucidate the crucial inversion of time in question, belied in the text by the notion of anachronism. The singular impulse underlying this forgetting, in itself nondescript and mute, signifies nothing, and admits no representable content. Our experiences as they are given in consciousness, such as thoughts, sporadic inclinations to speak, and perceptions, cannot contain any of this impulse's content. Indeed, strictly, it possesses none. In this sense and as a result, it is "anachronistic,"[31] in the terms of Klossowski's ambiguous phraseology: it never joins up with what is experienced, whether sensed, spoken or felt. It cannot be transmitted at the level of consciousness. In this sense, it is an impulse of a different time entirely. The present, constituted by the bombardment by stimuli in series and the empirical content they induce, is interrupted by an intensity of an entirely different order, which stands in no causal relations with the series of connected events which unfold before us in a relatively ordered and predictable fashion. These events – the cycles of waking and sleeping, consumption and digestion, work and play – establish successions which constitute a certain time, and it is relative to this time that these indiscernible fluctuations can be considered anachronistic. We attempt, Klossowski shows, to compensate for their intractability by equating them to fraudulent substitutes, either by describing them in a certain way or through the hypertrophy of desires erroneously considered to express them. In reality, they are equivalent to nothing. Their anachronism thus correlates with their *inequality* with anything present.

---

31 Klossowski, P. (1997). p. 80

The difficulty in thinking this circular structure, the emergence of an anachronistic event, is evident in Klossowski's own staging: "Even when I will not have forgotten that I had been precipitated outside myself in this life, I nevertheless had forgotten that I was thrown outside myself in another life – one in no way different from this life!"[32] Were I truly to recall an equivalent moment in a previous series, I would be such a moment, and not this moment. There is no applicable concept of distance, nor any qualitative resemblance, which could hold between different moments in which the vicious circle is revealed. Even in knowing that such moments have existed, and must exist henceforth, I could never remember them so long as I remain in the present moment, in my present life, whilst knowing that such moments must have occurred, in a life which must therefore be identical. As much as the edict of the vicious circle proclaims the necessity of untold previous and subsequent similar existences, at the exact peak of the intensity which produces it, it excites its own eschewal and forgetting. In order to return to the moment, one must separate from all previous identical moments; in order for the movement predicted by the revelation to be true, the revelation must be escaped. The revelation is in this sense the very form of the agent's movement itself – an unstable singularity or repelling point, and thus a series which must be explored in order for the present to be truly established. It is not, therefore, as a simple consequence of the agent's transition from one moment to another that forgetting is invoked as an important notion in these sequences in the text, but as a *necessary* result of the vicious circle.

These relations between the vicious circle and forgetting, forgetting and various temporal structures, temporal structures and the anachronism which consecrates Klossowski's typology of moral evaluations, are all components of the development of the inversion of time which is among the fundamental commitments of the temporality of *Nietzsche and the Vicious Circle*, and which we now endeavour to reach.

5.6 Reversal of Anachronism

The preceding remarks summarise the differences between the two temporal structures which are presupposed by Klosswoski's reflections on the reversal of time played out by Nietzsche. The following remarks provide an account of how these reflections themselves unfold. This reversal originates in the passage which appears abridged above:

---

[32] Klossowski, P. (1997). p. 59

5.6 Reversal of Anachronism — 127

> Depending on the strength of its intensity, however, this singular state, though anachronistic in relation to the institutional level of gregariousness, can bring about a de-actualization of that institution itself and denounce it in turn as anachronistic. That every reality as such comes to be de-actualized in relation to the singular case, that the resulting emotion seizes the subject's behaviour and forces it into action – this is an adventure that can modify the course of events, following a circuit of chance which Nietzsche will make the dimension of his thought. To the extent that he isolates its periodicity in history, the plan for a conspiracy appears under the sign of the vicious circle.[33]

Although the anachronism is initially the name for the structural differences between the two temporal dynamics, and specifically the failure of previous experiences to conform to present conditions, here it simply denotes whichever of the two structures is less prominent or dominant. In a state of extremal intensity, the present becomes anachronistic, with its de-actualisation. But, crucially, how can a reversal of time, the concept in scope, be constituted from the distinction between two temporal structures?

Consider the following reasoning. Ordinarily, the present is the primary mode which grounds the determination of events in time. Any event may be considered a member of a series of present moments with a definite location. This event's power to determine other events is conferred by its position in the series: each present exerts an influence over the events subsequent to it, and thus of a greater value in the series, either due to their pure rank or their distance from a specified event. Subsequent events have no power to influence those prior to them, and which influence their later equivalents. On this view, Nietzsche comments,

> Our intellect is completely incapable of grasping the diversity of an intelligent synthetic interaction, not to mention producing one, like the digestive process. It is the synthetic interaction of *several intellects!* Wherever *I* find life, I find this synthetic interaction! And there is also a sovereign in these numerous intellects! But as soon as we seek to comprehend organic actions that would be executed with the assistance of several intellects, they become completely incomprehensible.[34]

Two principles are espoused in this passage which militate against these conceptions of which kinds of events are capable of influencing each other, according to their temporal location. The intelligent synthetic interaction is, as an interaction, a collection of series of events obeying some relations of determination. Insofar as the interaction is synthetic, these series culminate in terms or elements com-

---

33 Klossowski, P. (1997). p. 80
34 Klossowski, P. (1997). p. 35

mon to all series involved in the synthesis – just as, following the digestive process, a collection of digested molecules may be synthesised and conglomerated with the organism's tissues, having originated in entirely different foods (and thus in different series of events). Insofar as the interaction is intelligent, the process must be regarded as determined throughout by the synthesised *result*. The independence of the series from each other prior to their synthesis, such as in digestion, does not preclude their being influenced by their final terms. These events are *acted on by the future*. Its direction inverted, the form of the causal relations obeyed by these series' terms is what our intellect is "completely incapable of grasping" in the Nietzschean epistemic.

Secondly, we find in this passage the principle of temporal complexity (which has appeared in a variety of modern works as the notion of "templexity")[35]. The interaction draws upon several "intellects," each of which is defined by the way in which it brings about each series' gravitation towards the result (such as the synthesised molecules' coalescence with a pre-existing aggregate, following the digestive process). Our inability to fathom interactions of this nature is no incidental result of the privation of a given faculty, but the rigorously necessary consequence of the inverted causality at work in the synthesis: the tendencies governing the interaction are not derivable only from states within this synthesis' parameters. The outcome or "sovereign" to whose ends the interaction is directed is not deducible from the elements combined in this interaction. The synthesis of cells which sustain the epithelial or muscular tissues, for instance, from a multitude of nutritive sources catalysed in digestion, is not a process exhaustively describable in terms of the elements undergoing the interaction – namely, the sources themselves. Nor, Nietzsche contends, can such a process be accounted for by the sole conjunction of (a) a description of these sources or elements with only (b) the faculties which digest and synthesise them. At any point in time during the interaction, not only (a) and (b), but supplementary futural conditions, determine it. Nietzsche's commitments in this context presuppose the possibility of a process whose organising principles are themselves temporal, distributed over the events which constitute the process. Such processes are what is meant by the above term "templexity." Aside from the templexities assignable to physiological processes Nietzsche investigated, S. Malik and A. Avanessian adduce as further evidence of the growing importance of phenomena describable in terms of templexities a range of others. The prevalence of financial derivatives used to extract value from anticipated as opposed to completed production, pre-emptive military interventions which recursively produce the en-

---

35 Land, N. (2014); see also Avanessian, A. and Malik, S. (n. d.).

emies whose aggressions are invoked as retroactive provocations, and predictive algorithms which generate targeted advertising based on desires which are entirely synthetic and projected, all constitute examples of this inversion scaled up to the social and industrial levels.[36]

These considerations allow us to develop in outline the logical form of this temporal inversion, and of action by and out of the future of the sort implied by Nietzsche's writings. Consider a series of non-simultaneous events which we may crudely represent with some distinct characters $ABCD$. If we accept, contra Klossowski, that these events are assignable determinate time values, it follows that at least one of these events possesses the (possibly joint) maximum of all their values. Call this value τ. Let us say that this series culminates in an event Z at time $\tau + \omega$, where the latter variable is non-negative and non-zero. Klossowski's relevant thesis, alleging a temporal inversion of sorts, addresses the question as to whether this event is deducible from $ABCD$, or indeed from $ABCD$ together with some set φ of supplementary conditions, all given at a time no greater than τ. Given these assumptions, does the conjunction or union of $ABCD$ with φ entail Z?

As a point of comparison, in the Humean philosophy of causality, only the *constant conjunction* of $ABCD$ with the result Z, together with subjective principles of association which fixate the mind upon Z given all these conditions, can produce such a result from the presentation $ABCD$. But if such conjunctions and associative principles were subsumed within the supplementary conditions, this modified Humeanism would affirm that Z is so entailed. Alternatively, in the

---

36 Avanessian, A. and Malik, S. (n. d.). In addition, in his *Templexity: Disordered Loops through Shanghai Time*, N. Land – who is among the other modern thinkers whose work enables us to bring the characteristics of templexity to bear in this context – states templexity to be "indistinguishable from unbounded real recursion." If this notion of templexity is equated with temporal complexity, and in turn with the intelligent synthetic interactions of Nietzsche's prophecies, then this definition should be reconcilable with the temporality of the vicious circle of which it is one of the principal expressions. The recursive dynamic asserted by Land is the outcome of the following triad of relationships: Firstly, the present precedes the future in time, just as in a given fluctuation, the past of the individual signifies in and with the present. Secondly, insofar as any sign depends on fluctuations which may arise in the future, this present is determined only after the future arrives. The future, in turn, and thirdly, is determined only after the past of the future passes. Thus, whilst the present is past relative to the future it precedes, and thus determines the future and contains its conditions, these conditions are not given before the future, but in and with the future itself. The conditions for the future's emergence are thus determined in and with the future, but if the future occurs only after its past has passed, and this past in turn includes the present which precedes it, the present seems to depend on the future it creates. Returning to the context of Klossowski's argument, we can make these conceptual outlines much more exact.

Kantian philosophy of causality, the connections imposed on the manifold of intuition by the understanding's categories replace such principles or conditions, conferring determinacy on appearances, as opposed to the mere subjective associability of Humeanism. Common to these classical positions is the avowal of the deducibility of Z from its antecedent conditions $ABCD$ together with φ. This deducibility is the mark of the position Klossowski aims to weaken with the notion of temporal inversion. The intelligent synthetic interaction, consequently, will deny this deducibility.

From this insistence on the derivability of future conditions, such as Z, from solely antecedent conditions, an additional proposition follows. In the ordered set of events constituted by $\{A, B, C, D, Z\}$ or $\{A, B, C, D, Z\} \cup \varphi$ the time value assignable to any member of the set $\{A, B, C, D\}$ is lower than that of Z. This is the simple meaning of the order of events in time which was assumed in this proof. In order for the derivability of Z from these conditions to follow from this straightforward assertion, the order of *determination* of these events must be equated to their *temporal* order. For any event whose position in the series of these events' occurrence (a temporal series) is n, n denotes also their position in that series constituted by the *order* in which they are *given*. Past events not only occur before, but are given and determined before the future. With this assumption, at the point of occurrence of Z, all prior events (including $\{A, B, C, D, \dot{Z}\} \cup \varphi$) have been given in appearance. If it is the case, then, as such an argument contends, that Z is derivable from this union in the sense that these conditions being given Z is itself determined, the mere fact of occurring prior to Z entails its givenness or determination being similarly prior.

It is undeniable that, once $\{A, B, C, D\} \cup \varphi$ is determined, Z is determined, so long as one assumes that this set of events entails Z. This is simply what logical entailment means; once these events are determined, their consequents are determined. But if Z were to be given or determined before these other events, no such entailment or other such logical relationship need hold. Only if one adduces the quite additional premise that these two orders are isomorphic – only if one assumes it to be impossible for Z to be determined before the events which are ranked before it in time – can the derivability of Z follow. Only then could it follow from the mere and indeed incontrovertible fact that the putative logical consequences of temporally earlier events are temporally later than these events that they were given before them, and thus that, from the hypothesis assumed at the start of the derivation, Z follows. If $\{A, B, C, D\} \cup \varphi$ entails Z, once Z has appeared after this union, this union is determined; being determined, it entails Z. Symbolically:

$$((((\{A,B,C,D\} \cup \varphi \vDash Z) \wedge T = t_Z) \to Z) \to (((T = t_Z \wedge Z \wedge (t_{\{A,B,C,D\} \cup \varphi} < t_Z)) \vDash A,B,C,D\} \cup \varphi)$$

In contrast to this position, for Klossowski as for Nietzsche, there must be a thoroughgoing separation of the order of events and the ordering process itself: their temporal order cannot be assimilated to the order in which they acquire determinacy. In any given moment, or hypothesised temporal position, the order that appears camouflages the order of appearance. Klossowski reproduces the following passage from the notebooks:

> This apparent conformity to a goal is simply subsequent to this will to power unfolding in every event; the becoming-strongest brings with itself organizations that have a certain resemblance to a plan of finality: the apparent goals are not intentional, but once the supremacy over a lesser power is attained, and the latter is made to work on behalf of the greatest, a hierarchical order of organization must take on the appearance of an order of means and ends.[37]

The order of events is distinct from the ordering process, as is the appearing order from the order of appearance. This principle underpins the denial that the order in which the members of $\{A, B, C, D, Z\}$ are given equates to their properly temporal order, and the concomitant denial of the derivability of Z from its antecedents.

Correlatively, the insistence (on the part of the view Nietzsche intends on inverting) on the *unilateral* dependency of future conditions, such as Z, on antecedent conditions, no less requires a supplementary presumption, just as does the calculability of the future in terms of the past. According to the classical logics outlined above, the future depends on the past, but there is no converse relation of the past to the future. The *asymmetry* inherent in the *order* of these events justifies the *asymmetry* of their *dependency*. This asymmetry of dependency makes it unilateral, or non-reciprocal, in the sense that the past does not depend on the future as the future does the past. Past events precede future events, and future events only ever follow past events, and so it is thought that the past produces the future. But in order to pass from the hypothesis that Z follows certain events in time to a hypothesis asserting its dependence on these events, now conceived as its antecedent conditions, one must additionally infer from this order in time an order of events' dependencies on one another.

There is, therefore, a pair of contentions which are indirectly confronted and refuted by the intelligent synthetic interactions of Nietzsche's.

---

[37] Klossowski, P. (1997). p. 118

A) Parallelism Thesis: The order of events in time parallels the order in which they are given or determined.
B) Asymmetry Thesis: The asymmetry implied by this order of events entails the asymmetry of the dependency of the future on the past.

Can Nietzsche's implicit denial of these inferences be translated into the context of his specific claim, made previously, which concerns the subterranean intelligence at work in synthesis? As an example, Nietzsche claims the digestive process as an example of this kind of intelligent synthetic interaction. For this, we would require two demonstrations: firstly, to justify Nietzsche's reflection that this process manifests a dependency of the past on the future – contrary to the thesis concerning asymmetry – and secondly to justify his posit of an ordering process distinct from the order produced, and incongruous with the order which appears as a result.

This distinction may be illustrated by this case (one incarnated perhaps all too frequently by Nietzsche's own valetudinary states). It may seem that the characteristics of the molecules which pass through the gastrointestinal tract, together with the faculties collectively constituted by the digestive organs – performing catalysis, peristalsis, bile secretion, i. a. – are sufficient to fix a destiny for these molecules. An exhaustive knowledge of these molecules' states ought, then, to yield a prediction of their evolution. Relative to an observation made during the process, there can be no doubt that this passage precedes its result in time (so long as the possibility of significantly distinct frames of reference is debarred). Does this then imply that they are *determined* in an equivalent order? Or, as is tantamount, does it imply that the *ordering process* follows the *order produced*? Firstly, at the level of sensation, this is certainly not the case; the sensations of the digestive process ignore the enormously greater part of it, and from the paucity of the signs which reach consciousness nobody could so comprehensively predict the fate of such a rich diversity of molecules as are involved. Often, at the phenomenological level – that is, the level of the comparison between the processes occurring in the enteric regions and our sensations of them, which was Nietzsche's case study – our judgement of whether a particular substance was nutritious or not, or readily digestible or not, is often something which occurs long after the ingestion or imbibition which, understood fully, supposedly could have predicted them. In such cases, it is neither the true that the results were deducible from previously given conditions (for there were no such conditions), nor that the order in which the different elements of the process were *given* is the same as their order in time.

However, it may be thought that instead of concerning sensations predictability may be recovered at an appropriate level of microscopic reduction, such as is proper to physics. Framed in accordance with the principles of microscopic dynamics, the constituent molecules of the process occupy states in a phase space whose evolution is describable in terms of prescribed laws. Then, an appropriate set of initial conditions, in terms of such quantities as the momentum and position of all the molecules in the process, would be thought to specify their fate. Putting aside the entropic or information-theoretic impediments to attaining such a specification, it is nonetheless hardly trivial to draw from the fact that the states of these particles precede their eventual synthesis the result that it derives from them, and not the converse. Of course, not only these states, but laws of their evolution, are required in order to formulate such predictions; one must not only gather information about the present states of the semi-digested molecules, but about their dynamical behaviour. These connect the states to their outcomes. Insofar as these laws are empirical, they may have been constituted by the repetition of these initial states, followed by their final states, with the requisite regularity to have been inductively intuited. But nor, in this case, is there an asymmetric dependency of the results (the distribution of molecules taken to be final) on the initial conditions (the distribution of molecules at the beginning of the process). At the level of the microscopic dynamics governing the sub-systems of these states, taken as inspiration for the 18th-Century pronouncements of universal deterministic calculability, there is nothing which prevents previous states being calculated from, and in this sense, produced or discovered by, subsequent ones. Calculation is as symmetric as the variable, time, in terms of which it is made. Indeed, the quickening accumulation of cosmological knowledge in contemporary scientific research programmes has led to the discovery of vastly richer ancestral phenomena than were ever previously anticipated, in a manner decidedly incommensurate with future predictability over comparable time-scales. Our exponentiating abilities to gradate time and garner knowledge about cosmological history has by no means been accompanied with an equivalent trend in the opposing temporal "direction."[38] Nor, returning to Nietzsche's example, is there a parallelism between the order in which the different stages of digestion occur and the order at which these stages are given. These conditions may be apprehended or determined, for instance, by inference from a plurality of measurements, long after the time which is retroactively imposed upon them. As a result, the two theses – asymmetry and parallelism – are supplanted by this case, which Nietzsche baptises as intelligent synthetic interaction. The conditions of this interaction lie in the as yet unformed intellect constituted by the assimilation of its ingredients: the synthesised result conducts the process of synthesis, enabling

---

38 Land, N. (2014).

the circumspect and conspiratorial guises of the return, while the real causes of events lie inaccessible to them, usurping the order of things which is apparent ordinarily. It is chiefly this dynamic, which embodies the reversal of time which constitutes this first element of the vicious circle's temporality.

The anachronism which separates two conceptions of time – the time of present conditions, as linear successions of extensive durations, and the time of the singular case, as discontinuous cycles of indeterminate fluctuations – provides the foundation for the inversion of time which distinguishes Klossowski's central tenets, as a result of the undoing of fixed temporal orders. The notion of an intelligent synthetic interaction, then, incarnates this reversal prophesised in "The Euphoria of Turin," and opens up the possibility of a logical formulation of Klossowski's rejoinder to the causal schema. With the intelligent synthetic interaction, the order of events can no longer be equated with their order of production: one's contemplation of events as past and their distribution of values in time is distinct from the order in which they are determined. Past states no longer exert exclusive and asymmetric causal power over future events; it is instead exchanged circuitously and multilaterally. Whilst the order of events in time constitutes a series of demarcations, or oppositional exclusions, between events which occur before and after one another, and thus events which are future or past relative to others, no such relation applies to the manner in which these events are given. We may believe in certain influences as the cause of their action upon us: we may represent events leading up to the present, furnishing the appearance of an order; but the order of events, in their appearance and in their determinacy, is the *reverse:* what appears as past relative to a moment, and as its cause, is in fact its consequence, "transformed" so as to produce the external world – transformed, that is, into a stable and permanent construction, which we construe as the past and locate in series before the present. The past is neither permanent, construed as once and for all, nor irreversible, construed as accomplished or complete. The retroactive or reverberant projection of this suddenly apparent order, out of the order of the events' actual production, is, then, the concretion of this reversal of time.

5.7 Distinction of the Nietzschean and Kantian Positions

Nietzsche's reversal of time turns on a thesis separating the way in which events are *ordered* and the ordering process, or the process which determines them. Relying on the passive participle to delineate the status of these events, the order is taken as something which is imposed upon them, rather than a spontaneous outcome of some independent events. If this apparent order is to be rigorously distinguished from their order independent of appearance, and if the conditions of the formation of this order lie in a process incongruous with this order, we must ask to what extent Klossowski is not drawing a distinction simply between appearance and reality, between the subject's imposition of order upon appearances and the events ordered, and thus between two terms which presuppose the employment of idealistic categories. Is this not a repetition of the transcendental idealism developed by Kant, in the aftermath of the Lockean and Humean species of empiricism and their concomitant theories of sensation? The position according to which the senses play a role in structuring appearances was not pioneered by Nietzsche. With Kant's project, and with space and time as formal intuitions and forms of intuition, the external world is subject to the conditions of space and time laid out in the Refutation of Idealism and Transcendental Aesthetic. Relations between external bodies, and externality itself, require the forms of sense, and prior (indeed *a priori*) sets of relations in which they can relate. Indeed, neither the externality of experience, nor the order of events, are independent of intuition in Kant. From this point of view, it seems like the central characteristics of the temporal inversion in Klossowski's analysis do not advance us beyond the quite traditional positions and formulations of transcendental philosophy. They perpetuate the critical idealism.

However, the Kantian reversal implied by the *apriority* of space and time, and therefore of the structuring of sensations by the organism's receptive faculties, in relation to events in space and time, is not ultimately comparable to the reversal in the above extract from "The Euphoria of Turin." In Kant, *apriority* is a broadly threefold notion: a representation is *a priori* if it is (i) independent of experience, (ii) presupposed by experience, and (iii) attributable to the constitution of the mind. Initially, then, the priority of the structure over the content of sensibility is not a mark of temporal priority. Indeed, time is the form of all appearances of inner sense, meaning events can occur at certain times – but their organisation in time is not itself a temporal process. Intuition as form, and specific intuitions, are thus of a different order. That Klossowski asserts a distinction between the ordering process and the events ordered, and imputes to the latter the origin of a particular temporality, does not imply an idealism with respect to the latter, the intervention of the mind in its formation, or its independence of experience. Whilst the difference between events in time and the process conditioning the appearance of their order is common to Nietzsche and Kant, in Kant these are *cognitive* structures separate from events, not attributes of events themselves. In the latter case, the production of events is a process immanent to the events produced, not a transcendental structure intelligible independent of them and schematised to them from without. The Kantian distinction could never, therefore, accommodate a description of this difference in terms of an inversion or reversal, since the conditions for the ordering it effects are not themselves an order. With Nietzsche, it is not merely that the logical or deterministic order of the manifold is imposed; actual states belonging to the manifold are reversed.

5.8 Parody

The status of parody is perhaps an under-emphasised one in many parts of *Nietzsche and the Vicious Circle*, in view of the weight the study accords to the *dramatic* character of the revelations which occurred to Nietzsche in his later years. Klossowski's study is divided between the scientific and the lived perspectives on the doctrine of eternal return, which is to say its dramatic and logocentric qualities and manifestations. Despite its evident occupation with the drama of the vicious circle, strewn as it is with excerpts from Nietzsche's correspondence and sustained evocations both of his epiphanous and delirious episodes, only one real remark is dedicated to the role of parody in the circle's temporality. Yet Klossowski dedicated the majority of a lecture, given in 1957 to the *College de Philosophie*, to the parodic character of the Nietzschean experience, in one of the somewhat rare instances of his other scholarship being brought to publishable light. In this text, parody is entwined with the very core of the temporality of the vicious circle, as well as the inversion of the institutional code to which it owes its origin. This entwinement has two main aspects.

First of all, the fortuity which the individual agent exhibits, under the conditions which reveal to it the vicious circle, itself amounts to a kind of parody.

> We believe we choose freely to be what we are, but not being what *we are*, we are in fact constrained to play a role – and thus to play the role of what *we are outside ourselves*. We are never where *we are*, but always where we are only the actor of *this other* that *we are*. The role represents the fortuitousness in the necessity of destiny.[39]

The individual, with its belief in a fixed history, believes in its own conscious and free choice to be itself; the subject of the vicious circle is always elsewhere, a de-actualised entity dispersed in the future and past. We are actors, as conscious signs, of simulacra of our impulses. Parody thus corresponds to the fact that, "We cannot not will, but we can never will something other than a role."[40] No authenticity could be constituted through the code of signs, but only imitation.

---

39 Klossowski, P. (2007). p. 116
40 Klossowski, P. (2007). p. 116

This passage is thus a now-familiar reassertion of the opposition of fluctuation to stasis, of intensity to the code of signs.

However, there is a second and more intricate aspect to parody in the lecture, which admits a more comprehensive link to the semiotic reflections that predominate in talk of the vicious circle.

> Even when we do not know how to share its mode of understanding, our pathos does not thereby prevent us from understanding ourselves. For where such sudden satisfactions, coupled with the absence of any rational motive, come from – for instance, when I laugh or cry, seemingly without reason, before some spectacle such as those offered by the view of a suddenly discovered landscape or of tidal pools at the edge of the ocean?[41]

Here, Klossowski develops a line of argument which parallels the additional note appended to the *Mercure de France* edition (1969) of his full-length study.[42] Both the additional note, and this section in *Nietzsche, Polytheism and Parody* complicate the relation between impulsive intensity and conscious signs, which earlier in *Nietzsche in the Vicious Circle* appears to be a straightforward opposition between authentic and inauthentic expressions of fluctuations, with opposite characteristics – fluidity over against stasis, specificity over against indeterminacy, etc. The two are no longer opposite orders of signs or proto-signs, but obverses of the same impulse. Accordingly, in the additional note, the intellect which exerts restraint on the impulses is itself an impulse. A similar, but more significant relationship is developed in the above passage. Pathos, or impulse, is not given to us in a lucid way by the signs relayed to consciousness, but it nevertheless "does not prevent us from understanding ourselves." Outbursts of emotion such as laughter, though apparently in reaction to events that befall us, may seem to provide rare snapshots of the untrammelled activity of the impulse.

> Something is laughing or crying in us that, by making use of us, is robbing us of ourselves and concealing us from ourselves, but which, by making use of us, is concealing itself. Does this mean that this something was not *present* otherwise than in the tears and laughter?[43]

The surfacing of an outburst in consciousness conceals us from ourselves in that it refuses to adopt the volitional guises of agency, but it no less dissimulates the underlying impulse of which, it may be suspected, it is the transparent expression. The laughter itself is the knowledge of the simultaneous obscurity and hegemony of the impulse: the outburst itself communicates the necessity of ex-

---

41 Klossowski, P. (2007). p. 111
42 Klossowski, P. (1978). pp. 359–367
43 Klossowski, P. (2007). p. 111

pressing a movement which is concealed beyond consciousness. The impulse creates its own dissimulation, just as the third chapter argued that it creates its own obverse, and its own constraint.

> But this most essential aspect of myself, which is made manifest in this way, corresponds to an image hidden in the full light of consciousness, an image that appears to me as inverted and that arrives late in the goal-oriented perspective, which wants to lend as much consciousness as possible to this laughter or these tears. Thus there must be a necessity that wills me to laugh or cry as if I were laughing or crying freely.[44]

The manifestation, however constituted, in consciousness of the impulse which the very transparency of consciousness disguises – the vividness and sensory detail of the scene whose hilarity ostensibly elicits the agent's reaction, the activity of the agent in perceiving and appraising it as this or that – is an inversion of the impulses which interpret it as an opportunity for the outburst. The image of impulsive fluctuation in consciousness is an inversion.

But if this vague and inverted manifestation of the impulse is its only manifestation, and thus is entire being, then we can only conclude that it is as the inversion of these signs that it is defined at all. The necessity that impels us to consciousness of our outbursts of necessity is

> the very *same* necessity that inverts night into day, which inverts sleep into wakefulness where consciousness posits its goal ... Is this not the same necessity that will re-invert the images of the day into those of night? To live and think in the goal-oriented perspective is to distance myself from what is most essential in me, or from the necessity that testifies, within me, to my deepest need. To want to recuperate this most essential part of myself amounts to living backwards from my consciousness, and therefore *I will put all my will and confidence in the necessity that has made me laugh and cry without any motive.*[45]

Klossowski is therefore committed to a reciprocal inversion between consciousness and the impulsive intensity. Conscious signs are inversions of the subterranean impulse, but the inversion, or re-inversion, of conscious goals – that is, conscious interpretations of impulses, or impulses insofar as they are spuriously conscious – is the route Nietzsche takes in order to resuscitate their authenticity, and to express them fully.

Consciousness thus stages the simulation of that which it inverts, but the impulse itself is only the inverted condition of these simulations, the phantasm whose image they mirror. The absurd circularity of this co-dependency can

---

44 Klossowski, P. (2007). p. 111
45 Klossowski, P. (2007). p. 112

only be described as a parody, and the doctrine which asserts the latter inversion as a "law" can only be as much of a simulacrum as any other conscious inversion – "a *simulacrum of a doctrine*, whose parodic character gives an account of *hilarity* as an attribute of existence,"[46] parodic since "one dissimulates the fact that the role one plays refers to existence itself" and yet "what one dissimulates is the fact that one is nothing other than existence."[47]

The outbursts of emotion that appear to render subterranean impulses visible function as case examples in this text in just the same way as in *Nietzsche and the Vicious Circle*. The chain of inversions, re-inversions, and inversions of re-inversions that results from the interplay between these two, or between intensity and sign, is what justifies Klossowski's usages of the term "parody" in relation to this drama. But how do these considerations justify the temporal significance which this work imparts to this parody, and which is our current concern? In "The Euphoria of Turin," the vision of the vicious circle is described as "the parody of a recollection of an event."[48] Klossowski openly asserts an intimate relationship between the inversion of consciousness for the sake of the impulses, and the law of the vicious circle. "Everything that rises up into the full light of consciousness rises up upside down – the images of night are reversed in the mirror of conscious thought. Later we will see that there is a necessity deeply inscribed in the law of being that is explicated as the universal wheel, the image of eternity."[49] Where does the connection between these two factors come from? How does the parody of the individual's history, and the parody of the impulses by signs, imply the parody of a recollection of an event – and then the law of the vicious circle?

The relations between the various different terms here parallel other terms which are by now familiar. The parodic status of the individual's history presupposes the deactualisation of this history which occurs in the circle, and the fortuitous individual which results. Klossowski's remarks about the individual's disingenuous adoption of occupations and vocations in the industrial world, and the conscious and retrospective efforts to conceal their arbitrariness, presuppose the fortuity of these commitments, relative to all the possibilities which could have befallen the individual instead. The individual's actions are a parody due and only due to this fortuity. But if this fortuity is triggered by the isolated moment of the vicious circle, and in this moment series of series are projected

---

46 Klossowski, P. (2007). p. 121
47 Klossowski, P. (2007). p. 109
48 Klossowski, P. (1997). p. 252
49 Klossowski, P. (2007). p. 109

and retrojected in place of the individual's history, and as a reconstruction – in Heidegger's terms, a "gathering," or according to Klossowski a recollection – thus a "parody of a recollection of an event."⁵⁰

This, then, explains the important relationship between parody and return: the dramatic and ironic character of Nietzsche's identification with a multiplicity of personages and panjandra, and the blooming of a plurality of gods on the altar of the dead God, emerge from the temporality of the vicious circle, and the individual's fortuity, which destroys individual history, because it destroys the permanence and the completeness of events. In the *Nietzsche, Polytheism and Parody* lecture, Klossowski summarises these relations in this way:

> Nietzsche saw that the mental conditions for such an "exit" lay in the *forgetting* (of the historical situation) that was preliminary to the act of *creating:* in *forgetting*, humans subcome to the past as their *future*, which takes the *figure of the past*. It is in this way that the *past comes to* them in what they create; for what they believe they create in this way does not come to them from the present, but is only the pronunciation of a prior possibility in the momentary forgetting of the (historically determined) present.⁵¹

Here, the well-known concepts of possibility and time's inversion are held to derive from that of forgetting, just as in the full study of Nietzsche, *forgetting* is the starting point for the entire exposition of the vicious circle:

> But what is the function of forgetting in this revelation? More specifically, is not forgetting the source as well as the indispensable condition not only for the revelation of the Eternal Return, but also for the sudden transformation of the identity of the person to whom it is revealed?⁵²

The indispensable priority of forgetting in Klossowski's argument leads to a problem. Is Nietzsche's position not refuted by the ability of the organism to incorporate and retain traces of previous excitations, or by the fact that the conscious and unconscious mind is equipped with a memory? How can we explain our ability to preserve and retain previous experiences, if, as Klossowski affirms, we necessarily forget from one state to another – not just in the minor sense that significations differ from presentation to presentation, but in the deeper sense that the knowledge of time's camouflaged structure itself appears and disappears? We have that forgetting obviates the indexical function of signs, but here it appears to be incompatible with any notion of preservation. This incom-

---

50 Klossowski, P. (1997). p. 252
51 Klossowski, P. (2007). p. 103
52 Klossowski, P. (1997). p. 56

patibility seems to be precisely the meaning of the deactualisation of the agent, the usurpation of individual history, and the rebuttal of permanence and completeness predicted by the vicious circle. Preservation, moreover, seems necessary for synthesis and memory; without it, not only would a "rhapsodic"[53] and indeterminate anarchy of experience seem to follow ineluctably; all distinct moments would be completely independent, and would need to possess no content possessed by any other. By way of a rejoinder to this possibility, not only does Klossowski not contemplate the possibility that forgetting and memory might exclude each-other; puzzlingly, he asserts its contrary: forgetting itself amounts to a kind of memory.

5.9 Forgetting and Memory: Coalescence

It is in the following passage that the supposed antipodes, forgetting and memory, coalesce:

> At the moment the Eternal Return is revealed to me, I cease to be myself *hic et nunc* and am susceptible to becoming innumerable others, knowing that I shall forget this revelation once I am outside the memory of myself; this forgetting forms the object of my present willing; for such a forgetting would amount to a memory outside my own limits: and my present consciousness will be established only in the forgetting of my other possible identities.[54]

Between the intensity of the revelatory moment and its diminution, the knowledge of the vicious circle's structure is relinquished, and the manifestation of the series, substituted in this moment for the individual's history, is forgotten. This forgetting places the individual agent "outside the memory of itself" – outside, that is, the memory of the kind of alien selfhood it attains in this exceptional moment. Then, however, the surprising equivalence between forgetting and memory is indicated by the usage of the term "équivaudra." Relinquishing this knowledge and the deactualising imagery of the series entails forgetting, but it is the *memory* of a prior state of ignorance of this knowledge – knowledge which must be attained in order for the revelation to be re-established – which one forgets with a view to remembering. More specifically, forgetting occurs first with the individual's submission to the vicious circle, and is thus the forgetting of the individual's present state in favour of a series. The compulsion

---

53 Kant, I. (1929). A81/B106
54 Klossowski, P. (1997). p. 58

to forget has, however, two aspects. Not only would forgetting propel the individual into an entirely new state, in which a *different* series of events would appear to the individual as the elements of its history; in addition, this forgetting aims to re-establish the revelatory moment, following the inevitable labyrinth of non-revelatory moments, in a trajectory known only because of the individual's *memory* of previous such moments. Forgetting amounts to a memory, not in that the state forgotten is the state remembered, but in as much as the memory of this state's absence brings about the forgetting of the present: one advances because one remembers. Forgetting of the present is not therefore the memory of the present, but the memory of a state which must be regarded as quite distinct.

In this culminating reasoning, Klossowski goes as far as to effectively discard the distinction between past and future. If it is indeed the case that forgetting and memory are basically equipollent, any act of forgetting a present state in order to explore some other series must no less be regarded as a memory of such a series. For any individual state S, and for any set of states in series γ, leaving S for γ may seem to amount to a passage in a certain direction in time. If, however, as the vicious circle prescribes, γ is a memory every bit as much as S is forgotten by the agent, γ also lies in the past of the agent. No event or series of events belongs therefore solely to the past or the future and not both, if the latter are conceived simplistically as sets of events positioned ahead of or behind the present. Conversely, as distant as a given memory may be, the vicious circle proclaims its inevitable resurgence in a future fluctuation.

Do these considerations produce such an extreme result as a refutation of the divide between past and future? In and of itself, neither the thesis that all events in the past recur in the future, nor the thesis that all future events have already passed by, entails this result. From the fact that all events in the past occur also in the future, and that all future events have done so already, it follows no more that there is no distinction between the two, or between the differing directions they constitute in time, than it does from the fact that one set of elements is equipped with a determinate ordering that another set of these same elements with a *different* ordering must be identical. Time is not, surely, indifferent to the order of the elements it effects. Consider, for instance, the following partial sequence: ...*PQRSTPQRSTPQRST*... This string is constituted by repeated sub-strings, and preceded and followed by further unspecified sub-strings. If we locate a certain state of the agent at the second occurrence of Q in this string, and consider the agent to be aware, sensibly or intellectually, of the sub-string *PQRST* as self-attributable states, there would still be a distinction between the elements *RST* and the element *P* from the perspective of the agent, notwithstanding that every occurrence of every element in this sequence is both preceded and followed by a separate occurrence of the same element. At *Q*, it is not the case that the recurrence of all of these elements elsewhere in the string renders all directions indifferent and equivalent. Ahead of *Q* lies *RST*, before it *P*: *RST* is futural at *Q*, and *P* past.

However, far from reinforcing the distinction between two directions in time, this reasoning assumes precisely what is placed into question by Klossowski's critique. The principle exposited in the previous section concerning the inversion of time, taken from his "Attempt at a Scientific Explanation of the Eternal Return," was the following one: The order of events in a given moment is distinct from the process by which they are ordered. As a result, the order which appears in this moment cannot originate a parallel order of appearance. This distinction, however, is exactly what must be collapsed in order for representations such as ...*PQRSTPQRSTPQRST*... to enable past and future to be meaningfully opposed. One must identify the order of these elements and the order in which they are given. The fact that one sub-string precedes another, as *P* does *RST*, does not require the appearance of *P* to precede the appearance of *RST*, but merely that they are so ordered: the order of appearance need not conform to the appearing order. To infer from the position at *Q* the order *PQRST* is not to attribute permanent positions to each of these elements. In knowing or glimpsing the sequence of states *PQRST* at *Q*, the agent is not for this reason furnished with two independent sub-strings, *P* and *RST*, each intrinsically and essentially located, akin to time-stamps.[55] No attribute of the appearance(s) of these sub-strings confines them to separate enclaves, which could be assimilated to different directions in time. These events are sorted or arranged at a particular way at *Q* in a way which cannot be simply equated with their appearance independent of *Q*. The moment in which the ordering occurs is quite separate from the appearance of the moment ordered. Consequently, further, these events cannot be accorded permanent positions in time; this would require that such a position be constant and not variable, and that *Q* and subsequent events have no bearing on their value – an impossibility so long as these values, functions of the order appearing at *Q*, are determined at *Q*, unlike the order of appearance.

If the order of the elements of the series *PQRST* is specific to *Q* in this sense, the existence of strings such as ...*PQRSTPQRSTPQRST*... does not evidence a disjunction between past and future, such as would undermine the coalescence of the two we have entertained in this section. This disjunction would legitimate the separability of the string ...*PQRSTP* from the string *RSTPQRST*..., since these are the two series whose different orderings (of the same elements) respectively represent past and future. But if these are unitary features of one moment

---

[55] King, P. (1995). p. 535

Q, no asymmetry or break exists between a forward-looking receptivity and a backward-looking receptivity such as could tell these two series apart, one as past and the other as future. There is no sense in which retrospection allows us to access or receive events with certain time values, and in which anticipation furnishes events with later ones. These events occur, or recur, at *Q*, all at the same time.

In order to account formally for reasoning of this sort, a different kind of series must be posited. A series such as *PQRST* thought to constitute a specific permutation of events is not sufficient as a specification of the order in which these elements are actually given. Firstly, any series is the coruscation of a particular point in time. The series inhabits a temporal dimension, and obeys an appropriate set of relations, seemingly just as a set of locations might be organised along the axis of a spatial dimension. But if the points which produce series are themselves given in series, a second dimension is involved – a dimension which would involve not only a series, but a series of series, each of whose members could be distinct. In previous chapters, the substitution of series of series in the place of series corresponded to the deactualisation of the individual with a determinate history. Here, it is cast in its temporal aspect.

These formulations can be made more precise if transposed into the terms, now well established interpretative tools in the metaphysics of time, originally introduced to the tradition by J. M. E. McTaggart. Consider a series of events in time, such as *PQRST* or *MNOP*, tokens of a particular type of series. Firstly, the A-series is "the series of positions running from the far past through the near past to the present, and then from the present to the near future and the far future."[56] Secondly, the B-series is "the series of positions which runs from earlier to later."[57] By virtue of these definitions, the A-series designates the mutually incompatible predicates "present," "past" and "future," whose inherence in each moment, McTaggart claims, is required for temporal change. The B-series consists in constant, invariable or "permanent" relations of anteriority or posteriority between whichever terms participate in it. The C-series of events is defined implicitly, not as a series of positions or relations, but as an ordination of moments, or events. *PQRST* and *MNOP* are instances of this kind of series. For McTaggart, when conjoined with the A-series, this C-series yields the B-series, although he notes that this conjunction is subject to the limitation of being an invertible series, failing to discriminate between *PQRST* and *TSRQP*, or *MNOP* and *PONM*, unlike the B-series. This aside, an allocation of a position – a member of

---

56 McTaggart, J. (1908).
57 McTaggart, J. (1908).

the A-series – to each moment – a member of the C-series – is sufficient to specify for any pair of moments which is anterior to the other. Overall, then, we have a series of events, a series of their positions, and a derivative series of their binary relations (being earlier or later than another) – respectively C-, A- and B-.

The salient feature of this structuring of various kinds of series for Klossowski's argument is the following. McTaggart claims:

> The A-series, together with the C-series, is sufficient to give us time. For in order to get change, and change in a given direction, it is sufficient that one position in the C-series should be Present, to the exclusion of all others, and that this characteristic of presentness should pass along the series in such a way that all positions on the one side of the Present have been present, and all positions on the other side of it will be present.[58]

Now if, as is Klossowski's contention, a *series* is no less the content of a given point in time than is the moment which occupies it, such a sufficiency (of A-series and C-series for time) can never obtain. It is not enough that each element in the C-series progressively traverses, or is traversed by, various positions in the A-series. The conjunction of the C-series with the A-series is the conjunction of a set of tensed positions together with a set of events. In McTaggart's staging, for a series of events *PQRST* and a series of associable positions $x_1, x_2, \ldots, x_n$, the conjunction of these two series can be interpreted in two ways.

Firstly, if we construe the positions to constitute present moments, the x_i effectively designate which of the elements of *PQRST* are present. The conjunction of the series fails to constitute time in Klossowski's theory, since it amounts only to a set of couples $\{x_i, P\}, \{x_j, Q\}, \ldots, \{x_k, T\}$ which defines a series of independent present moments: P is present at x_i, Q is present at x_j etc. Klossowski's assertions are unamenable to such a series, insofar as they concern series of series, that is, series as the contents of each and every moment, themselves comprising further series, in turn. These couples fix only which of the series' moments is present at a given moment, leaving indeterminate the status of the others. By contrast, Klossowski alleges that, at a point in time, not only a single and isolated present moment is given but a series, such as appears at the privileged moment of the vicious circle's revelation. Secondly, however, and alternatively, we may construe the positions X_n described by McTaggart, not as present moments attributable only to one position, but as the various positions in series which some particular moment or event may assume. This interpretation, however, is no more successful a description of Klossowski's approach than the previous. Simplistically, these explain a range of possible positions occupied by a *given* moment, but

---

58 McTaggart, J. (1908).

offer no account of how a range for other moments could be specified, nor the innumerable plurality of orphan blocks not contained within this privileged moment. One moment's journey from position to position, for instance from the future to the past, is not sufficient for time.

Accounting for the genesis of a *series* at every point is more tenably envisioned as requiring a kind of Cartesian product $S_x \times X_n$, where $X_n = x_1, x_2, ..., x_n$ and $S_x = PQRST$. This produces a set of elements $\{(P,x_1),(P,x_2),...,(P,x_n),(Q,x_1), (Q,x_2),...,(Q,x_n),...,(T,x_n)\}$. In this product, we would be given not only each moment or event at the present time, but also at a series of other times. This would be to deny the premise that the content of a given point in time can be exhaustively delineated by attaching to a singular element (such as P or Q or M or N) another variable (such as the x_i) which *alone* determines when this term corresponds to something which actually exists and is real.

In order for the distinction between past and future to be maintained, it must be possible to demonstrate an asymmetry somewhere in the series concerned. Past and future cannot be distinguished by whether or not they contain different elements. For Klossowski, the elements they contain are the same. For them to be distinct in spite of this fact, there must be some other fact, concerning perhaps their order or nature, which marks them out as uniquely past or future in any case. The distinction could be, for instance, based on the repetition of different permutations of the elements contained by both in one compared with the other. Isolating from the series *PQRST* the moment *Q*, it is obvious that, whether or not *RST* occurs before *Q* as well as after it, and whether or not *P* occurs after *Q* no less than before, it remains the case that these occur in a different order before and after *Q*. But nor can this function as the basis for such a distinction. Once the difference between the order of events and the order in which they are given is articulated, the isolation of Q in the series *PQRST* does not permit a fissure or cleft between two directions in the series. At *Q*, *PQRST* is produced as the series of which *Q* is an element. From the fact that, at *Q*, a distinction is formulable between events before and after *Q*, it does not follow that events are ordered in such a way permanently, or independent of *Q*. The semblance of these elements produced at *Q* is produced in one moment, not distributed over the elements the semblance resembles. Being given together, no separation of these elements from each other can thus be made in such a manner as to divide them according to the directions in time they furnish. These directions can be opposed, and past and future separated, only if these events before and after can be excluded from one another by this kind of separation. Laconically, the process of ordering $(Q, PQRST)$ is not equivalent to the order which results (P, Q, R, S, T). This principle, established in the previous section, is in this way the basis for Klossowski's tenet that the past and the future effectively coalesce.

5.10 Consistency and Repetition

It follows directly from the above that any degree of consistency in the presentation of such a series, over more than just one moment – concretely, the consistency with which we recall and affirm that certain events happened at certain times, and in a certain order – is a result of the repetition of this presentation across distinct moments, not of stasis or permanence. If it is indeed the case that the process of ordering is not equivalent to the order which results, and if series are internal to a certain moment, several conclusions follow. That one is able to recall a previously extant event under certain conditions, and to locate this event in an appropriate series, by affixing to it an approximate date and time, or by describing the events adjacent to it, is by no means proof that this event occupies a determinate position in time. Nor is it deducible from these phenomena that the temporal series containing this event is determined independent of this recollection. It is rather proof that this event is relatively reproducible. The recollection, like the attendant series, is the manifestation of the return of these events. Were such recollections, which may be formalised in terms of these kinds of series, connections or relations to previous independent moments instead, these connections or relations could only be construed as events with an already determined position, now reflected into the present: I now remember an event which occurred before, as a predecessor of the present, and in doing so rank this moment which has appeared, ordered before the present, as appearing before the present too. Nietzsche's principle, to the contrary, is that the order in which events are ranked differs from their provenance.

The concept of temporal position, besieged at almost every step of Klossowski's reasoning, is thus exchanged for the concept of repetition. Memories which purport to confer data about events' positions in time are in fact new occurrences of them, over series of series. But, more notably, there is no intrinsic difference between the event's own fluctuation and its anticipation or recollection – between, that is, the faintness of a memory, said faintness ostensibly owing to the imperfection of the agent's synthetic powers, and the uncertainty latent in the approaching future, or its premonition. Equivalently, there is no such thing as an original or archetype proper to a fluctuation of which premonitions or recollections are the shadows. The repetition that replaces position is not, therefore, the repetition of an original case, nor indeed the teleological anticipation of a future one, but rather the repetition of nothing other than repetition.

By way of comparison, kinds of relations between events which are the upshot of Klossowski's intricate constructions, such as this recursive relation of repetition to repetition, have been expounded formally in the work of Deleuze. According to Deleuze, in distinguishing events, such as the members of the series above, we establish differences, in the broadest possible sense of the term: two or more events are given and distinguish themselves. Deleuze's specific notion of difference is defined in the following way. Difference is a state in which something distinguishes itself, but in which that from which that which distinguishes itself distinguishes itself *does not* distinguish itself from that which distinguishes itself: "Imagine something which distinguishes itself – and yet that from which it distinguishes itself does not distinguish itself from it."[59] Difference is thus a distinction which is non-reciprocal, non-mutual, asymmetric and unilateral. Does the vicious circle exemplify this difference? Does the way in which repetition replaces consistency of past and future events do so? Firstly, by way of an affirmative response, there can be no oppositional distinction between on the one hand the event which conditions its results, and on the other the event which retroactively projects its conditions into something prior, under the conditions of the circle. In order to see this, we can note that events standing in causal relations, for example, fulfil a dyadic schema which is oppositional – albeit opposition being a logical relation between propositions which entail each-other's falsity, this thesis is more properly cast in terms of exclusion: only one of the events can occur at once, so one's occurrence excludes the other's. This opposition or exclusion is reciprocal, symmetric and mutual. In the vicious circle, however, the series containing these events as terms is presented at once, at the culmination of intensity. These cannot, therefore, be *reciprocally* or *mutually* different, in the manner of an *opposition*. Secondly, and consequently, these events are not at the fundamental level primarily distinguished *from* each-other. Difference or distinction *from* one event to another is difference *between* them. Difference between is distinct from the kind of unilateral difference addressed by this exegesis. Events are distinguished as a result of fluctuations of intensity, which generate the series which allow them to be compared. Events distinguish themselves as events, not from one another as the other's exclusive condition or exclusive consequence, but rather from the vicious circle: the multiplication of events into an eternal series of interpenetrating terms. The content of an event, together with its dependencies, is dispersed far into the future and past. By virtue of these two features, therefore, this notion of difference informs a related notion of repetition which serves to further explain the figure of the circle latent in Klossowski's narrative. Deleuze defines repetition as that which difference inhabits, that is: "Difference inhabits repetition."[60] Repetition thus acquires all the characteristics of difference. It is unilateral, not reciprocal. In

---

59 Deleuze, G. (2004). p. 28
60 Deleuze, G. (2004). p. 76

5.10 Consistency and Repetition — 149

the circle, every event is a repetition in this way and not a repetition of another similar, analogous or qualitatively similar event.[61]

These considerations, moreover, demonstrate the limitations of conceiving the necessity of returning with the aid of the crude image of a series. In the figure of a series of states, each element is identified by its qualitative characteristics, both with itself and with its numerically distinct equivalents. Each element would then be a state which possesses a relatively coherent mass of sensory content by virtue of which it has the properties it does. A closed sequence of such elements constitutes the individual. Accordingly, the repetition of these elements in the circuitous drama undergone by Nietzsche, and the return of the individual which results, would imply the *qualitative resemblance* of these elements' *instances at different times*. Time, construed either as a variable independent of these states, or as a variable emergent from them, separates the tokens or instances of elements which recur – thus also the sequence they compose. But, regarded as an economy of such elements and such a sequence, the vicious circle is erroneously conceived. The return signified by the circle is not the periodic re-exploration of bundles of resemblant qualities, as if occurrences of characters in a string, or sequences of states in an abstract space: ...*PQRSTPQRSTPQRST*... Firstly, the states which are the subjects of the circle's return have nothing to do with quality.

> In turn, having passed through the entire series, this dissolved soul must itself return, that is, it must *return to the degree of the soul's tonality in which the law of the Circle was revealed to it.*[62]

The point at which an element returns qua individual state is not the return of qualities, but the "return to the degree of the soul's tonality" in which a particular kind of knowledge is revealed (namely the nomological aspects of the circle). This degree is indifferent to the qualities which feature in the individual's experience – just as is the circle's exogenous fortuity or chance, which is "but one thing at each of the moments ... of which it is composed."[63] Accordingly, the necessitarian impetus of the circle is not formulable in terms of the constancy of the inter-cyclic qualitative resemblance of the elements, but the "*necessity for the individual to live again in a series of* different *individualities.*"[64] Were the circle's structure tantamount to the elements' qualitative identity from cycle to

---

61 Land, N. (1992). p. 15
62 Klossowski, P. (1997). p. 71
63 Klossowski, P. (1997). p. 72
64 Klossowski, P. (1997). p. 98

cycle, such a statement would be impossible to explain: no identical sets of elements can constitute truly different individualities. Secondly, there is no question of time instituting the *progressive* return of these elements, whether or not conceived as an independent variable. Any progression connotes a state which another state follows through time. Time passes from the past into the future, with future events protractedly passing. If memory and forgetting, premonition and recollection, and past and future are inseparable, progressions of this sort can no longer be picked out: the distinction between past and future on which the structure of the progression rests no longer exists. Saying that time moves in both directions in this sense amounts to the statement that time has no direction at all, and certainly no tendencies describable as bilateral progressions, which continuously would carry events out of the future and force them to recede into the past.

There are, therefore, two aspects to the unilateral differences in time construed in the context of the vicious circle's structure and revelation. Firstly, the revelation of the circle is not distinguished qualitatively from other non-revelatory moments, but by virtue of the degree of intensity which produces it. Secondly, the collapse of the distinction between past and future and their integration, following Klossowski's reflections on memory and forgetting, means the characterisation of the return in terms of progression is similarly untenable.

In review, therefore, Klossowski's attempt to collapse the distinction of future and past follows the following route:

Forgetting is the condition for the future; memory is the condition for the past. Forgetting amounts to a memory, so past and future conditions, regarded as groups of events, contain one another. If the order of these events is distinct from the process which orders them, the order in which an agent positions them at a given moment has no bearing on the order in which they appear, are given, or acquire determinacy. Consequently, we cannot separate such sets of events into independent sub-sets, or represent them as separate strings or sequences. Not only is all past content also futural, and all futural content also past; they are also inseparable, and cannot be prised into the differently ordered or permuted fragments that might reinstate the caesural or fissile quality of the present – its reflection, that is, of two essentially different modes of time, which are now substantively unitary. Inevitably, with these remarks, we encounter the extensively analysed images developed in *Thus Spoke Zarathustra*, such as the gate of the moment, where two seemingly opposed paths curve back into one another in eternity, like the lines of magnetic field which emanate from a bar, or the concentric circles which radiate from disturbances on the surface of a pool.

5.11 The Excentric Calendar

The crystallisation of this coalescence of past and future in a formula marks the culmination of the study, as well as Nietsche's spiralling cerebral dissolution, in the final chapter preceding his *Additional Note:* For Nietzsche, "Yesterday became today, the day before yesterday spilled over into tomorrow." The present could no longer be held apart as an element independent of its conditions and predecessors, but, deactualising in the intensity of the vicious circle, suddenly accommodated a convergent series. In a "brief interval of time" – indeed, however brief an interval time – Nietzsche could never reduce the present beyond a minimum of complexity. It was unavoidably a series. The present, thus nothing more than a presentation of multifarious contents, merged with the past, whose displaced fluctuations returned and repeated themselves in this presentation. Prevailing within the horizon of the sensuous was a selective simultaneity: groups of events fluctuated together regardless of their point of origin. None of these events maintained a position in an original series, as if their new fluctuations were degenerate attempts to access them, which could survive their reflux in this new series, as if a fortuitous archival patchwork. Yesterday thus becomes today. But if yesterday is to become today, then the day before yesterday must become the day after tomorrow. The past in general – the prehistory of the series which includes both fluctuations and traces of fluctuations, reanimated to some degree – can be understood only as what the agent must similarly reanimate in order for it to be real. The scope of the present expands, serialising into streams of events, or waves of greater and greater amplitude, but the prehistories jettisoned by these fluctuations remain buried and immobile. In order for them to emerge afresh, a deeper intensification of these series is needed. "The instant is multiplied. It is no longer one instant but many ... a specular multiplication."[65] In the future, a new intensification can re-excite this prehistory. The prehistory thus becomes its futural potential fluctuation, spilling over into "the day after tomorrow." This formula therefore reiterates the logic of the foregoing argument: the past is identified with the future, as memory with forgetting.

It may be observed that residues of the Bergsonian account of the pure past are displayed by the formula according to which the individual's prehistory merges with its future. If yesterday (like tomorrow) is identified with series which become present, as well as with the circuits which the agent can bring into consciousness, the day before yesterday can only be construed as a more general past. To assert that the day before yesterday becomes the day after to-

---

[65] Castanet, H. (2014). p. 111

morrow is, then, to assert a relationship between the past in general, or the pure past, and the future.

J. Williams' staging is instructive in developing the connection between these two thinkers, which may assist in contextualising Klossowski's idiosyncratic formulations. Beginning from first principles, he compacts Bergson's contributions into three theses:

1. "The past must be contemporaneous with the present that it was."
2. "All the past must coexist with the new present in relation to which it is past."
3. "The pure element of the past pre-exists the passing present."[66]

According to the first two theses, the past is in a sense one. Although Williams is fastidious in separating contemporaneity from simultaneity, the past being contemporaneous with the present that it was implies that the past, in general, is contemporaneous with any particular present. The past is therefore contemporaneous with all past presents, and so the whole of the past with itself. Were only part of the past contemporaneous with the present, the past would not be the pure past, or the past in general. In this way, it is temporally unitary. Consequently, all the past must coexist with the new present in relation to which it is past, per the second and third propositions is appended almost as an axiom – if the passing present passes into the past, the past must pre-exist it. Converted into Bergson's terminology, then, the fact that significations depend on fluctuations, or equivalently the fact that events are relative to the series in which they appear, equates to the claim that the past and the present are *contemporaneous* and *coexisting*. Just as Bergson claimed contemplating the content of duration, in the intensity of the circle, the present becomes merely a capacity to receive the same contents at another point in time. Simultaneously forward and backward looking, the agent of the circle can only evaluate its present experience as potential memories to be relived and, indeed, premonitions which will have been fulfilled. The gravity of the moment in its intensity is its inspiration of the sense that it must be recalled and relived. This grounds the parallel between the positions of Bergson and Klossowski: the past and the present are contemporaneous and coexist, just as the day before yesterday passes over into the day after tomorrow, according to an eccentric and irrational calendar.

In the *Genealogy of Morals*, this exchange between present and past is latent in Nietzsche's discussion of the formation of memory:

---

[66] Williams, J. (2011). p. 63.

5.11 The Excentric Calendar   153

> A thing must be burnt in so that it stays in the memory: only that which continues to *hurt* stays in the memory ... When man decided he had to make a memory for himself, it never happened without blood, torments and sacrifices.[67]

In fact, Nietzsche's theory of mnemotechnics cannot be grasped without its integral of all three aspects of time, not simply present and past. On the one hand, since memory is not a result of a natural retentiveness, or the default state of the organism of which forgetting is the privation, it presupposes the infliction of present violence. In this sense, memory is simply a present event: the infliction of violence. However, it is also the *resurgence* of a moment whose presence has now *past*. It is therefore both the memory of a present event and a past one: a past present, or present past – depending on whether one characterises this violence as a present state of suffering past, or the past state of present suffering. But such a memory is equally futural. In the present act of "burning in" a memory, a present which will be recovered as past, what is burned in is a future in which this memory will be present as a recollection. "Far from being a dimension of time, the past is the synthesis of the whole of time and the present and future are only its dimensions."[68] But although both Deleuze and Nietzsche privilege the past as the synthesis in which the other two temporal dimensions inhere – respectively, in this excerpt which reflects on the status of the past, and in the *Genealogy*'s arguments focusing on *memory* – the vicious circle accommodates nothing of this. All three modes of time are equivalent, and all three inevitably become conflated, in the loss of coherence inflicted by the vicious circle.

When Nietzsche refers to the power of resistance or strength to resist he refers to nothing more than this commitment to memory. His crippling illnesses appeared to him only as potential triumphs, from a point of view in which his health had been regained. The destruction of his personal and familial relationships only magnetised a position in time where this destruction would be seen as a source of creative energy and philosophical impetus. His genetic endowment – both in the sense of his physiology and in the sense of his familial milieu – was never experienced, but always already a memory, a situation into which he was thrown passively. What is essential to emphasise is that this equivalence between past, present and future, closely related to the marriage of memory and forgetting previously expounded, is distinct from the pre-critical banality that the present will become past and was previously future. Rather, the present, *as present*, *is* all three *at once*. It is not that each event in time instantiates three contradic-

---

[67] Nietzsche, F. (2006). p. 38
[68] Deleuze, G. (2004). p. 111

tory predicates, or that it *successively* assumes different relative positions in a series of moments. It is rather that distinguishing, at any position, in any series, between any of these positions, is incompatible with the vicious circle.

The Nietzschean analysis of the formation of memory is therefore taken up and extended in Klossowski's study, and paralleled in the concepts of Bergson, as an important forerunner. The status of the pure past in *Matter and Memory*, as contemporaneous with the present, is fruitfully comparable to the role of memory in the *Genealogy*. Neither allow the extrication of past from present modes of time. But in Klossowski, this inextricability is not limited to these two, but granted also to the future.[69]

5.12 Order and Disorientation

Much of the propositions adduced to demonstrate the coalescence of past and future in this section presuppose the analysis carried out more fully in the section preceding it – The Inversion of Time – and, in particular, the distinction of the order of events and the process which orders them. However, the ramifications of this distinction are not confined to this coalescence. From the formula which captures the merging of yesterday with tomorrow, and the reversals of time in this chapter, two further propositions follow. These lead to a further re-evaluation – here, one which relates to the way in which events are ordered.

Y) Recurrences of events in present series cannot be assigned an original fluctuation
Z) Recurrences of events in present series occur at variable distances from other events

Y) follows since, if yesterday becomes today, and the day before yesterday the day after tomorrow, there is no sense to the notion of origin. Organising events into series – the form assumed by moments in time devoid of an accumulation of intensity – means each event is endowed with a determinate time value. The deictic term "yesterday" denotes all events with hypothesised time values lower than the point of reference present, just as does "tomorrow" all events with

---

[69] Williams, J. (2011). p. 64. As regards another point of difference between these otherwise similar positions, for Klossowski, the present does not subsist other than as past, as a result of the deactualization inherent in the circle – whereas Williams, reading Bergson through Deleuze, rejects the complete *identity* of present and past, referring to contemporaneity rather than a provocative simultaneity

greater such hypothesised values. Now, the proposition Y) is such as to stipulate a Gaussian or modular arithmetic in respect of these time values: they are determinable only as increments of a cycle. By way of justification, consider any possibly original fluctuation and any event which reproduces it (thus as its trace). The latter *ex hypothesi* possesses the greater time value of the pair. Yet, however these values are assigned, if at some point there exists a modulus, albeit unspecified, making congruent all those values in this series separated by multiples of it, and therefore equivalent, there can be no original fluctuation: the original is congruent with an event of even lesser value, and thus prior. Y) is derived by contradiction.

Z), secondly, distinguishes the vicious circle from a periodic mechanism or regular cycle. A *regular* (non-vicious) deterministic (non-circular) cycle can be construed as a series of states, each defined in terms of certain variables (such as position and momentum, or temperature, pressure and other macroscopic parameters). More importantly, in such a case, the intra-cyclic relations of elements are constant over iterations of the cycle. Assuming the existence of more than one cycle, the relations of the events in any individual cycle – including their order – coincide with those of any other. Z), by contrast, pertains to a circular movement which nonetheless does not maintain constant relations over iterations. Comparing the various formulations of the circle's topology in the text of Klossowski's study, we find this distinction in the difference between Lou de Salomé's gloss of the vicious circle revealed to Nietzsche and the latter's own communications of the doctrine. Stymied by its psychoanalytical content, de Salomé's surmisal neglected

> the necessity for the individual to live again in a series of different individualities. Hence the richness of the return: to *will* to be *other* than you are in order to become what you are ... not the idea of reliving the same sufferings sempiternally, as Lou interpreted it, but rather the loss of reason under the sign of the Vicious Circle.[70]

The mechanistic conceptual architecture supporting this purely cyclical conception must be resolutely separated from the real dynamic of the circle lived by Nietzsche, and the derivation of Z) as a consequence. Following the analysis of possibility described before, this dynamic multiplies its subject's identity, through the deactualising effects of interpretation. It is not its unitary reproduction. Being one's self – or, leaving out any references to the self, an event being given – requires serialisation. The self multiplies, only becoming itself through different resonances of itself. The circularity implicit in the priority of recursion

---

70 Klossowski, P. (1997). p. 98

in time over occurrence – that is, the priority of events which possibilise and multiply in order to be themselves over positions which are indexed – is not therefore cyclicality. Firstly, the subject of the *cycle* is a series (of determinate elements). By contrast, the subject of the *circle* (specifically) is any event in general, as opposed a fixed series of them: the deactualisation and multiplication of any given event is the movement of the vicious circle. It is for this reason that *series of series*, as opposed to the mere series of events, are the result of the return. The latter equate to an individual's history, but the former to its evisceration. Secondly, and correlatively, the circle is as much an internal feature of its subject event as cyclicality is external to the events within a given cycle. From the appearance of any given event in a cycle, nothing implies its necessary return in subsequent ones, nor those which predate it. The identity of this event with its equivalents in other cycles, and therefore its membership of the cycle at all, is a relation *between* it and another.

The circle, however, as this deactualisation and multiplication, excites any and all events qua events, possessing the force of the requisite maximum of intensity. The circularity which belongs to them collectively is thus no external or secondary characteristic, but an internal mechanism: the events' interpretation of themselves. It therefore reflects the *internal* qualitative differentiation of the events subjected to it, not the *external* relations to qualitatively identical events in other cycles. The cycle's identical elements are displaced from one another by a period of defined length, but the circle's undefined locations are, by contrast, series which converge whenever their terms resonate. With such a circularity, there is no question of the same elements in the same order recurring inter-cyclically. This latter recurrence requires external relations between elements, permanently localised constituents, and a determinate period separating them, ensuring their order and positions are preserved from cycle to cycle. The fact that the *same* elements occur at these same positions, and in this same order, derives from the exact qualitative resemblance they exhibit with respect to their equivalents in other cycles. The vicious circle eschews each of these characteristics.

Accordingly, Z) asserts the *variability* of distances of each event from other events in the series. With a cycle such as . . . *IJKLMIJKLMIJKLM* . . ., the period of the cycle corresponds to the fact that five events elapse. It is thus determinate and constant. Moreover, it is this interpretation of the vicious circle that serves to underpin the claim that events are ordered invariably. With the vicious circle accurately envisaged, however, a break is posed with this determinate and constant order. Insofar as the events which show up with the intensity of the circle's fluctuation can be identified with elements, their positions are not permanent, but pure functions of fluctuations: after the occurrence of *K* in the sub-sequence *IJK*, we cannot assume that its location in time is fixed – just as the consistency of its location depends entirely on its repetition. But if its position is not fixed, and the fixity of this position is a necessary condition for both (a) the fixity of the order of the sub-sequence, and (b) the fixity of the distances between the elements, then Z) follows directly. Distances between events and their orders vary in the circle – just as they did in Nietzsche's person.

In the scattered landscapes of the Nietzschean biography, we are presented not with a continuum of well-ordered and consistent scenes but with combinations of series, whose terms are presented in a variable order. In Nietzsche's childhood, we find the conscious and unconscious presages of the delirium he was eventually to enact and so re-enact, such as in the deranged screams which engulfed his dreams of returning to his family as an invalid. In a separate affectation which itself was to become just as much a premonition, he dreamed of his father's demise and burial, later not merely recalling, but embodying it himself with the unshakeable affliction of his physical decline. Nietzsche thus involuntarily relived scenes from his childhood and upbringing which interceded during his period in Turin. These reversals and inversions of the consensus order of events, and the subversion of the very feasibility of an originating event and its derivative re-enactment, were consecrated in Nietzsche's conception of his own birth and ancestrality, extrapolated up as far as the phylogenetic order. The vulnerability and frailty that ended his father's life early were transposed into fears of his own infirmity. The rarity and fragility of life could only inflate its value in Nietzsche's eyes. Nietzsche's father, responsible for the trauma which rarefied Nietzsche's own life, was in this way responsible for its value, and therefore for life itself, to the one who posited life's coincidence with its interpreted value. But Nietzsche's hypochondriac mother – to him, a dolorous and morbid ancestral node – was swept aside from the picture in favour of Nietzsche himself, as his own mother – the life affirming counterpart of the afflicted father. The conditions, causes and origins of the widest span of events in Nietzsche's life – his very birth and death – thus came to be seen as simultaneous with, and dependent on, fluctuations in his bodily states, resonances of memory and forgetting, and his always under-determined destiny.

In this way, Nietzsche's childhood premonitions could signify only once they manifested themselves later in his life, in a repetition of their pre-existence: the signified intensity merged with the trace of itself. The significance of these experiences, and their formative aspects, emerged long after childhood had receded into the seemingly distant past, yet their resurgence was nothing other than what this past had always been. Recounting the way in which Nietzsche refers to these events in his autobiographical notes, Klossowski asks, "How could this lugubrious note, chosen here to recreate the ambience of puerile terror in these pages, not take on its signification at the end of Nietzsche's lucid life?"[71] How could the significations of these events do other than to repeat one another, despite their seeming localisation in different regions of time? "This dual descent, as it were, from both the highest and the lowest rung of the ladder of life, at the same time a *decadent* and a *beginning* – this, if anything, explains that neutrality, that freedom from all partiality in relation to the total problem of life, that perhaps distinguishes me."[72] The decadence which provoked Nietzsche's incessant cathexis was his inescapable tendency to "be determined by one's environment,"[73] at least to a basic degree: his dependency on his family, the parochialism of his upbringing, and his incurable physical ailments all subverted his plans to emancipate fluctuations of intensity and deliver them from the impasses of time, place and history. At once the unwitting product of inescapable endogenous constraints and the exogenous progenitor of a kind of emancipation, his descent was "dual" – simultaneously a beginning and an end, towards the environment which conditioned him, and away from it as its product, as well as towards the ramifications of his work and life, and away from it as its prototype. The events whose premonitions and consequences Nietzsche experienced occurred neither before the latter nor after the former. No fixed order, but only a *variable* one, can be assigned to these parts of exchanges between conditions and results.

5.13 From Intention to Intensity

> There are only the consequences of something unforeseen, and because something can be calculated afterwards does not mean that it is necessary. In this case, a goal is reached only by a combination of random events.[74]

In the chapter following the introduction to this work, the semiotic of intensity was affiliated with an attack on intentional states and volitions, of the sort which Nietzsche never tired of promoting in his notebooks and published works, such as the *Genealogy*. The critique of intentionality was an integral consequence of the semiotic underlay to the vicious circle. It is, however, only after a long discussion of the temporal implications of this semiotic that this critique can be fully exposited. Moreover, Klossowski is led to explain what "Nietzsche sought

---

71 Klossowski, P. (1997). p. 180
72 Klossowski, P. (1997). p. 172
73 Klossowski, P. (1997). p. 91
74 Klossowski, P. (1997). p. 105

from the experience of the *Return of all things* – namely, *to lead intention back to intensity.*"⁷⁵

Nietzsche himself assembles a number of propositions for an attack on intentionality which advance propositions about causality and temporality, as opposed to semiotic, psycho-linguistic, psychoanalytical or physiological ones, and which we are now in a stronger position to understand, following this chapter's study.

> In this regard, 'purpose' requires a more vigorous critique: one must understand that an action *is never caused by a purpose*; that *purpose* and *means* are *interpretations* whereby certain points in an event are emphasized and selected at the expense of other points, which, indeed, form the majority ...⁷⁶

1) No action is caused by a purpose.

From the perspective of the semiotic, every purpose is an interpretation, and thus a type of sign, that is, an abbreviation of a fluctuation by the institutional code. All conscious actions are conditional on these fluctuations. Could one not maintain the existence of a parallel series of events, occurring at the level of consciousness, which nonetheless permit causal relations? Simply that A causes B and C causes D does not, surely, prohibit that B cause D. Be then the relations among the impulses what they may, actions and purposes, intentions and decisions could relate among themselves in some other way, it may be thought. But since all signs are abbreviations of intensities, and such intensities never cease to fluctuate, there is no possibility of any parallelism between two series of events: the only events are fluctuations, and signs are traces of them, like a "pale image," lacking efficacy. In this regard, Nietzsche appeals to criteria of *authenticity* to denigrate abbreviations of fluctuations in relation to what they abbreviate (at times endorsing an ideational view of intensities almost Platonist in nature).

From the correlative perspective of the metaphysics of time expounded in this chapter, it is no more defensible to consider purposes to be fundamental drivers of events. If the causes of events are functions of the events themselves, the kinds of pre-existing purposes on which outcomes must exclusively depend in order to be efficacious purposes at all are not tenable drivers of processes of agency or intention. Consequently:

---

75 Klossowski, P. (1997). p. 112
76 Klossowski, P. (1997). p. 51

> Why could 'a purpose' not be an *epiphenomenon* in the series of changes in the activating forces that bring about the purposive action – a pale image sketched in consciousness beforehand that serves to orient us concerning events, even as a symptom of events, *not* as their cause? – But with this we have criticized *the will itself* – *is* it not an illusion to take for a cause that which rises to consciousness as an act of will? Are not all phenomena of consciousness merely terminal phenomena, final links in a chain, but apparently conditioning one another in their succession on one level of consciousness?[77]

2) Intention is an epiphenomenon.

> This apparent conformity to a goal *is simply subsequent to this will to power unfolding in every event*; – the becoming-strongest brings with itself organizations that have a certain resemblance to a plan of finality: – the apparent goals are not intentional, but once the supremacy over a lesser power is attained, and the latter is made to work on behalf of the greatest, a hierarchical order of organization must take on the appearance of an order of means and ends.[78]

3) Purpose and means are strictly dependent on the events which produce them.

The drive is richer in content than its schematisation as a coupling of means and end. From this point of view, in constructing an intention, the institutional code filters out the greater part of what occurs among the impulses, mapping them to their metonyms. This proposition, however, does not yet require that there is any *qualitative* difference between signs and intensity.

> Every single time something is done with a purpose in view, something fundamentally different and other occurs ... every purposive action is like the supposed purposiveness of the heat the sun gives off: the enormously greater part is squandered ...[79]

4) No intended outcome is ever realised.

This thesis involves an equivocation: it regards not only the difference between the intention at the level of consciousness and the outcome at the same level, but also the difference between the conscious intention and the unconscious or subterranean outcome in intensity. Not only, then, is there a disagreement between the signifying intention of a goal and the actual outcome, an obvious con-

---

[77] Klossowski, P. (1997). p. 52
[78] KSA 12, 9[91] = WP 552
[79] Klossowski, P. (1997). p. 51

sequence of the preceding thesis; the representations of goals and those of their attainments differ in principle.

Thus, since the representation of a goal (or any intentional referent) derives from one excitation, and the attainment of something from another, these two representations do not generally coincide. Conformity to a goal – the interpretation of an intensity – is imposed retrospectively, as a perspective of attainment; the goal before and after this attainment are thus incomparable. The symmetry of this incomparability means that, conversely,

5) No realised outcome is ever intended.

Therefore, at the root of the translation of intention into intensity is a temporal category, as well as the semiotic perspective.

In this relationship between intentionality into intensity, the temporality of intensity inverts and eventually replaces causality. This is demonstrable from the parallels between the semiotic and temporal aspects of this translation. In order for this replacement to be subsumed under the rubric of tracing "intention back to intensity,"[80] there must be a connection between causality and intensity. If intention emerges from intensity and its fluctuations, and this emergence parallels the way intensity is expressed in causality also, what is the relation between causality and intention? These categories accommodate a small number of superficial structural comparisons, such as have inspired the theories of intentionality in terms of causal relations between objects and intentional mental states. But in *Thus Spoke Zarathustra* these two are accorded a bizarre and exceptional relationship. Zarathustra's proclamations on redemption focus on the inability of the will to will backwards: "Backwards the will is unable to will; that it cannot break time and time's desire – that is the will's loneliest sorrow."[81] In Klossowski's terms, the irreversible character of past events, as supplied in present series, is the responsibility of deficiencies of the will. Nietzsche's strain of voluntarism thus fuses temporality and intention: "The will projects its powerlessness on time, and in this way gives time its *irreversible* character: the will cannot reverse *the flow of time*."[82] The philosophy of time corresponding to the semiotic of the institutional code, which proclaims the irreversibility of time, is also therefore associated with the inability to will the past. Characteristics belonging to one imply that analogous characteristics must belong to the other. Temporal considerations

---

80 Klossowski, P. (1997). p. 112
81 Nietzsche, F. (2005). p. 121
82 Klossowski, P. (1997). p. 67

and those of agency are in this way closely connected and assigned a central importance.

More precisely, in Land's exegesis of Nietzsche, intentional conceptions of agency become *sufficient conditions* for certain temporal constraints. The latter camouflage the manifestations of folk propositions about time's structure.

> An inadequately-interrogated conception of agency can disguise itself as a logical conclusion about the shape of time ... Certain deeply-rooted intuitions about human agency, it might be suspected, exercise surreptitious authority in respect to tolerable conceptions of time. A dogmatic presumption of empirical human freedom ... has not only survived the supposedly irresistible onslaught of mechanical determinism, but has even maintained its dominion over the basic (temporal-causal) structures of scientific explanation, which have been pre-programmed for conformity with its dramatic criteria. This is, recognizably, the Nietzschean skepsis.[83]

Temporal relationships, such as the irreversibility of one event with respect to another, covertly express intentional states: powerlessness, in Zarathustra's voluntarism.

So what are the ultimate implications of these observations for the notion of intentionality? Intentions must be defined, in Brentano's terms, by the intrinsic directedness of a mental phenomenon, or "reference to a content, direction to an object."[84] In earlier chapters' comparisons between the institutional semiotic and fluctuations of intensity, this intentionality was understood in terms of two aspects. Firstly, intentionality is the result of a filtration process in which fluctuations lose intensive content. Secondly, they reduce the dynamism of these fluctuations of intensity to static oppositions between mental states and their referents. Now, if intentional states are sufficient for temporal ones, as Land and Klossowski follow Nietzsche in suggesting, some component of intentional behaviour must be convertible into *an irreversible temporal structure*.

Intentional states, defined by an intrinsic relatedness, bring about as necessity the objects to which they refer. An intentional act, by extension, has two components: an intentional state followed by the (presumed) result of the act intended to actualise or realise this state. The proposition refuted by the Nietzschean skepsis is the proposition that *intentional states stand in causal relations with or are sufficient conditions for their results*. The intentional state being given, its actualisation must follow. The former, as a result, explain or account for the latter. Moreover, this relationship is asymmetric; whereas intentional states account for what we assume to be their consequences, these have only a nugatory

---

[83] Land, N. (2014). 8.2
[84] Brentano, F. (2009). p. xvii

converse role in return. This asymmetry of dependency between intentions and actual results is the analogue at the level of agency of irreversibility at the level of time. Being unable to undo or redo actions previously undertaken is the correlate of a conception of intentional behaviour according to which events follow from the intentions, or desires, wishes and decisions of a sovereign individual. Given a certain set of intentional initial conditions, real actions are inexorable ramifications. Intentionality is here comparable to the role of the will in passages from *Zarathustra*. The will's inability to will a certain class of events, its submissive indifference to them, gives the impression of irreversibility, just as does the sufficiency, but not necessity, of intentions for actions. Not only, then, is a logical relation being asserted between intentionality and temporality. Time in turn brings causality to the admixture, by virtue of their dual implication in the "basic (temporal-causal) structures of scientific explanation."[85]

What is the import of the previous analysis of the temporality of the vicious circle, once its complicity with intentionality is exposed? Once the vicious circle is fully expounded, the distinction between past and future brought into question, and the permanence of events' locations relaxed and displaced, all events circulate in a variable order. Irreversibility cannot be reconciled with the vicious circle. The separation of intentional act and consequence cannot be sustained without permanence, indexation and a categorical divide between past and future, all of which the circle refuses. The one-way dependency of past conditions on future ones is, in addition, incompatible with the standpoint of the circle whence dependencies are not organised by direction, and conditions are never pre-established. But if irreversibility cannot be reconciled with this temporality, and irreversibility follows from intentionality, or the states which coincide with it, intentionality cannot be upheld in the face of the vicious circle.

The necessary condition for a state of affairs to function as an explanation, is given seminally by Hempel and Oppenheim in the following terms: "An explanation is not fully adequate unless its *explanans*, if taken account of in time, could have served as a basis for predicting the phenomenon under consideration."[86] Since no such predictions are possible, this condition is not fulfilled in the case of intentionality as here conceived, voiding its explanatory role. It follows for the proposition that intentional states are sufficient conditions for their results, that outcomes can be explained by reference to states of mental agency which are their sufficient conditions, that it can only be jettisoned.

---

85 Land, N. (2014). 8.2
86 Hempel, C. and Oppenheim, P. (1948). pp. 135–175

If intentional mental states, such as aims, purposes, goals and desires, are not sufficient for and explanatory of what we take to be their results, what is their status? The textual evidence for Nietzsche's position is vast:

> Finally: why could 'a purpose' not be an epiphenomenon in the series of changes in the activating forces that bring about the purposive action – a pale image sketched in consciousness beforehand that serves to orient us concerning events, even as a symptom of events, not as their cause? ... Are not all phenomena of consciousness merely terminal phenomena, final links in a chain, but apparently conditioning one another in their succession on one level of consciousness?[87]

No longer efficacious, intentional states are epiphenomenal: emergent and derivative features of the real forces driving events, and, as such, "symptoms" not "causes." Their role as conditions is merely apparent, as a result of the successions they constitute. Orfali reaches a similar conclusion, referring to events – in this case, dream-like events – which, "in their principal and immutable aspects," are "by no means a function of a precise goal," but rather "can be prolonged as such ... indefinitely."[88] Just as Orfali assigns to these repetitions a "temporal structure" proper to them, so is the fundamentally temporal thrust of these theses about intentionality explicit in Nietzsche's writings:

> This apparent conformity to a goal is simply subsequent to this will to power unfolding in every event; the becoming-strongest brings with itself organizations that have a certain resemblance to a plan of finality: the apparent goals are not intentional, but once the supremacy over a lesser power is attained, and the latter is made to work on behalf of the greatest, a hierarchical order of organization must take on the appearance of an order of means and ends.[89]

The conformity of a state of affairs to a pre-fabricated intention, of *explanandum* to *explanans*,[90] is *subsequent* to the forces belied by these epiphenomena: causality is posited in reverse by what we assume to be its aftermath. This is an alternative formulation of the thesis of the inversion of time. The supremacy over a lesser power is a particular state of various impulsive forces, which confront each other in moments of fluctuation of intensity. The impulsive interpretation which endows an event with signification (and its qualitative characteristics) is a function of its dominance or servitude in relation to other impulsive interpretations. The horizontal or extensive order of successive events is therefore an epipheno-

---

87 Klossowski, P. (1997). p. 52
88 Orfali, I. (1983). p. 269
89 Klossowski, P. (1997). p. 118
90 Hempel, C. and Oppenheim, P. (1948). pp. 135–175

menon of the vertical or intensive order of actors in a hierarchy. The chronological order of the couples cause-effect and *explanans-explanandum* is inverted in favour of the dominion of forces, where antecedent conditions are part of their ends.

In conclusion, therefore, intentionality bears an essential relation to the temporal structures which arise in the analysis of the vicious circle, no less than the structures of signs. Intentionality implies a certain view on time and, by extension, causality. Intentional structures of agency correspond to beliefs about the irreversibility of the past which are considered and rejected (by Zarathustra) as being inconsistent with the temporality of the circle. From a semiotic standpoint, the stabilising and filtering proclivities of the institutional code are the chief implications of intentionality. Understood from the vantage of temporality, however, we can see that, in the strength of the fluctuations proper to the vicious circle, intentionality is not a feature of agency.

5.14 Conclusion: Summary of Propositions

From an analytical standpoint, Klossowski's metaphysical commitments in the context of the philosophy of time can be distilled into several sets of propositions. It is the principal aim of each of the sections in this chapter to formulate an explanation of a set of them.

The inversion of time targets the exclusive or asymmetric dependency of past on future, such as is exemplified by the causal schema referred to in "The Euphoria of Turin." This intricate argument involves a number of unusual premises gathered together below:

I. The time of the impulses is asynchronous with the present.
II. It is false to claim that *permanence* is a feature of signs, and equally false to assert their *completeness* with respect to all those characteristics which can be veridically attributed to them.
III. All characteristics of the event, whenever they are anticipated or recalled, occur in and with the presentation of the event.
IV. Intelligent synthetic interaction is the organising principle of events in the vicious circle, in which they can be acted on by the future.
V. It is false to claim that the order of events in time parallels the order in which they are given or determined, or to claim that the asymmetry implied by this order of events entails the asymmetry of the dependency of the future on the past.

VI. The order of events is distinct from the ordering process, as is the appearing order from the order of appearance.
VII. There must be a thoroughgoing separation of the order of events and the ordering process itself.

The following account, the foundation of the analysis of the vicious circle, revolves around the coalescence of forgetting and memory.

VIII. Forgetting amounts to a memory.
IX. Conceived more generally, past and future themselves coalesce.
X. Repetition replaces consistency in our apprehension of events.

As a consequence of the propositions advanced in these two sections, Klossowski is additionally committed to the variability of the order of events organised by the dynamic of the circle, as well as the following two propositions:

XI. Recurrences of events in present series cannot be assigned an original fluctuation.
XII. Recurrences of events in present series occur at variable distances from other events.

Finally, having reconceived the close relationship between the causal-temporal structures and the intentional structures of human agency, we attempted to review the second chapter's inchoate critique of intentionality in light of these statements:

XIII. No action is caused by a purpose.
XIV. Intention is an epiphenomenon.
XV. Purpose and means are strictly dependent on the events which produce them.
XVI. No intended outcome is ever realised.
XVII. No realised outcome is ever intended.

These sentences synopsise Klossowski's philosophy of time, as related in and through the apotheosis of *Nietzsche and the Vicious Circle*.

6 Conclusion

Klossowski's analysis of the Nietzschean philosophy presents four main lines of attack on what it takes to be tenets of occidental metaphysics. Ordered thematically, *Nietzsche and the Vicious Circle* juxtaposes close readings of *Nachlass* fragments, letters and published works with borderline psychoanalytical reconstructions of the privileged, if not personal, Nietzschean experiences which generated them. Although these experiences, or his attempts to describe them, are brought in as the raw material to be analysed, and as the evidence for the philosophical commitments Klossowski attributes to Nietzsche, it has been the contention of the present work that the logic of *Nietzsche and the Vicious Circle*, taken in conjunction with a number of other texts, largely proceeds in a fashion more reminiscent of foundationalist philosophical approaches than the aphoristic one proper to this raw material itself.

Firstly, said present work attempts to establish a distinction between two semiotics, on the basis of an assortment of oppositions: the representational vs. the sub-representational, the authentic vs. the inauthentic, fluctuation vs. stasis, determinacy vs. indeterminacy, the distinct vs. the indistinct, the clear vs. the confused. The second chapter explores these oppositions, and attempts to identify similar approaches outside of Klossowski's tradition, such as the thermal physicists from whom the notion of intensity was borrowed, and such as Peirce's triadic semiotic, with its infinite semiosis and hierarchical structure. The third turns to Klossowski's deflationary or deconstructive philosophy of the self, with Descartes as the principal point of contrast. The chapter attempts to resolve what the experienced reader of *Nietzsche and the Vicious Circle* no doubt recognises as a *prima facie* patent incoherence, namely Klossowski's definition of the self in terms of the highest degree of intensity – and yet also the lowest degree of intensity – and also develops comparisons with other thinkers, such as Freud.

In the fourth chapter, Klossowski's revisions to the connection between possibility and actuality follow directly from the fate befalling the subject of the vicious circle – a fate which Klossowski describes as a deactualisation and subsequent multiplication of its identity. This chapter's foils include Peirce, Silverstein, and scientific theorists whose work on ergodicity provides a useful counterpoint for Nietzsche's aborted attempts to translate his metaphysical speculations into a dynamical context. Finally, the temporality of the vicious circle, latent throughout *Nietzsche and the Vicious Circle* and indeed many of Klossowski's other works, is addressed directly.

Deriving the particular commitments of each chapter and each theme from the principles established at the beginning of the study (the principles of the semiotic of intensity) has been a methodological principle consistently employed in this interpretation of Klossowski. Although the "raw material" of the Nietzschean experience – the fluctuations of intensity belied by sensate content, visual representations, or philosophical writings – may or may not have stood in causal or other relations with the concepts Klossowski extracts from his corpus in his study, we here assume that such relations can be separated from the logical and semantic relations which Klossowski's propositions together express, whether or not Nietzsche himself would have endorsed such a separation, or even believed it to be feasible. Such a separation is the *sine qua non* of an analytical approach to the text which, this current work contends, is likely the most immediate precursor to improving the accessibility of Klossowski's discourse.

This approach is evident from the close relations which have been asserted between the semiotic of intensity and the central elements of each chapter. For instance, the attack on various conceptions of the self from the Cartesian philosophy through to its 20th-Century adherents and detractors is presented on the basis of the circuitous behaviour of the impulses articulated in the chapter preceding it. Aiming at nothing other than themselves, and creating the epiphenomenal aims and goals of the intellect as their own obverse, they refuse the permanent history allotted to the individual which Klossowski takes to be chimerical, in place of a notion of fortuity. The denial of the coexistence of consciousness and unconsciousness, one of Klossowski's foremost commitments in his analysis of the self, relies on the previous chapter's claims, especially the claim that the activity or inactivity of all signs or designations is an exclusive function of the prevailing excitations – of the fluctuation of intensity – as well as the claim that these excitations are inconstant, discontinuous. This discontinuity on the part of fluctuations is deployed again in the comparison of Nietzsche's with Kant's conceptions of the relation of the subject to experience.

A number of other examples are available. The topological metaphors which underpin the semiotic of intensity in the beginning – division, separation and rejoining – evoke the circularity which later becomes an explicit characteristic of this semiotic, once the vicious circle is defined as the coincidence of intensity with its trace. This occurs in the fourth chapter, which considers the notions of fortuity and possibility in *Nietzsche and the Vicious Circle*. In this chapter, the circular movement of the impulses in the formation of signs manifests itself in the merging of intensity with the trace of intensity, and the collapse of the distinction between originary and non-originary sign. Specifically, the Nietzschean thesis that all signification is interpretation is adduced in order to derive a rejoinder to indexical signification – to the fixity or constancy of the relationship between signs to events. Since signification is the signification of events, since such signification requires interpretation, and since interpretation can neither be permanent nor impart determinacy to events, signification for Klossowski ends up signifying possibilities. Interpretation itself is a clear artefact of the underlying semiotic principles, reflecting the intentional or taking-as structure of fluctuations of intensity. All of these circular figures and theories of fortuity and possibility thus implicate either the vicious circle or its equally circular semiotic underpinnings.

The content of the fifth chapter, with its focus on the temporality of the vicious circle, stands in perhaps the clearest logical relations with the semiotic groundwork. If signs are themselves events, the behaviours attributed to signs by the semiotic resurface at the temporal level – events relate temporally to fluctuations as signs do linguistically, making the event the theoretical counterpart of signification from the viewpoint of time. It is the fluctuating nature of the impulses that undoes the dual properties of permanence and completeness attributed to time by the folk metaphysics of time. The circular structure which generates infinite semiosis – the definition of the sign in terms of traces of fluctuations – applies equally to the movement of events in time. And, by way of further illustration, the notion of anachronism which becomes a central principle organising Klossowski's perspectives on time, and in particular the chapter "The Origin of Four Criteria," rests on the distinctions between singular (authentic) intensive states and the gregarious significations imposed by the institutional code: the difference between the latter and the former is used to explain the temporal difference between an originary fluctuation of intensity, the vestige of an impulse from some other epoch, and "present conditions"[1] (the conditions of the present moment).

In this regard, the connections drawn here between the semiotic of intensity and central themes of Klossowski's writings on Nietzsche may strike the reader as incongruous with much of their tone. *Nietzsche and the Vicious Circle* is hardly surmisable as a minimalistic set of principles and maxims distilled to their metaphysical essence. Biographical speculations and narrative loops intervene between focused analysis of Nietzsche's philosophical writings, many of which richly characterise and dissect everything from oneiric experiences of childhood and personal relationships to hypochondria and fondness for nature and outdoor exploration. "The Consultation of the Paternal Shadow," for instance, presents an extended deconstruction and reconstruction of a highly particular and parochial premonition Nietzsche relates on two occasions in his teenage years.

---

[1] Klossowski, P. (1997). p. 80

"The Most Beautiful Invention of the Sick" chronicles Nietzsche's problematisation of the distinction between sickness and health, inspired by his own persistent and severe physical ailments. Klossowski's accounts of these experiences and landscapes are not purely instrumental to the broader didactic purposes of *Nietzsche and the Vicious Circle*, nor, arguably, ancillary or subordinate in any way at all. So to what extent can a critical, analytical, propositional reconstruction, reorganising as it does what it takes to be Klossowski's circuitously avowed, if not altogether camouflaged, philosophical commitments into the form of premises and arguments and logical sequences, and emphasising the architecture of this work, especially the dependency of body of the text on the foundations laid in the opening chapters, above its occasional meandering tendencies, be credible, in view of these other elements?

The non-assertoric passages in *Nietzsche and the Vicious Circle* are central as opposed to peripheral – as central as is the argumentation. The characteristics imputed to the singular experiences labelled "fluctuations of intensity" and used as a foundation for all the philosophical conclusions exhibited herein comprise only one perspective on these experiences. Thus the same impulse, the same system of signs and thought, which denounces the mendacity of the institutional code in relation to the impulses it conceals must thereby denounce itself (just as the intellect is defined as the obverse of any impulse in general), being just as mendacious, with regard to both the impulses and this mendacity itself.

As Smith notes in the introduction to his translation of *Nietzsche et le cercle vicieux*, Klossowski more or less abjured philosophical writing after the publication of *La monnaie vivante*.[2] Artistic and literary interests consumed his time, as they had throughout the fifties and sixties with the publication of *La vocation suspendue*, *Roberte ce soir*, *La révocation de l' édit de Nantes*, and *Le Baphomet*. Would the author of these texts be the same author of the principles-based account of Nietzsche's philosophy of language and time? This would seem to further diminish the motivation for the approach taken here.

In his *Anamnèses*, dedicated to Klossowski's largely unexcavated literary works as well as his philosophical studies, Thierry Tremblay attributes their muted reception and limited exegesis to the *in-principle* intractability of this opus.

> Klossowski's readers will be only partly surprised by the modest impact his works have enjoyed since the author's life. Literary journals have barely dedicated any thematic issues to him, very few critical works, and relatively few recent articles.[3]

---

2 Klossowski, P. (1997). p. ix
3 Tremblay, T. (2012). p. 9

Klossowski is without a doubt a hermetic author. This aspect has been insufficiently emphasised when, over and over again, the difficulty of grasping his works has been mentioned.[4]

Tremblay follows Camus' own (not entirely ironic) proclamation that Klossowski is engaged in a wilful "enterprise of reader demoralisation,"[5] and, by consequence, contends that Klossowski's is "An *oeuvre* which proceeds like a grimoire; in a sense, a magical *oeuvre*, whose coat of arms is determined by the identification of the symbols it assembles."[6] Taking *Nietzsche and the Vicious Circle* as one among a collection of fantasies, incantations, and parables casts a very different light on his endeavours. What have been described here as notions or concepts – simulacrum, sign, intensity, fluctuation – might be better and more broadly cast as symbols which do not accommodate traditional logical relations, which may or may not even be consistent with one another, and which can be attributed truth values only as much as could any *story*. The kinds of problems posed with regard to the semiotic of intensity, such as its analogies with other theorists, its location on the spectrum between metaphysical, scientific, genealogical, meta-ethical and psychoanalytical registers, its internal consistency, and whether and what philosophical sense can be made of it at all, recede into comparative insignificance from this point of view. Indeed, the perspective suggested by Camus extremises these sophistical characteristics to the point that Klossowski becomes an outright obscurantist. Similarly, Castanet holds as far as *Nietzsche and the Vicious Circle* is concerned that, "Some passages verge on the unreadable."[7] Consequently, for Tremblay, the "first task is a work of identification."[8] and not, therefore, one which would involve the isolation of philosophical commitments, the reconstruction of arguments, the imputation of specific theses to Klossowski, or their critical analysis. Indeed, Tremblay's "second task will consist in closely grasping the *modus operandi* of Klossowski's texts," a task Tremblay proposes to accomplish "with recourse to a dualism of body and mind, beginning from a certain sovereignty of spirituality exercised over a matter which the spirit signs."[9] Yet this should not be construed as an admission that the arcane character of Klossowski's theoretical texts could be dispelled straightforwardly, by a traditional exegesis, by immediate reduction to formal theses.

---

4 Tremblay, T. (2012). p. 9
5 Tremblay, T. (2012). p. 10
6 Tremblay, T. (2012). p. 10
7 Castanet, H. (2014). p. 78
8 Tremblay, T. (2012). p. 10
9 Tremblay, T. (2012). p. 10

Klossowski's philosophical *opus* is, for Tremblay, no less imbued with fiction than his novels are philosophical. Tremblay finds in Klossowski's Nietzsche a counter-movement to ontology, which presents chaos, nature *"without a framework,"*[10] "general disarray,"[11] as the consequence of the death of God, and the Nietzschean abnegation of the self, of causality, of representation and extensity: "ontological catastrophe."[12] His intricate descriptions of Nietzsche's social and familial travails, recurring dreams, and valetudinary illnesses, his close readings of his correspondence, account of his mental breakdown, and other biographical interludes, such as the waves on the lakes Nietzsche observed for long periods, used to construct the metaphors of fluctuation and repetition which populate *Nietzsche and the Vicious Circle*, or such as the open squares of Turin in which the "interpretative availability"[13] of then-past experiences allowed Nietzsche to reanimate them in his final hallucinatory breakdown, would then amount not to pathetic fallacy or metaphor for a fully articulated philosophical position, but rather the object of study itself: Nietzsche's disintegration into multiple personae.

Does the methodology espoused in this study therefore not fall foul of Tremblay's attuned analysis of the implications of Klossowski's idiosyncrasies? Did Klossowski intend to formulate philosophical propositions at all, or instead to parody these propositions, just as he refers to the vicious circle and the eternal return, not as doctrines, but as their simulacra?

> Nietzsche's own mode of expression ... would now diverge in two directions that were foreign to each other. First, there was the pure poetic creation, the parabolic expression of his experience, through the character of Zarathustra – a creation in which Lou no doubt played a decisive role by trying to dissuade him from an explanation based on the discoveries of science. But this poem, with its dithyrambic style, was essentially a book of sentences whose bombastic movement alternates with riddles and their resolution in images: a *mise-en-scène* of the *thought* in wordplays and similitudes. It would later become apparent that Zarathustra is a buffoon in the guise of a false prophet, an imposter proclaiming the simulacrum of a doctrine.[14]

For his philosophy to be little more than an extension of his fiction, an attempt to formalise or explain the fantasies, dreams and experiences which prompted his work as a writer and an artist, is surely for the credibility of an analytical ex-

---

10 Tremblay, T. (2012). p. 200
11 Tremblay, T. (2012). p. 200
12 Tremblay, T. (2012). p. 203
13 Klossowski, P. (1997). p. 251
14 Klossowski, P. (1997). p. 99

egesis of Klossowski to wane in favour of Tremblay's *repérage*. Klossowski would then be seen to have left philosophy behind, just as Nietzsche conceived of art, or artistic activity proper, as a means of overcoming defunct epistemology. As Tremblay thus affirms, in contrast to the discourse of the philosopher, "The privilege of artistic activity would be to not hide the powers (*puissances*), prosperous or harmful, to not neglect the importance of experience, to not lead the phenomenon back to its ideality."[15] And, in such a case, Klossowski's superficially philosophical work would be regarded as sibylline or hermetic mysticism, not as credible ontology. As proponents of a reading of this work inclined towards the latter, we would find ourselves among the authors Tremblay accuses of neglecting this dimension of Klossowski's thought unduly, proponents, perhaps, of a facile conversion of fiction to academia. Were this conversion extended to Nietzsche in turn, we can only speculate about the extent to which it might elicit the disquietude of various scholars who might take his experimental, aphoristic and occasionally meandering style to resist analytical methodology.

In addition to this sceptical perspective, Tremblay offers his own understanding of Klossowski as a thinker motivated by a type of concern rather foreign to those recited in this study:[16] Klossowski's thought is inseparable from his religious orientation – a complicated and circuitously avowed orientation Tremblay locates in various ambivalent statements and biographical notes – ultimately consecrated in the dualism he then alleges between mind and body. The significance of the eternal return, chaos, and critique of the self are for Tremblay intimately tied to the death of God: "When Nietzsche announces that *God is dead*, this amounts to saying that Nietzsche must necessarily lose his own identity."[17]

It is tempting to speculate as to whether Klossowski's interest in these elements of the Nietzschean philosophy stemmed from a more fundamental interest in the question of a deity: was it Nietzsche's heretical stance from a traditional Christian perspective, his antagonistic figure of the anti-Christ, that aroused Klossowski's interest, and should *Nietzsche and the Vicious Circle* be regarded as an exercise in alternative theology? Regardless of the applicability or inapplicability of this distinction to Nietzsche, such a proposition may well lead us to further doubt the viability of a construal of Klossowski himself as metaphysician, scholar, or analytical philosopher.

---

15 Tremblay, T. (2012). p. 196
16 I am grateful to Christian Kerslake for discussion of this matter, as well as for drawing my attention to the importance of Tremblay's contributions to the religious and Gnostic aspects of Klossowski's thought.
17 Klossowski, P. (2007). p. 117

Tremblay is not the only commentator to problematise the classification of Klossowski's work, which veers over and back over the borders between a number of disciplines in a strangely classical tone. Kevin Clark, in his *On Pierre Klossowski and the Problem of Transcription*, insists on the inseparability of the fictional and literal, figural and conceptual modes of expression in Klossowski's opus.

> Far from suggesting an abandonment of thought in favour of some more intuitive way of apprehending the real, Klossowski, in taking the Idea as myth or fiction, intends to restore thought to an authentic and autonomous way of *seeing* … A first step … consists in discovering the inseparability as well as the acute conflict between the fictional image and literal interpretation.[18]

> Klossowski seems singularly unwilling, or unable, to make the choice between a figural mode of expression and a conceptual one.[19]

Both of these two modes are implicated in *Nietzsche and the Vicious Circle*, where extracting the narrative from other elements of the work is at times almost impossible. For instance, the opening sequences of the third chapter ("The Experience of the Eternal Return") slip between reproductions of Nietzsche's letters to Gast, biography, and theory-fiction, and from the third to the first person. Does this near-inseparability necessitate metaphysical propositions pregnant with fiction, denying them determinate truth values? Consider the following remarks from Kevin Clark's *On Pierre Klossowski and the Problem of Transcription*:

> What Klossowski calls the "secret of the incommunicable" should be sharply distinguished from any mystical or romantic claims of the ineffable, reposing on metaphors of obscurity. Mystery and explanation are not mutually antagonistic, but increase in direct proportion to each other …[20]

Although *prima facie* a reflection on two tendencies of Klossowksi's writing, such as the figural and the literal, Clark's account provides the basis for unlocking a much more fundamental distinction. For if these two tendencies are the elements of a distinction which is meaningful at all, it is because they display different aspects of the attempt to convert into language the fluctuations of intensity which pertain to the domain of the impulses, thereby shedding light on the very core of Klossowski's project, namely to discover the conditions

---

[18] Clark, K. (1982). pp. 827–828
[19] Clark, K. (1982). p. 828
[20] Clark, K. (1982). p. 837

under which experience can be spoken about at all. When asking whether Klossowski can be a philosopher, whether philosophers can write about Klossowski at all legitimately, or whether Klossowski the metaphysician compromises Klossowski the artist or the mystic to an intolerable degree, we are asking a question which is only on the surface about the relationship between philosophy and art, and which is more fundamentally about the relationship between intensity and sign, especially the signs which Nietzsche and Klossowski used to describe them. Clark's discussion of the fictional and the literal, of the figural and the conceptual, or of seeing and thinking, can thus be gleaned as a proxy for the relation between intensity and sign. The status of our own interpretation will thus turn on the status of this relation, already analysed at length in this essay. But this analysis appears only to support Tremblay's suspicion: does the exegesis of Klossowski falsify his hermetic tendencies in the same way that the code of signs falsifies and abbreviates fluctuations of intensity? Or does the relationship between sign and intensity in fact accommodate Klossowski's semiotic in a way which also implies the legitimacy of this project, to grasp and rebuild his work in spite of its forays into seeming mysticism, forays which are so strongly emphasised by Tremblay?

The incommunicability, muteness and singularity of fluctuations of intensity are the characteristics on which Klossowski's very theory rests – at least, the way we have structured it. They are the basis for the semiotic of intensity and its ramifications at various orders, in various other philosophical contexts, whether the philosophy of identity, self, causality, and time. For this incommunicability, muteness and singularity to be unanalysable would be to vitiate the semiotic's foundation; such would therefore be the justification for consigning Klossowski's discourse to the "mystical or romantic ... reposing on metaphors of obscurity."[21] Clark's position implies that, to the contrary, this sweeping conclusion amounts to an overstatement. Mystery and explanation, or intensity and sign – the components of this study – are not two distinct states or semiotics each of which prevails only if the other does not.

> The incommunicable exists only insofar as it is circumscribed by a theory of the incommunicable, which, as its contrary, must either reduce it to nothing or produce a mere negative image of it. The greater the correspondence between the phenomenon and its explanation, the greater become the internal contradictions of the latter; on the other hand, the greater its gain in logical coherence, the more the theory risks becoming itself the exclusion of its own object.[22]

---

21 Clark, K. (1982). p. 837
22 Clark, K. (1982). p. 838

Far from being independent of its description, the incommunicable exists only insofar as it is circumscribed by a theory of the incommunicable, placing the two in an unbreakable relationship (at times suggestive of dialectical negation, in spite of Klossowski's protestations).[23] The incommunicable, intensity however singular, does not belong outside the world or the bounds of language. Were it to so belong, our interpretation of intensity would be compelled to honour the maxims of the *Tractatus Logico-Philosophicus* mentioned at the very beginning of this study: it would be incumbent upon us to describe only what exists within the world and to pass over in silence everything else besides.[24] Cast, alternatively, in Kantian terms, intensity must not be conflated with the noumenon in Kant's positive sense – that is, an object or experience of some kind which would be comprehensible but for our absolute lack of a certain faculty, namely the kind of intuition which only a mystic might possess. Construing intensity in this way would go hand-in-hand with the rebuttal to the analytical-philosophical, principles-based approach to Klossowski's work, supporting the tendency to take him to be a hermetic author. A trade-off exists between intensity ("phenomenon," in Clark's looser use of the term) and sign – that is, description of intensity ("explanation") – but not an outright exclusion. This would preclude description entirely.

This is the sense in which Clark's work allows us to mitigate the irredeemably mystical elements of Klossowski's opus. Scholars are at liberty to extract its philosophical contents more or less as they would any others', because the intensity or, more broadly, the phantasm, does not interdict description absolutely. Rather, it requires and presupposes description, in just the way that the intellect, as the obverse of any impulse (which gives rise to fluctuations of intensity), is itself a product of the impulses. The semiotic of intensity does not attempt to anchor meaning in primitive experiences, in the way the foil of Wittgenstein's argument from private language, alluded to in the opening chapters, takes immediate private sensations to ground signification. It is not therefore the kind of semiotic which collapses because of the unintelligibility of its object; nor, consequently, is scholarship focused on it misdirected. Yet to argue that the radicle of Klossowski's theory, fluctuations of intensity, are not independent of the theory's descriptions, as we do here, is to argue vaguely, and risks failing to capture the singular elements of Klossowski's thought. The structuralist movement, the reaction to positivism, Peirce's semiotic – none of these, nor numerous other recent movements in and around the philosophy of language, would naively affirm the

---

[23] Klossowski, P. (1997). p. 12
[24] Wittgenstein, L. (1922). 7

independence of intensity (or Clark's "phenomenon") from theory or explanation. As such, were the extent of Klossowski's innovation his resistance to this affirmation, it would be no innovation at all; in such a case there would be little originality or distinctiveness about his contributions to recent philosophy of language. Thus, if we are to use Clark's account of the incommunicable and its description as the basis for an account of Klossowski's competing styles, and therefore to demonstrate the validity of our own approach to these styles, this line of argument must be refined.

Denying that a perfect correspondence between intensity and the theory's description could coexist with the coherence of this description is not simply to assert the theory-ladenness of the former, or to present a trite rehash of the conclusions of structuralist thinkers. Klossowski's position, conveyed by Clark, is not reducible to the straightforward rejection of correspondences between signs and their objects, or to the refusal to equate signification and reference. What is there that is distinctive about this position, and in what way is it germane given the methodological questions posed above?

Clark's assertion that the incommunicable demands to be communicated in a theory concerning it is underpinned by Klossowski's own assertion that Nietzsche's theorising about his impulsive movements was willed by the impulses themselves: "the producer of the 'concept,' namely the intellect, is used as a *tool* by this arbitrary 'incoherence.'"[25] Indeed, Klossowski says that it is "necessary" that this theorising take place, at the impulses' behest.[26] This gives us insight into the relation between the incoherence (the impulsive fluctuation) and its description, which distinguishes Klossowski's stance, in the following way:

> From the mood (impulse and repulsion) to the idea, from the idea to its declarative formulation, the conversion of the mute phantasm into speech is brought about. For the phantasm never tells us why it is willed by our impulses. We interpret it under the constraint of our environment, which is so well installed in us by its own signs that, by means of these signs, we never have done with declaring to ourselves what the impulse can indeed will: this is the phantasm. But under its own constraint we simulate what it 'means' for our declaration: this is the simulacrum.[27]

The notion of simulation is the element which differentiates Klossowski's position from the more familiar and somewhat less ambitious thesis that descriptions of experience are dependent on theory. This dependency is evident from

---

25 Klossowski, P. (1997). p. 255
26 Klossowski, P. (1997). p. 255
27 Klossowski, P. (1997). p. 260

the first statements in this extract: impulse and its repulsion is converted circuitously into an idea, and communicated in speech or writing. From this alone it is obvious enough that the two are not independent. Insofar, however, as under its own constraint we simulate what it means for our declaration, we enact this impulse *only* in accordance with the declaration. The impulse thus stages and acts out this interpretation of the impulse, with this speech or writing as its theoretical representation, mirroring discontinuous fluctuations of intensity at the level of apparent human agency. It is thus distinguished by "claiming not to stabilize what it presents of an experience and what it says of it: far from excluding the contradictory, it naturally implies it. For if the simulacrum tricks on the notional plane, this is because it mimics faithfully that part which is incommunicable."[28]

Klossowski thus claims that all action compelled through thought is a simulation of this thought by the impulse – never a faithful expression, but a simulation of an invariably *false* interpretation which "tricks." In doing so, it fluctuates just like the original intensity, but as perceptible content which can subsequently be cognised, it is represented and described by the stationary code of signs. Thus Nietzsche's madness letters jump between the guises of as many personae as there were ways for his impulses to interpret his "physiognomy,"[29] whether Alexander, Caesar, Lord Bacon, Shakespeare, Voltaire, Napoleon or Dionysus. Thus also the various expressions of the doctrine of the eternal return, or various doctrines under the rubric of the eternal return, attempted to concretise a fluctuating phantasm which had become a catch-all for Nietzsche's inspiration and his mode of philosophising, both at the level of Nietzsche's own *discourse* on the one hand, which in his published and unpublished work is referred to consistently as a definitive philosophical commitment, and as a scientific principle, and on the other hand at the level of his *behaviour*, spiralling as it did into invalidity. This is, indeed, how Nietzsche also viewed his own attempts to simulate or fabulate meta-ethical criteria.[30] Between the world of the intensity and that of signs and thoughts, the discontinuity analysed in previous chapters entails a fundamental discordance between the actions agents intend to carry out and the impulses they purportedly sate. For Klossowski, this is the distinctive meaning of the simulacrum.

The perversity of this behaviour lies not so much in the linguistic or formal representation of impulses, in their ossification and abbreviation by signs, but by the disingenuousness implied by the agent's desire to stage a knowingly

---

28 Klossowski, P. (1995). p. 148
29 Klossowski, P. (1997). p. 248
30 Klossowski, P. (1997). p. 132

false codification of impulsive intensity. This is the way in which the intensity overcomes its singularity or incommunicability and finds a comprehensible, communicable equivalent. Hence one of the primary motivations for Klossowski's investigations into perversion: to demonstrate the pervert not simply to be the one who allows the obscenity of his singular impulse to dictate his behaviour unchecked, but to demonstrate instead that it is unleashed in response to checks on such behaviour. *Sade My Neighbour*, for instance, testifies to this dynamic. The singular and incommunicable perverse impulse can remain inexplicable and incommunicable, manifesting itself obscurely (if at all) in an unaccountable heinous act (such as the abuses described by Sade), but it can also manifest itself at the discursive level by giving rise to a *gesture* which simulates this impulse in accordance with what Klossowski describes as the "norms"[31] governing the agent's behaviour. The agent can therefore be identified, held responsible, his motives accounted for, and his lack of moral fibre located in a particular set of deviant inclinations – rejections of a moral code, religious apostasy, or whatever other pathologies:

> Sade invents a type of pervert who speaks with his singular gesture *in the name of generality* ... But the singular gesture of the pervert is precisely not the gesture formed in the medium of generality that may accompany speech, is sometimes substituted for the word, and sometimes even contradicts it. The singular gesture of the pervert *empties all content out of speech at once, since it is by itself the whole of existence for him.*[32]
>
> For the pervert who speaks, the obstacle is not to be singular but to belong to generality in his own singularity. How can he overcome this obstacle? ... The singularity of the gesture is re-established without its opaqueness being in any way cleared up. The only one to have to show the validity of his gesture, the pervert makes haste to perform that gesture.[33]

This, then, is the chief identifiable respect in which incoherent and incommunicable intensity demands its own representation at the level of consciousness – by a description formulated in the code of signs, whether in the form of Nietzsche's scrawled self-diagnoses, Klossowski's phantasmic paintings, or philosophers' exegeses of whatever metaphysical contents can be extracted from them. Fluctuating intensity simulates the meaning of its own misrepresentation. The simulation (encapsulated in a gesture or act) reproduces the variability of intensity, but remains amenable to description, perception, or other representation. The gesture or act can then be accounted for as intentional behaviour.

---

[31] Klossowski, P. (1992). p. 6
[32] Klossowski, P. (1992). p. 26
[33] Klossowski, P. (1992). p. 27

Klossowski never provides a definitive explanation for the mysterious tendency on the part of intensity to be circumscribed in this way, to manifest itself in consciousness, or to be theorised about or described. Whilst he meticulously catalogues the numerous illusions to which the unwitting agent falls prey as a result of these manifestations – the failure to acknowledge the discontinuity of its existence, the impotence of what it misinterprets to be intentional capacities, the ephemerality of its own identity and the indeterminacy of its past and future – their provenance is never made clear. The necessity not only for intensity to be enslaved and domesticated by the forces of representation, under the rubric of the code of signs, but for intensity to actively bring about its own enslavement, has the status not of a theorem but of an axiom in his work. Nor, in *Sade My Neighbour*, is it made clear why exactly the perverse impulse must maintain a certain relationship with thought, that is why it must deliberately subvert a moral code, rather than just discharging itself in a wanton act without the diversion through the intellect, whilst it would only be the world of institutional norms which takes it upon itself to intrude on the domain of the impulses in an attempt to analyse the behaviour of the deviant. Nor, in *Living Currency*, does Klossowski ever completely unveil why certain desires motivate an agent to labour in search of the currency that he alleges to be the economic counterpart of language. These features of intensity are among the obstinately mystical components of these texts. But what is more relevant to our current purposes – to assess how applicable the style of analysis attempted in this study can be to Klossowski's opus, and to *Nietzsche and the Vicious Circle* in particular, by means of the general relationship between intensity and signs, including those of Klossowski's own discourse – is the fact that intensity compels its own interpretation at all.

This proposition allows us to grasp that apparently incommunicable fluctuations of intensity must be circumscribed by a description or "theory" of the incommunicable, as Clark contends. This is moreover the kernel of a resolution to the problem of how to put together a meaningful philosophical commentary on the experiences Klossowski's work really concerns, namely just these fluctuations. The relation, then, between this present study and Klossowski's work mirrors the relation between the latter and fluctuations of intensity. No codification of intensity, including Klossowski's writings on his and Nietzsche's experiences – *a fortiori this* writing – could ever *reproduce* intensity itself, as has by now been argued repeatedly. However severely the style of Klossowski's writing deviates from traditional philosophical discourse, however frequently it makes use of alternative material – letters, notebooks and sheer speculations – it could never capture the impulses as it might describe representational content. But given this in principle impossibility, it is no more an objection to the analytical philosopher's incursion upon Klossowski's corpus that such an incursion might not lead to a complete reading, and might discount its poetic, fictional or hermetic inclinations, than it would be valid to demand of this corpus that it pass over the movements of intensity, simulacrum and phantasm in silence.

Nietzsche's attempts to transcribe his experiences occurred in unpredictable and spasmodic bursts, produced inconsistent scrawled aphorisms and poetry, and abandoned traditional modes of philosophical expression. Klossowski's own, in and aside from his confrontation with Nietzsche, spanned art and literature, creative and philosophical writing, gregariousness and muteness. Since his adoption of an analytical style is only episodic, there are inevitable constraints on his writings' ability to convey these fluctuations of intensity, an elementary ontological unit inasmuch as one exists in his work. Accordingly, his alternation between different media and only occasional foray into philosophical scholarship invites a range of interpretative styles and responses. But whilst privileged focus on the mystical and non-philosophical elements of his work may seem to be the proper response at first, especially to followers of Tremblay, this alternation by no means gives cause for abandoning the exegetical tradition to which this present study claims to subscribe. The same compulsion which compelled Klossowski's multifarious depictions of what Nietzsche took to be his singular experiences compels us to articulate in turn their ramifications for any philosophy rooted in experience. In the same sense in which Klossowski supposes he may have written a "*false* study"[34] we might suppose ours to be incomplete, not only because of the obvious possibility for interpretation and reinterpretation of any work, but especially in view of the in principle elusiveness of its subject matter. In spite of this incompleteness, it is no less legitimate for us to hope to make Nietzsche "speak in 'us'"[35] as it is for Klossowski to do so, even if it is only simulacra of doctrines which result. The same falsification of the impulses which Klossowski alleges occurs in thought may well hold between his esoteric, hermetic and religious tendencies on the one hand, and our reproduction of them on the other. But this does not undermine the critical philosopher's ambitions, which remain a rigorous consequence of them.

> If these sovereign moments are so many examples of the discontinuous and of the flight of being, then as soon as mediation considers them as its object, it reconstitutes all the unsuspected stages that pathos burned in its sudden appearance–and the language of a process that is only suitable for vulgar operations does nothing here but conceal the modalities of the absence of thought, under the pretext of describing them and reflecting them in con-

---

34 Klossowski, P. (1992). p. xiv.
35 Klossowski, P. (1992). p. xiv.

sciousness, and thus seeks to lend to pathos, in itself discontinuous, the greatest continuity possible, just as it seeks to reintegrate the most being possible. Thus because (notional) language makes the study and the search for the sovereign moment contradictory, inaccessible by its sudden appearance, there where silence imposes itself, the simulacrum imposes itself at the same time.[36]

---

36 Klossowski, P. (1995). p. 153

References

Albert, D. (2000). *Time and Chance*. Cambridge: Harvard University Press.
Ansell-Pearson, K. (2000). A Superior Existentialism. *Pli* 9. pp. 248–256.
Atkin, A. (2013). Peirce's Theory of Signs. *The Stanford Encyclopedia of Philosophy*. Edited by E. N. Zalta. Available from: https://plato.stanford.edu/archives/sum2013/entries/peirce-semiotics/ Accessed 26th September 2019.
Avanessian, A. and Malik, S. The Time-Complex. *DIS Magazine*. Available from: http://dismagazine.com/discussion/81924/the-time-complex-postcontemporary/ Accessed 26th September 2019.
Babich, B. (1999). *Nietzsche, Epistemology, and Philosophy of Science*. Dordrecht: Kluwer.
Boltzmann, L. (2015). On the Relationship Between the Second Fundamental Theorem of the Mechanical Theory of Heat and the Probability Calculations Regarding the Conditions for Thermal Equilibrium. Translated by K. Sharp and F. Matschinsky. *Entropy* 17 (4). pp. 1971–2009.
Boscovich, R. (1922). *A Theory of Natural Philosophy*. Chicago: Open Court.
Brentano, F. (2009). *Psychology from an Empirical Standpoint*. Edited by L. McAlister. Taylor & Francis.
Brown, H., Myrvold, W. and Uffink, J. (2009). Boltzmann's H-Theorem, Its Discontents, and the Birth of Statistical Mechanics. *Studies in History and Philosophy of Modern Physics* 40. pp. 174–191.
Burnet, J. (1920). *Fragments of Parmenides*. Translated by J. Burnet.
Callender, C. (2016). Thermodynamic Asymmetry in Time. *The Stanford Encyclopedia of Philosophy*. Edited by E. N. Zalta. Available from: https://plato.stanford.edu/archives/win2016/entries/time-thermo/ Accessed 1st November 2019.
Castanet, H. (2014). *Pierre Klossowski: The Pantomime of Spirits*. Bern: Peter Lang.
Clark, K. (1982). On Pierre Klossowski and the Problem of Transcription. *MLN* 97 (4). pp. 827–839.
Crary, J. (1995). *Techniques of the Observer: On Vision and Modernity in the Nineteenth Century*. Cambridge: MIT Press.
De Oliveira, C. and Werlang, T. (2006). Ergodic Hypothesis in Classical Statistical Mechanics. *Revista Brasileira de Ensino de Fisica* 29 (2). pp. 189–201.
Deleuze, G. (1984). *Kant's Critical Philosophy: The Doctrine of the Faculties*. Translated by H. Tomlinson and B. Habberjam. London: Athlone.
Deleuze, G. (1986). *Nietzsche and Philosophy*. Translated by H. Tomlinson. London: Athlone.
Deleuze, G. (2004) *Difference and Repetition*. Translated by Paul Patton. London: Athlone.
Della Rocca, M. (2008). *Spinoza*. New York: Routledge.
Descartes, R. (2008). *Meditations on First Philosophy*. Oxford: Oxford University Press.
Dries, M. (2008). Nietzsche's Critique of Staticism: Introduction to Nietzsche on Time and History. In: Dries, M. (ed.). *Nietzsche on Time and History*. Berlin: Walter de Gruyter. pp. 1–22.
Earman, J. (2006). The "Past Hypothesis": Not Even False. *Studies in the History and Philosophy of Physics* 37. pp. 399–430.
Eco, U. (1983). *The Role of the Reader: Explorations in the Semiotics of Texts*. Bloomington: Indiana University Press.

Faulkner, J. (2007). The Vision, the Riddle, and the Vicious Circle: Pierre Klossowski Reading Nietzsche's Sick Body through Sade's Perversion. *Textual Practice* 21 (1). pp. 43–69.
Freud, S. (2015). *Beyond the Pleasure Principle*. Translated by J. Strachey. New York: Dover.
Grenon, P. (2006). Temporal Qualification and Change with First-Order Binary Predicates. In: Bennett, B. and Fellbaum, C. (eds.). *4th International Conference on Formal Ontology in Information Systems*. Amsterdam: IOS PRESS. pp. 155–166.
Heidegger, M. (1991a). *Nietzsche*. Vol. I. Edited by D. F. Krell. New York: HarperCollins.
Heidegger, M. (1991b). *Nietzsche*. Vol. II. Edited by D. F. Krell. New York: HarperCollins.
Heidegger, M. (1991c). *Nietzsche*. Vol. III. Edited by D. F. Krell. New York: HarperCollins.
Heidegger, M. (1991d). *Nietzsche*. Vol. IV. Edited by D. F. Krell. New York: HarperCollins.
Helgeson, J. (2011). What Cannot Be Said: Notes on Early French Wittgenstein Reception. *Paragraph* 34 (3). pp. 338–357. Available from: http://www.jstor.org/stable/43263808 Accessed 9th July 2019.
Hempel, C. and Oppenheim, P. (1948). Studies in the Logic of Explanation. *Philosophy of Science* 15 (2). pp. 135–175.
Howell, R. (1992). *Kant's Transcendental Deduction*. Dordrecht: Kluwer.
Hume, D. (1969). *A Treatise of Human Nature*. Edited by E. C. Mossner. London: Penguin.
James, I. (2001). Klossowski, Nietzsche and the Fortuitous Body. *Romance Studies* 19 (1). pp. 59–70.
Jowett, B. (2015). *Plato's Parmenides*. Aeterna Press.
Kant, I. (1929). *Critique of Pure Reason*. Translated by N. K. Smith. London: Macmillan.
Kaufmann, W. (1974). *Nietzsche: Philosopher, Psychologist, Antichrist*. Princeton: Princeton University Press.
Kellner, D. (1998). *Nietzsche and the Vicious Circle: Review*. Available from: https://pages.gseis.ucla.edu/faculty/kellner/Illumina%20Folder/kell23.htm. Accessed: 23rd August 2019.
King, P. (1995). Other Times. *The Australasian Journal of Philosophy* 73 (4). pp. 532–547.
Klossowski, P. (1963). *Un Si Funeste Désir*. Paris: Gallimard.
Klossowski, P. (1973). Circulus Vitiosus. In: De Gandillac, M. and Pautrat, D. (eds.). *Nietzsche Aujourd'hui*. Vol. 2. Paris: Union Générale d'Editions. pp. 91–121.
Klossowski, P. (1978). *Nietzsche et le cercle vicieux*. Paris: Mercure de France.
Klossowski, P. (1992). *Sade My Neighbour*. Translated by A. Lingis. London: Quartet.
Klossowski, P. (1995). Of the Simulacrum in Georges Bataille's Communication. In: Boldt-Irons, L. (ed.). *On Bataille: Critical Essays*. Albany: State University of New York. pp. 147–155.
Klossowski, P. (1997). *Nietzsche and the Vicious Circle*. Translated by D. Smith. London: Athlone.
Klossowski, P. (2007). *Such a Deathly Desire*. Translated by R. Ford. Albany: State University of New York Press.
Klossowski, P. (2017). *Living Currency*. Edited by V. Cisney, N. Morar and D. Smith. London: Bloomsbury.
Klossowski, P. *Living Currency*. Translated by J. Levinson. Available from: https://monoskop.org/images/b/b0/Klossowski_Pierre_Living_Currency.pdf. Accessed 1st October 2017.

Kojève, A. (1980). *Introduction to the Reading of Hegel: Lectures on the Phenomenology of Spirit*. Translated by J. Nichols, Jr. Edited by A. Bloom. Ithaca and London: Cornell University Press.
Land, N. (1992). *A Thirst for Annihilation: George Bataille and Virulent Nihilism*. London: Routledge.
Land, N. (2011) *Fanged Noumena: Collected Writings 1987–2007*. Edited by R. Brassier and R. Mackay. Falmouth and New York: Urbanomic and Sequence Press.
Land, N. (2014). *Templexity: Disordered Loops Through Shanghai Time*. Urbananatomy Electronic.
Laurence, S. (1996). A Chomskian Alternative to Convention-Based Semantics. *Mind* 105. pp. 269–301.
Leibniz, G. (2005). *New Essays on Human Understanding*. Edited by J. Bennett. Cambridge: Cambridge University Press.
Locke, J. (1999). *An Essay Concerning Human Understanding*. Pennsylvania: Pennsylvania State University.
Logos Group (2014). *Peirce, Eco and Infinite Semiosis*. Available from: http://courses.logos.it/EN/2_20.html#2 Accessed 23rd August 2019.
Malabou, C. (2005). *The Future of Hegel: Plasticity, Temporality and Dialectic*. Translated by L. During. Oxford: Routledge.
Malabou, C. (2016). *Before Tomorrow*. Translated by C. Shread. Cambridge: Polity.
McTaggart, J. (1908). The Unreality of Time. *Mind* 17 (68). pp. 457–474.
Meillassoux, Q. (2008). *After Finitude: An Essay on the Necessity of Contingency*. Translated by R. Brassier. London: Bloomsbury.
Mill, J. (2011). *A System of Logic*. Adelaide: University of Adelaide.
Moore, A. (2012). *The Evolution of Modern Metaphysics: Making Sense of Things*. Cambridge: Cambridge University Press.
Nietzsche, F. (1968). *The Will to Power*. Translated by W. Kaufmann and R. Hollingdale. New York: Random House.
Nietzsche, Friedrich (1999). *Sämtliche Werke. Kritische Studienausgabe in 15 Bänden*. Edited by G. Colli and M. Montinari. Munich, Berlin and New York: DTV and Walter de Gruyter.
Nietzsche, F. (2005). *Thus Spoke Zarathustra*. Translated by G. Parker. Oxford: Oxford University Press.
Nietzsche, F. (2006). *On the Genealogy of Morality*. Translated by C. Diethe. Cambridge: Cambridge University Press.
Orfali, I. (1983). *Fiction érogène à partir de Klossowski*. Stockholm: Skoglunds Tryckeri.
Peirce, C. S. (1997). *Collected Papers of Charles Sanders Peirce*. Vol 1. Edited by C. Hartshorne, P. Weiss and A. Burks. Cambridge, MA: Harvard University Press.
Peirce, C. S. (1998). *The Essential Peirce: Selected Philosophical Writings*. Vol. 2. The Peirce Edition Project. Bloomington: Indiana University Press.
Pereboom, D. (2014). Kant's Transcendental Arguments. *The Stanford Encyclopedia of Philosophy*. Edited by E. N. Zalta. Available from: https://plato.stanford.edu/archives/fall2014/entries/kant-transcendental/. Accessed 21st March 2019.
Sheehan, T. (1975). Heidegger, Aristotle and Phenomenology. *Philosophy Today* 19 (2). pp. 87–94.

Silverstein, M. (1976). Shifters, Linguistic Categories and Cultural Description. In: Basso, K. and Selby, H. (eds.). *Meaning in Anthropology.* Albuquerque: University of New Mexico Press. pp. 11–55.

Smith, D. (2005). Klossowski's Reading of Nietzsche: Impulses, Phantasms, Simulacra, Stereotypes. *Diacritics* 35 (1). pp. 8–21.

Smith. I. (2011). *Freud – Complete Works.* Available from: https://www.valas.fr/IMG/pdf/Freud_Complete_Works.pdf. Accessed 24th June 2017.

Stambaugh, J. (1972). *Nietzsche's Thought of Eternal Return.* Baltimore: Johns Hopkins University Press.

Tolman, R. (1917). The Measurable Quantities of Physics. *Phys. Rev.* 9 (3). pp. 237–253.

Tolman, R. (1938). *The Principles of Statistical Mechanics.* Oxford: Clarendon Press.

Tremblay, T. (2012). *Anamnèses: Essai sur l'oeuvre de Pierre Klossowski.* Paris: Hermann.

Van Cleve, J. (1999). *Problems from Kant.* Oxford: Oxford University Press.

Williams, J. (2011). *Gilles Deleuze's Philosophy of Time: A Critical Introduction and Guide.* Edinburgh: Edinburgh University Press.

Wilson, M. (1977). Confused Ideas. *Rice University Studies* 63. Available from: https://scholarship.rice.edu/bitstream/handle/1911/63299/article_RIP634_part7.pdf?sequence=1 Accessed 24th August 2019.

Wittgenstein, L. (1922). *Tractatus Logico-Philosophicus.* Translated by C. K. Ogden. London: Kegan Paul.

Wittgenstein, L. (2001) *Philosophical Investigations.* Translated by G. E. M. Anscombe. Singapore: Blackwell.

Index of Names

Ansell-Pearson, K.   5, 6, 10, 73
Atkin, A.   35
Avanessian, A.   137

Bataille, G.   113
Bergson, H.   6, 20, 21, 22, 23, 28, 161, 162, 163
Boltzmann, L.   71
Boscovich, R.   10, 74
Boyle, R.   10, 70
Brentano, F.   172
Brown, H.   73

Camus, A.   182
Cantor, G.   105
Castanet, H.   182
Chomsky, N.   29
Clark, K.   185, 187, 188

De Salomé, L.   68
Deleuze, G.   5, 9, 20, 23, 54, 157, 158, 163
Descartes, R.   20, 28, 54, 85, 87, 91, 93, 179
Dühring, E.   70

Eco, U.   33, 37, 38, 57, 87

Freud, S.   30, 41, 42, 55, 60, 66, 178

Gauss, C.   164
Groddeck, G.   55

Heidegger, M.   9, 12, 54, 93, 113, 148
Helmholtz, H.   27
Hempel, C.   173
Howell, R.   81
Hume   27, 28, 41, 111, 138, 143
Husserl, E.   93

Jaspers, K.   113

Kant, I.   20, 21, 22, 23, 27, 41, 45, 46, 51, 67, 81, 82, 83, 84, 138, 143, 144, 187

Kellner, D.   8
Kelvin, W.   10, 70

Land, N.   137, 171, 172
Laplace, P.   70, 73
Laurence, S.   31
Leibniz, G.   7, 22, 28
Locke, J.   20, 67, 143
Löwith, K.   113

Malik, S.   137
McTaggart, J.   126, 153, 154, 155
Meillassoux, Q.   104
Mill, J.   73
Muller, J.   27
Myrvold, W.   73

Oppenheim, P.   173
Orfali, I.   89, 90, 174

Parmenides   15, 16, 17
Peirce, C.   8, 32, 33, 34, 35, 36, 37, 38, 39, 87, 95, 178
Poincaré, H.   73, 74, 98

Rée, P.   68
Russell, B.   20

Sade, D.   190
Silverstein, M.   96, 178
Smith, D.   5, 7, 58, 61, 65
Socrates   15
Spinoza, B.   115
Stambaugh, J.   55

Tremblay, T.   50, 68, 182, 183, 184, 186

Uffink, J.   73

Van Cleve, J.   81

Whitlock, G.   74

Williams, J. 161
Wittgenstein, L. 8, 19, 20, 31, 87, 188

Zeno 15

Index of Subjects

Abbreviation   38, 40, 41, 43, 45, 165, 181
Anachronism   82, 120, 121, 122, 123, 125, 127, 130, 131
Apperception   78, 79, 80
Asymmetry   136, 137, 153
Asynchrony   11

Causality   4, 6, 85, 94, 99, 107, 110, 112, 114, 115, 116, 117, 119, 132, 133, 134, 139, 163, 164, 165, 166, 170, 172
Chance   7, 8
Conspiracy   82
Corporeality   4, 25, 39, 48, 56, 57, 60, 83
Deactualisation   9

Desire   41, 45, 130, 134
Determinism   67, 85, 94, 107, 132, 160
Discontinuity   4, 41, 76, 77, 78, 81, 82, 83, 107, 115, 126, 139, 174, 184

Epiphenomena   10
Extensivity   17, 19, 29, 122

Forgetting   112, 116, 121, 127, 128, 129, 130, 146, 147, 156, 157, 171
Fortuity   10, 66, 69, 71, 72, 73, 74, 86, 95, 96, 97, 98, 145, 174, 175

Genesis   47

Identity   4, 10, 64, 91, 96, 97, 98, 99, 100, 107, 125, 127, 129, 161
Indeterminacy   4, 6, 86, 87, 95, 96, 98, 99, 106, 108, 112, 113, 123, 124, 134, 139, 142, 151, 156, 162, 173
Individuality   4, 10, 98, 100, 125, 127, 147, 155, 161
Infinite Semiosis   30, 34, 37, 88, 115
Intentionality   5, 12, 44, 45, 87, 89, 164, 165, 166, 167, 168, 169, 171
Interpretation   6, 9, 30, 31, 36, 89, 90, 91, 98, 99, 161, 175, 184

Mechanism   11, 67, 73, 85, 94, 101, 113, 138, 161
Memory   112, 116, 121, 146, 147, 152, 156, 157, 158, 159, 171
Mereology   26, 57
Meta-ethics   46, 120
Monism   21, 51

Necessity   6

Order (temporal)   11, 12, 117, 118, 120, 123, 124, 132, 134, 136, 139, 140, 145, 148, 150, 152, 153, 156, 160, 162, 164
Organic   28, 66, 69, 71

Parody,   141, 144
Permanence   13, 40, 44, 91, 92, 97, 102, 112, 116, 117, 118, 119, 122, 139, 150, 168, 175
Phantasm   35, 36, 82, 144, 187
Possibility   10
Particularity   9
Probability   67, 68, 71, 94, 101
Process   24
Psychoanalysis   7, 62, 63, 164, 173

Quality   18, 19
Quantity   18, 19

Recurrence   12, 14, 94, 128, 130, 148
Repetition   12, 14, 24, 28, 100, 119, 128, 138, 146, 152, 153, 154, 162, 163, 171
Representation   27, 42, 48, 49, 74, 79, 81, 104, 130, 166, 173, 186
Reversibility   139, 140, 141, 167, 168

Self   8, 32, 51, 52, 53, 55, 60, 66, 73, 74, 79, 82, 83, 107
Sensation   5, 14, 17, 18, 20, 25, 33, 34, 38, 39, 81, 88, 108, 113, 116, 128, 137, 140, 174
Simulacrum   6, 142, 144, 177, 178, 184, 185, 187, 188

Singularity 6, 49, 91, 96, 105, 107, 111, 120, 121, 124, 125, 130, 131, 139, 175, 185
Sleep 56, 64
Space 5, 17, 18, 19, 20, 42, 43, 54, 76, 92, 140
Self 6
Subjectivity 6
Succession (temporal) 123, 124, 126, 130, 169
Synthesis 132, 137, 139, 146

Templexity 133

Temporal Order 137
Thermodynamics 17, 19, 111
Trace 24, 26, 27, 32, 84, 85, 94, 96, 100, 102, 129, 146
Transcendental 25, 80, 140
Triad 30

Verticality 37, 59, 128, 170
Vision 42

Waves 23, 87, 102, 126, 156, 157, 178